CRITICAL INSIGHTS

The American Comic Book

CRITICAL INSIGHTS

The American Comic Book

Editor

Joseph Michael Sommers

Central Michigan University

SALEM PRESS

A Division of EBSCO Information Services, Inc.

Ipswich, Massachusetts

GREY HOUSE PUBLISHING

Copyright © 2014 by Grey House Publishing, Inc.

All rights reserved. No part of this work may be used or reproduced in any
manner whatsoever or transmitted in any form or by any means, electronic or
mechanical, including photocopy, recording, or any information storage and
retrieval system, without written permission from the copyright owner. For
information, contact Grey House Publishing/Salem Press, 4919 Route 22, PO
Box 56, Amenia, NY 12501.

∞ The paper used in these volumes conforms to the American National Standard
for Permanence of Paper for Printed Library Materials, Z39.48-1992 (R1997).

Library of Congress Cataloging-in-Publication Data

The American comic book / editor, Joseph Michael Sommers, Central
  Michigan University. -- [First edition].

    pages ; cm. – (Critical Insights)

  Includes bibliographical references and index.
  ISBN: 978-1-61925-226-4

  1. Comic books, strips, etc.--United States--History and criticism. I. Sommers,
Joseph Michael, 1976- II. Series: Critical insights.

PN6725 .A44 2014
741.5/973

LCCN: 2014936877

First Printing

PRINTED IN THE UNITED STATES OF AMERICA

Contents

Resources

About This Volume

Joseph Michael Sommers

At the core of *Critical Insights: The American Comic Book* lies a set of relatively simple questions: Where, when, why, how, and to what extent did comics become so desperately important to an American people of any and all ages, creeds, and colors? While that list might seem somewhat journalistic by nature, and, in many ways, the essays contained within *do* offer fine reporting, the arguments proffered in this volume seek to reconceptualize the idea of comics and the culture of comics under the red, white, and blue umbrella of American discourse communities and social mores—which is not to say that between these covers lie all that there is to know about comics, not by a long shot.

For example, while the contributors and I sought to be as inclusive as possible between thirteen essays and an introduction, a conscious decision was made not to include a chapter on comics video games and adaptations of comics into interactive games. They're mentioned, of course, but, at some point, it was simply decided that to make the move from classic narratology (where an examination of narrative forms akin to reading and analyzing comics or comics movies is standard practice) to *ludology* (where game studies and active audience interaction within are par for the course) would likely take the anthology far astern of its intentions to cata catalogue the first seventy-five or so years of comics in America. We'll have to save the video games for the book's sequel. (Because to be American *necessitates* sequels.) All kidding aside, there is only so much any book can feature between its front matter and the index; this volume strives to start a conversation that will, hopefully, continue on for many years to come. To those ends, this is not merely a book that contains long-winded discussions of solrads and muscloma (for other such formalist comics nomenclature, please see: Mort Walker's *The Lexicon of Comicana*.). Rather, it really is a discussion of moments in time stemming back into the late nineteenth century and well into 2014, mere weeks before this book's publication. Moments where a recurring name, Fredric Wertham, sought to decimate comics culture by claiming it was harmful to children. If this book accounts for a real life super-villain, or, at least, a primary antagonist, it might be the man who falsified his research in an attempt to censor comics. Likewise, that censorship is documented from before the inception of the Comics Code Authority through the rise of the underground movement and the end of both. This book spans distance as well, from the offices of Joseph Pulitzer in New York City to the streets of Birmingham, Alabama, all the way into the line entering Hall H at San Diego's Convention Center and every place in between. We deal with ages gold, silver, bronze, and even rusty. We catalogue the movement of the comic book from a rolled up magazine kept in one's back pocket to one encased in Mylar for historical preservation to the tablet computer, where art became digitized and transferable. We challenge the notions of what a comics fan looks like and what her identity might be (not to mention how quickly it can change with a simple change of cosplay), and we do all of this daring greatly and audaciously.

What could be more American than that?

As such, the volume in your hands does many things, most of all, perhaps, to provoke further and greater conversations, both academic and fanatic, as those things are not mutually-exclusive. I start this conversation in the introduction, this prefatory note being very much part of that introduction. Here, I suggest that the scope and reach of comics has been largely shaped by a synergistic relationship with its ever-growing and ever-evolving fanbase—the lifeblood of the industry in all its myriad shapes, forms, and styles. Nowhere can this be seen better than at the industry's great parade of innovation and fan support, San Diego ComiCon International, where fans and producers of all things comics gather together in celebration of the medium.

From this point, we present four Critical Context essays with four distinctive points of view and egress for the comics scholar. Daniel Clark and Krystal Howard begin our discussion with a concise, but informative, history lesson on the medium. Their "The American Comic Book: a Brief History," offers the reader just that, a point of departure for understanding a magnificent and long history. Taking the reader abroad to start and quickly returning to American soil, they articulate the meteoric rise of comics from the strips of New York City's newspapers into the workings of the comic books now so familiar to the everyday reader. No essay of this size could ever hope to be all-inclusive, and that is not their purpose. Rather, the two survey key touchstone moments further elucidated in this volume, while situating a context for additional discussion.

On such discussion comes in the form of the first of two Kim Munson essays, this one entitled, "Hiding the Forbidden Fruit: Comics Censorship in the United States." It is a chapter primarily concerned with the reception of comic books, seemingly almost from their point of debut and hitting a pinnacle at that radical moment of concern in 1954, which stemmed from Fredric Wertham's publication of *Seduction of the Innocent*. The damage done in that year would take decades to repair, and Munson goes to great lengths to catalogue that history's moments both ugly and proud. However, as much damage as this chapter notes, many great advances arose from censoring of the medium, including the rise of underground comix and alternative comics as well as the lauded Comic Book Legal Defense Fund.

Daniel Lawson takes a more in-depth investigation of comics into our present moment in time with his chapter, "The Rhetorical Construction and Negotiation of Cultural Difference in American Nonfiction Comics." In it, Lawson takes a hard look at the rhetorical gestures and formalist attributes surrounding "othering discourses" at play in comics involving delicate real world subject matter. In particular, Lawson focuses his eye upon responses to comics in the aftermath of the events surrounding 9/11 in America. He investigates works by Art Spiegelman, Marjane Satrapi, Joe Sacco, and even the commissioned efforts of the 9/11 report (neither the first time nor likely the last, as other chapters show, that the United States government has requested help from the comics community to make sense of a difficult topic and situation). His conclusions articulate that both the visuals and the message of the books underpin otherwise veiled American cultural mores and systems of thought.

Our final Critical Context essay examines the power of comics as a part of and factor within American social policy. Matt Bryant Cheney's chapter, "US Comics, Moral Capital, and Social Change: 1954–2014," looks at the interplay between comics and major moments in American ethical debate. Furthering this book's discussion of the CCA stemming from Wertham's study, Cheney interpolates comic books within the larger socially-conscious narrative of US history, such as the Civil Rights Movement and the precursors to the War on Drugs. Likewise, he looks at some of the earlier instances where the US government specifically utilized comic books in an effort to promote messages fit and proper for youth culture. Fit and proper, possibly, only meaning that all might be judged on the correct side of history.

Moving past our Critical Contexts essays, I present a taxonomy of the medium itself with "Negotiating Popular Genres in Comic Books: an Impossible Mission. Against All Odds. Yet, Somehow, the Chapter Is Saved!" Less an argumentative chapter and more an encyclopedic listing of the popular genres and subgenres of American comics, the chapter seeks less to be inclusive, and more to comment and supplement the histories presented with some semblance of definition and connotation. (For, as the chapter articulates, it is rather difficult to pin down *anything* in comics definitively.) While neither intending to be an exhaustive list or a definitive one, the essay hinges on the principle that comics constitutes a tree bearing many different types of fruit; all I can offer by illustration are some representative features to help the reader distinguish the flavors and variety while trying to contextualize their form and development.

The next three chapters demand intertextualization as they form a larger triptych of readings that demand to be read in succession. Joseph Darowski's "The Improbability of Assignment: Arriving at a Golden Age of Comic Books," Matthew J. Smith's "The Silver Age Playbook: Minting the Modern Superhero," and Kyle Eveleth's, "Rust and Revitalization: the So-Called Bronze and Modern Age of Comics," are three essays that form one large look at the stratification

---

of comics history along three traditional periodic approaches: the Golden, Silver, and Bronze Ages. This periodization, the names most likely drawn, it is argued, from pricing guides and fandom itself before becoming academized, is as contentious as anything else argued in this volume, yet, all three writers take pains to place their arguments within the context of the time, the traditionally-bandied arguments, as well as the comic books themselves. Eveleth, in particular, makes a strong argument for both retrenchment of periodization of comics as, he argues, it is easily shown that the Bronze Age simultaneously never ended and fizzled out amidst radical ideological change in the mid-1980s.

Less contentious is Kim Munson's second chapter, "From the Mainstream to the Margins: Independent Comics Find a Voice," which examines the expansion of the comics industry both in light of the post-CCA collapse of many smaller independent publishers and the rise of underground, alternative, and creator-owned comics that developed in response to that implosion. Munson presents a cyclical history articulating troughs and peaks brought about less by the capital interests of the so-called 'Big Two' of Marvel Comics and DC Comics, rather, a desire to articulate stories drawn from more personal interests and investments.

It is at this point where we begin to experience a medial shift within our examination of the comic *book*. Philip Smith starts that journey by ostensibly removing the book from the comic in "From the Page to the Tablet: Digital Media and the Comic Book." This examination of the digitalization of the form builds on the groundbreaking work of names such as Scott McCloud, who, in *Reinventing Comics*, predicted this move from paper to the computer. As much as Munson's examination of the independent comics scene was shown to be motivated by less capitalistic means, Smith's argument shows the arrival at the digital frontier in comics as both servicing the industry's health from a monetary perspective as well as giving unknown names an opportunity to, essentially, self-publish.

Our final three chapters explore the boundaries and borders of comics in this present, very transmedial moment, in comics history;

Owen R. Horton and A. J. Shackelford's "Fantasy Elsewheres, Sutured Realities, and the End of Camp: Comics in Contemporary Film and Television" couches an analysis of the adaptation of comic book intellectual properties into both film and television within an examination of larger franchises, both successful and not. Forrest C. Helvie moves past the introduction's initial foray into Hall H with a historical analysis of the comics fan with his chapter "Comic Fandom Throughout the Ages," where he shows how comics sought to form a community across its history by capitalizing on all available forms of media. Finally, Katherine E. Whaley and Justin Wigard address a specific nexus of concern that Helvie articulates at the end of his chapter: the role and construction of women in what has been largely (mistakenly?) perceived as a field attenuated to a male audience. Their "Waiting for Wonder Woman: the Problematic History of Comic Book Women and Their Cinematic Doubles" interrogates comics both in filmic properties and books asking the simple, remarkably Joss Whedonesque question of: Where are all the women in comics and why can they not break through in this day and age?

On the American Comic Book_____

Joseph Michael Sommers

As I compose these words, comics fandom in America is radically amidst its annual pilgrimage to San Diego, CA, its very own Mecca, for the annual Comic-Con International, where, since 1970, fans, academics, creators, publishers, and devotees, young and old alike, gather for a week of discovery, community, and celebration of their love for the greater multiverse of all things known or related to comics. By day, many of them don ill-fitting and excruciatingly uncomfortable cosplays[1] that do not weather well standing in line with thousands of others wearing outfits that stand as application to Stan Winston's School of Character Arts, sometimes for well over twenty-four hours, just to gain access to Hall H, comics' ultimate cathedral, which, for fans, is a veritable "rocket ship made of cheers" (VanDerWerff). They will not weather this wait with anything remotely resembling discomfort or ill-will, unless you cut in line; that is strictly *verboten*. Rather, these citizens of the comics community will be on their best behavior, so as to gain audience with the celebrities of the medium, whether those stars are from the book, television, film, or video game industries. By night, with a stamina one cannot imagine a human might still muster, the citizen of Comic-Con will gather at any of a host of parties both formal and impromptu, recalling the day's events with a great mirth and cheer that would make Thor blush. On Friday of Comic-Con week, the industry's annual Will Eisner Comic Industry Awards, as of this writing in its twenty-sixth year, will prize and laud the finest books, creators, and even academic contributions to the field with the same pageantry one might expect of the Academy Awards or the BAFTAs.

Consider this our application to next year's event.

All this pomp and circumstance begs a very simple, if not obvious, question: Where did this all come from? Not comics or comicsdom—many preeminent scholars, such as Scott McCloud (*Understanding Comics*), Douglas Wolk (*Reading Comics*), Charles

Hatfield (*Alternative Comics*), and Bart Beaty (*Fredric Wertham and the Critique of Mass Culture*) have addressed comics' origins and culture to remarkable ends. Journalists, such as the indefatigable Tom Spurgeon (*The Comics Journal*), Jonah Weiland (*Comic Book Resources*), and Timothy Holder and Dan Nadel (*The Comics Journal*), make it their daily practice to catalogue and disseminate the minute-by-minute machinations of the industry to the lay reader via all possible communication portals. Even the nominal fan, the person who once (still?) stood in line to Hall H and now takes to the internet to break news stories and gossip about comics properties as both a means of living and a lifestyle, people such as Umberto Gonzalez—better known on Twitter as both @ElMayimbe and the bane of Marvel Studios producer Kevin Feige's life—and his colleagues at *Latino Review* have made a business of digging into the fandom's incessant need for more access, more points of entry into the omnipresence of comics in the twenty-first century. And before anyone openly wonders, "Wait. We're going to the internet fansites now as academic resources?" I'm not sure there is anything more distinctly American, as later chapters will address, than the fact that in the discussion of comics and its greater cosmology, fandom, and the fansites have become *as* important to the growth of the field as the academics and, arguably, the creators of the work. The real surprise might be the argument that they always have been.

For, if the "literary work" in comics is the book, or graphic novel, or video game, or television show or other filmic property, then all this discussion, academic, journalistic, fan gossip, etc. would likely be considered comics' "paratext," as Gerard Genette famously put it, or "what enables a text to become a book and to be offered as such to its readers and, more generally, to the public [. . .] a 'vestibule' that offers the world at large the possibility of either stepping inside or turning back" (1–2). The fan community, once resigned in voice largely to the letters columns oft no longer found in electronic versions of Marvel or DC Comics (at least on ComiXology), now shouts loudly at the industry in the internet talkback and fan websites of a largely unmediated digital frontier dedicated the endless mass of merchandise and information that is comics culture. Disney, the parent company of New York-based Marvel Comics, and Warner Brothers, likewise to Burbank, CA's DC Comics, may now own and control the day-to-day operations of the largest crafters and distributors of the medium, but the internet and the millions upon millions of fans who reside there ultimately exert control over those companies and the success and failure of the products they craft. The internet fandom, all these "heterogeneous groups of practices and discourses" (Genette 2), is both the ultimate paratext of the comics industry *and* an integral part, parcel, participant, and partner in and within the industry itself. As, whether it be Spurgeon or Beaty or Gonzalez, I'm willing to bet that none of them would be finessing their craft if they were not, now or at some meaningful moment of their lives, fans of comics. And, if not, someone please explain why, within fan circles, it makes any difference whatsoever whether the casting of Michael B. Jordan, a young man of color, as the character of *Fantastic Four*'s Johnny Storm, traditionally depicted as a young Caucasian, makes the internet fanbase already declare Josh Trank's filmic depiction of *FF* a "train wreck" (Lewis4510), while the casting of the late actor Michael Clarke Duncan as the also traditionally-depicted Caucasian character of the Kingpin in the critically-derided *Daredevil* was "perfect" (BaronZemo).

All of which brings us back to San Diego.

While it certainly is not the only large-scale comics convention in the world, San Diego's Comic-Con might serve as the perfect synecdoche for the state of the American Comics as it currently stands—which is exactly to state that comics are not necessarily just about comic *books* any more, nor have they been for a very long time; this book's title, possibly, has an inherent misnomer in it. Whether one traces the gravitation of the comics industry from the "direct sales" within the doors of an "insulated comic book shop" (D. Johnson 74) to the virtually limitless audience expansion of the comic book *vis-à-vis* ComiXology or something akin to *The Marvel Experience*, or even the "reimagining, restructuring, and relauching" (74) of entire characters and universes via adaption into the filmic sphere (and backwards retconing into the comic books themselves), comics have become what Henry Jenkins calls a "transmedia" experience, where comic narratives are told and unfurl over multiple platforms and media at the same time, not unlike a massive jigsaw puzzle of narrative content (20). Where once, a comics consumer might have to try and track the numerous books and their titles across a greater comics arc, now, they might have to do the same, but also incorporate a television show or four, such as Marvel will be doing with their Netflix initiative to bring *Daredevil*, *AKA Jessica Jones*, *Iron Fist*, and *Luke Cage* to the small screen as television series, only to reconvene them into a cross-population in what they believe will come across as *The Defenders* mini-series. This model, of course, mimics what the Marvel Cinematic Universe has already done building towards *The Avengers* (2012) and *The Avengers: Age of Ultron* (2015) incorporating movies, TV, video games, and, of course, comic books into a larger scale event that allows a participant more access based largely upon how much time and energy (not to mention pocket money) they have to expend on the narrative.

Fortunately, as noted elsewhere here, handling narrative time and evolution (mutation?) over actual time is something comics are particularly good at; as "characters and their histories underwent significant evolution at the hands of studio writers, who, in reintroducing these almost half-century-old characters to an expanded audience via film, sought to bring them into the zeitgeist of the post-9/11 moment" (Sommers 188). Mirroring that change in approach and development of comics and comics characters, America, short of abandoning stalwart shops, more institutions really, such as New York's own Midtown Comics, have greatly embraced the ease and accessibility of the shift to digital comics, whether that comes from an outright shift of abandoning paper through portals, such as ComiXology, or ordering their comics packaged by the story-arc through parent-site Amazon. While one might not say that the day has grown long and dark for the brick-and-mortar comic book store, one might find that store more successful if it were to host nightly role-playing games than live and die on box after box of now severely-devalued comics back issues and a major Wednesday influx of traffic with the week's new books. For whatever reason, the brick-and-mortar comic book store tries to avoid the same fate as the stand-alone music, trading card, or movie store by virtue of being a place that has expanded its inventory by the same manner that the medium has expanded its media: toys, collectables, clothing, DVDs, cosplay material, RPG cards and Heroclix figurines, among assorted and related ephemera; these likely occupy more of the store's shelves and walls than the comic books themselves.

The American Comic *Book* has become an odd deconstructed/reconstructed thing in the contemporary age. Deconstruction, a term crafted in the mid-1960s by philosopher Jacques Derrida, and, not ironically, beset with enough sliding meanings as to elude any single one, concerns notions of texts and textual creations outliving their creators and original intents to become new things, perhaps contradictory, and maybe greater than originally intended. So, whereby once a reader might contend, as one often does in adaptation study/ersatz film criticism that, "Yeah, the movie was okay, but it's NOWHERE near as good as the book," now, one must allow that there really isn't so much an adaptive moment of the comic book as the notion that there is no *outside* the comic book. Or, as Derrida once wrote, "There is no outside-text" (158); for us, this concerns the decentralization of the comic book as god concept for interpretation—the transcendental signifier of how character and character arc must be constructed on comics. This notion holds that, somehow, somewhere, over, in some cases, seventy-five-plus years of character and character development, there is some idea or construction of a true version of a character. Example: which Batman is *the* Batman? Bill Finger's original concept? Denny O'Neil's groundbreaking and defining visualizations? Frank Miller's Dark Knight? And which Dark Knight—the year-one Bats or the one who returned or the one who struck back or the "all star" who, quite infamously, settled this debate telling Robin "I'm the goddamn Batman." (Miller and Lee)? Batman may have been around for seventy-five years (and looks good for a septuagenarian), but he has not aged quite in that same diachronic manner, as comics time and comics reader time are significantly different.[2]

Comic books and their contents have evolved significantly from the eras in which they began, and to remain successful, they must. Their "development," I have written, "[allows] a truncated narrative to expand upon an established orthodoxy in comic books in an effort to preserve the core pre-text of the comic book's narrative history, while adapting it to a new chronotopal point in space and history alongside and with any baggage that comes with the change" (Sommers 193). Truth, this established orthodoxy in comic books, is as malleable a thing as a thing can be, as *truth* changes with time and space, particularly in America, where something can be hip today and gauche . . . later that same day. Once staid characters with inhabited histories lasting fifty–seventy-five-plus years (Spidey, Cap, . . . the entire Justice League) have become characters who can transmogrify every year and a half to two years, as is the case with Marvel's "Now" initiative where traditional comic numbering has given way to archetectonic shifts that give established characters new looks and new books every thirty–thirty-five issues.

Today, as of this writing, Captain America (Steve Rogers) has been robbed of his Super Soldier serum and sits as an old man; Thor and Loki (the younger, more mischievous, less evil one) quest for their sister, Angela (who used to reside in the pages of Image Comics' *Spawn* but has found her way into Marvel's books and a previously unknown tenth realm of Yggdrasil); and Iron Man is generally still busy being Iron Man, doing very Iron-Man-y, cum-Robert-Downey-Jr., things, such as restoring some sense of intelligence to the Hulk in recompense for juicing the gamma bomb that turned Bruce Banner into the Hulk in the first place (*Original Sin: Hulk vs. Iron Man 3*). In some months hence, where Sam Wilson was once the Falcon, the first mainstream African American superhero,[3] he will be the next iteration of Captain America, following in a long tradition of superheroes to don that mantle. Whereas Thor once was . . . several people actually, most recently, he was simply Thor Odinson without Donald Blake or other such secret or alternative identities, "Now," *she* is a new Thor of, as yet, undisclosed origin, while Thor Odinson has been found "unworthy" to bear Mjolnir . . . which may or may not have something to do with the fact that he seems to be sporting a bionic arm (Wheeler). Captain Marvel, Carol Danvers, is the former Ms. Marvel, and the new Ms. Marvel, Kamala Khan, is a teenager representing, to my mind, one, if not the first, Muslim American characters to headline her own monthly title. Iron Man? He'll remain Iron Man; he'll just be "Superior" and relocate to the West Coast. Some things rarely change. Tony Stark's persistent hubris seems to be one of those things (Ching).

On the DC side of the major publishers, the "Flashpoint"-inspired New 52 essentially took a 'greatest hits' package approach to the entirety of DCs continuity and gave it significant updates, costume changes (Both Batman and Superman *finally* both opted to wear their underwear beneath their tights.), some miraculous advances in spinal repair, an amalgamation with Jim Lee's Wildstorm Universe and a considerable bit of the Vertigo imprint . . . and the Joker cut off his own face so that he could wear it as a mask. DC, itself no stranger to retcons and updates of main stage characters that have been around since the dawning of the Golden Age of Comics, brought about their company revamp of their titles in an effort to couch their characters in the present moment akin to what Marvel did on film with their MCU, it being a collapsing of their 616-continuity and Ultimates line. Not coincidentally, DC's parent company, Warner Bros., has prepared an ambitious movie slate to capitalize and synchronize with the new direction of the comics, while also populating television across the dial with shows like *Constantine*, *Arrow*, *The Flash*, *Gotham*, and *Preacher*. As Richard Reynolds has so understatedly put it, "Superhero comics present [. . .] a body of contemporary mythology from which television and Hollywood have plundered material" (7). With aplomb.

All this still begs the obvious question: Why? So much change. So much reinvention of a medium and characters within that medium that has been in existence, most conservatively, going back to Richard Outcault's 1895 Yellow Kid and, possibly quite liberally from McCloud's perspective, over thirty-three centuries ago, to Egyptian hieroglyphs (14). Ultimately, short of the ludography inherent to interaction and play seen in video games, most comic books or movies or what have you, still adhere to Will

Eisner's notions of sequential art, an "ancient form or art, or method of expression [having] established an undeniable position in the popular culture of this century" (5). When Eisner wrote that in 1985, he spoke of the twentieth century as being at the cusp of transition into what is now generally regarded as the Modern Age of Comics. In this period, comics' heyday in America was considered to be in the World War II/immediate post-World War II period, when comics were considered by some to actually outstrip most all other forms of popular media. When put into today's context, when comics dominate *all* forms of media as a hinterland for the convergence culture of which Jenkins speaks, comics are likely at their zenith in terms of not just American cultural consumption, but global cultural consumption. And, from such lofty heights, comics bear the weight of pressurized evolution and diversification not necessarily as an opiate for the masses—rather, comics evolve alongside their youthful audience, who know no speed less than, as Marvel rightly acknowledges as, Now!

And yet, when a medium, theoretically, has reached its zenith, one considers whether it has the terminal velocity with which it can still ascend and reach further into the stars. (See: *Guardians of the Galaxy* [2014]. Marvel implores you to see it.) Will the industry plateau, or, as many fear, will the transmedial supersaturation of the market across all platforms cause what one assumes must entail an eventual decline? History suggests such a cycle of peaks and valleys. The current run of overwhelming success stretches back fifteen years to 1999's *The X-Men* in cinema, which seems to have been the harbinger of the rebirth of the phoenix (no pun intended) after the trough of the mid-90s, where the defection of the Image seven and the onslaught of foil comic book covers, super-sized issues, and general excess sucked the air out of the industry for a short while (*Super-Heroes,* Johnson 160–61). However, with what Marvel and Disney, under the creative direction of Joe Quesada and Kevin Feige, have begun seems sustained and balanced for at least a decade to come. Granted, with the incursion of the WB/DC slate of movies, three a year, and their current dominance in the home television and animated features market, not to mention the overall strength and longevity of their creations (recent quality control be damned), a comics geek would not be ill-advised to have concern that the comics bubble is approaching critical mass and may burst.

However, there is something to be noted about so-called geeks and the geek culture at large. To quote a Richard Donner vehicle, not *Superman*, "Goonies never say die" (*Goonies*). Or, to situate the argument a bit more within the desired discourse community, Jeffrey Johnson recalls the moment of clarity in his life, as a seven year old, where he realized that:

> What much of the American public still does not realize is that comic book superheroes are an important part of America's social fabric. Since its creation in the 1930s, the superhero has become the United States dominant cultural icon. Superheroes quickly expanded from their comic book origins to become a part of nearly every portion if American culture and society. (1)

Further, Johnson reminds us that "as American society change[s] so [does] its heroes" (37); comics, with their weekly release dates and individual titles with their monthly to bi-monthly ones, have always held a finger to the pulse of the current moment in American youth culture. When the times change, so do the comics. A prime example of this came in the previously mentioned WWII/post-WWII moment; as quickly as Captain America was punching Hitler square in the jaw on the cover of *Captain America 1*, with the arrival of the "nuclear fear" in the aftermath of WWII, Marvel dropped the jingoism and launched the Silver Age by way of embracing war-ending radiation: Peter Parker was bit by an irradiated spider, the Fantastic Four were bombarded with cosmic radiation, the Hulk was caught in the blast of a gamma bomb mishap etc. (J. Johnson 60). Essentially, comics reflected the cultural moment of America, processed it for young minds and disseminated it to a youth culture looking to embrace the moment and become imbricated within American culture one way or the other. It didn't hurt matters that those characters became younger to reflect the readership and provided them with characters who adolescents could empathize when facing similar problems.

Moments as such might never have seen as crucial a point in empathy as when America faced attack from a then unknown and faceless enemy on 9/11/2001. September 11 was a moment in recent American history when Americans knew fear and terror in a moment when they never thought they could be terrorized. Comics reflected this by showing their *Super*heroes working alongside real heroes, New York City's first responders; for example: "the post-9/11 *Amazing Spider-Man* #36 showed Spider-Man, along with other Marvel heroes and villains, working side by side with New York City first responders at Ground Zero" (Sommers 194). Who knew Dr. Doom could cry? Who knew Magneto might be welcomed as a savior, for once, for his abilities to shift and move large volumes of metal (Straczynski and Romita Jr. 9)? In that moment of a shared public trauma, there were no heroes and villains in comics; as J. Michael Straczynski wrote, "Because some things surpass rivalries and borders. Because the story of humanity is written not in towers but in tears. In the common coin of blood and bone [. . . .] Because even the worst of us, however scarred, are still human. Still feel. Still mourn the random death of innocents" (9). Sentiments expanded upon by Doom, a Latverian, and Magneto—a character who, in some comics, has actually killed millions of innocents (notably in New York City) due to his indifference towards *homo sapiens* when compared with *homo superior*—aren't consistent with Straczynski's words. However, such narrative consistencies are entirely irrelevant in the face of the greater collective message the comics community sought to deliver that day: Today, there are no heroes or villains. Today, there are just Americans, regardless from where they hail. And, today, they know great pain and great community with one another as we all try to heal.

Community in comics culture is a precious thing. Bradford W. Wright has called it a "comic book nation," and he places it quite distinctly in "the domain of young people, who inevitably outgrow them, recall them fondly, and then look at the comic books of their children and grandchildren with a mixture of bewilderment and, perhaps, concern" (xiii). Bradford W. Wright may not have recently visited San Diego (kidding, of course). But in his generational examination of this most distinctly American outlet of popular culture, Wright touches upon the idea that comics operate for youth (in all its ages) much like the New Journalism did for the adult reader: they posed the ability to take up and reflect "the social and political issues of the times"; speaking on the Bronze Age works of DC's *Green Lantern/Green Arrow*, "racism, poverty, political corruption, the 'generation gap', the plight of Native Americans, pollution, overpopulation, and religious cults" (Wright 227). Comic books have not turned their back upon a moment in American history as they are a resonant part of it. Functioning for the young and adolescent reader akin to what *The Daily Show* and *The Colbert Report* do for the adult reader, comics invoke powerful moments within a world where young people are often left to feel powerless, and then the comics, if only through narrative and imagination, empower them. That, perhaps, may be comics' great strength and unifying principle across the decades, changes in modality and form, and significance; they have the unique facet of giving the smallest of us an opportunity to enter into the greater adult discussion of being an American, even if only in story: fictional, semi-fictional, or non-fictional. There is a name for that sort of narrative.

Comic books are American mythology.

Not necessarily a concise set of cultural encodings structuralized into any sort of sacred pantheon, mind you. Some critics, like Geoff Klock, would likely reject such outright structural constructions as overly Jungian (9) if not entirely "tedious" (10), yet he would also readily contend that, in narratives that run fifty–seventy-five years, "reinterpretation becomes part of a survival code" (13). And, he would be right. For, at the most fundamental level, comics are the stories told to youth to help them make sense of a strange world growing ever stranger by the day. They aid youth of all ages in trying to comprehend a world full of changes and in constant motion and reinvention more so now than at any point in American history. The reason, I might suggest, that comics have become ubiquitous in the present moment, past the fact that it has finally become cost-effective to articulate amazing visual powers across a wide variety of media, is what Wright suggests on a more longitudinal plane: comics do not require one to outgrow them anymore. They are not the stuff of a radically-terminalized childhood bracketed between the borders of birth and the acquisition of a job affording one a 401K plan. Rather, with the rise and acceptance of children's and young adult literature as the stuff of a very malleable readership, with the rise of and overlap between toy makers and narrative makers, all of which might generally be couched under the term of world-building, the shame and dismissal of all of that might otherwise be considered juvenilia has been dismissed as geek chic. In the twenty-first century, comics offer a gateway into a state of endorsed permanent juvenescence. Unabashedly and without shame. You lose, Dr. Wertham.

And that takes us back, once again, to San Diego.

In an article for *Collider*, Matt Goldberg details a list of etiquette and advice on how one should and should not behave at San Diego Comic-Con International. At one point speaking on the fact that to Comic-Con (as verb) is very much to stand in line for what one wants to see at Comic-Con, he states quite clearly, "Learn to stop worrying and love the line," going on to say:

> The line isn't the worst thing ever. If you're waiting in line for a panel room, you can sit down, chat with friends, or even better, make new friends. Nerds get a bad rap for being anti-social, but the person next to you in line might be really cool. Strike up a conversation, share what you're excited to see, see if you're both part of the same fandom, and so forth. You're more than welcome to break out a book or a video game or what have you (but read on for why you should be careful about the electronics), and you probably will when you're waiting for hours in line. But you'll have a better time if you take some time out to chat with someone. Seeing the panel you're excited for is all well and good, but it's only a fraction of the full experience. (Goldberg)

The idea is clear and simple: have fun, make friends, and enjoy the show. Sometimes the show consists of sitting through panels in Hall H for hours awaiting any news on the upcoming Justice League movie, sometimes the show consists of navigating the convention floor dressed as a member of the Justice League looking at new products, action fictions, maquettes (*really* expensive action figures that you *do not* let your children play with), of the latest iteration of the Teenage Mutant Ninja Turtles, etc. It is a time and opportunity when grown men and women (and their children) can enjoy a second Halloween without fear and not arrest their development but revel, unadjudged, in their possibly second childhoods. And while one could easily point out that the entire spectacle of SDCC is the merchandizing of product and the generating of excitement for the next wave or slate of movies, games, television shows, and, oh yeah, comic books—Jean-Paul Gabilliet reminds that "publishers have always been more interested in selling copies of their publications than advancing the status of comics as an art form" (134). Pessimistic as that sounds, there is certainly some truth to that statement. Realistically speaking, though, what is more American than such outright commercialism?

For that matter, is there anything inherently wrong with the idea of walking through a recreation of *The Walking Dead*'s Terminus set from the AMC adaptation of the Image comic? Is a child's glee at being able to take a picture with a real life-sized version of Baymax from Disney's upcoming animated superhero movie *Big Hero 6* really that problematic? If donning an operational Oculus Rift headgear so as to reenact interfacing with Cerebro as Professor X does is wrong or playing with LEGO figurines from Star Wars is not right, then what exactly did Walt Disney build back in 1955? In his own words: "Disneyland is dedicated to the ideals, the dreams, and the hard facts that have created America, with the hope that it will be a source of joy and inspiration to all the world." If Disneyland is the house that the mouse built, might not SDCC be the Bacchanalia that American comics has fostered? And that's why this introduction to an anthology about the American Comic Book in all its myriad ways and forms is as much about and dedicated to the *fan* of the American Comic Book, without whom none of this wonderful madness and genius—in comics, there's little difference—would be possible. Because the real superheroes of comics are the people, the scores and generations of fans, who sought to dream a little differently and embrace the amazing fantasies afforded to them in monthlies that they could read, roll up into their back pocket, and trade with a friend.

Notes

1. For the uninitiated, read as a portmanteau of "costume" and "role play" of character design that the crafter wears as a temporary identity.
2. Hence Steve Rogers' man-out-of-time appeal, when he is literally thawed out of the Golden Age of Comics by the Avengers and transported into the Silver Age as a noble plot device of a by-gone era and comic book simultaneously.
3. Don't forget, the Black Panther hails from Wakanda.

Works Cited

BaronZemo. "Why I Think Michael Clarke Duncan Was The Perfect Kingpin." *ComicBookMovie.com.* 17 Nov. 2013. Web. 30 July 2014.

Ching, Albert. "'SUPERIOR IRON MAN' AND MORE HEADLINE MARVEL'S 'AVENGERS NOW'!" *Comic Book Resources.* 16 July 2014. Web. 30 July 2014.

Derrida, Jacques. *Of Grammatology*. Baltimore & London: John Hopkins UP, 1976.

Eisner, Will. *Comics & Sequential Art*. Tamarac, FL: Poorhouse, 1985.

Gabilliet, Jean-Paul, Bart Beaty, & Nick Nguyen. *Of Comics and Men: A Cultural History of American Comic Books*. Jackson: UP of Mississippi, 2010.

Genette, Gérard. *Paratexts: Thresholds of Interpretation*. Cambridge: Cambridge UP, 1997.

Goldberg, Matt. "A Guide to Comic-Con for First Time Attendees." *Collider*. 23 June 2012. Web. 30 July 2014. *The Goonies*. Dir. Richard Donner. Prod. Richard Donner and Harvey Bernhard. By Chris Columbus and Steven Spielberg. Perf. Sean Astin, Josh Brolin, & Jeff Cohen. Warner Bros., 1985.

Jenkins, Henry. *Convergence Culture: Where Old and New Media Collide*. New York: New York UP, 2006.

Johnson, Derek. "Will the Real Wolverine Please Stand Up: Marvel's Mutation from Monthlies to Movies." *Film and Comic Books*. Ed.

Ian Gordon, Mark Jancovich & Matthew P. McAllister. Jackson: UP of Mississippi, 2007. 64–85.

Johnson, Jeffrey K. *Super-history: Comic Book Superheroes and American Society, 1938 to the Present.* Jefferson, NC: McFarland, 2012.

Klock, Geoff. *How to Read Superhero Comics and Why.* New York: Continuum, 2002.

Lewis4510. "Michael B. Jordan: 'Fantastic Four' Reboot Is 'Not Your Typical Superhero Film'–Spinoff Online–TV, Film, and Entertainment News Daily." *Spinoff Online.* 18 July 2014. Web. 30 July 2014.

McCloud, Scott. *Understanding Comics.* New York: HarperPerennial, 1994.

Miller, Frank, & Jim Lee. *All Star Batman and Robin #2.* New York: DC Comics, 2002.

Reynolds, Richard. *Super Heroes: A Modern Mythology.* Jackson: U of Mississippi, 1994.

Sommers, Joseph Michael. "The Traumatic Revision of Marvel's *Spider-Man*: From 1960s Dime-Store Comic Book to Post-9/11 Moody Motion Picture Franchise." *Children's Literature Association Quarterly* 37.2 (2012): 188–209.

Straczynski, J. Michael, & John Romita Jr. *The Amazing Spider-Man #36.* New York: Marvel Comics, 2002.

VanDerWerff, Todd. "A Day Inside Comic-Con's Hall H: Worshiping in the Ultimate Movie Church." *Grantland.* 22 July 2013. Web. 30 July 2014.

Waid, Mark, & Kieron Gillian. *Original Sin Hulk Vs. Iron Man #2.* New York: Marvel Comics, 2014, Reynolds, Richard. *Super Heroes: A Modern Mythology.* Jackson: U of Mississippi, 1994.

Wheeler, Andrew. "A Female Thor, A Black Captain America: What Does It All Mean?" *Comics Alliance.* 17 July 2014. Web. 30 July 2014.

Wright, Bradford W. *Comic Book Nation: The Transformation of Youth Culture in America.* Baltimore: Johns Hopkins UP, 2001.

CRITICAL
CONTEXTS

The American Comic Book: a Brief History
Daniel Clark & Krystal Howard

Interestingly enough, the American comic book neither originated in America nor did it develop in a vacuum. Some diverse and distant antecedents to American comics may be seen in the drawings of political cartoonists, such as Thomas Nast (1840–1902), who, in addition to using his political cartoons to target the corruption of Tammany Hall's William "Boss" Tweed and the institution of slavery, is often credited with popularizing the images of Uncle Sam, the Democratic Party's symbol of the donkey, and creating the Republican Party's symbol of the elephant. Likewise, another indirect antecedent to American comic books was the dime novel. With improvements in the nation's education system and increased literacy rates, dime novels, such as those published by Beadle and Adams, filled a growing need for reading material for the working classes starting in the 1860s. Dime novels presented sensationalized tales of heroism, mystery, and adventure. They were often illustrated with woodcut drawings and were just as often publically condemned by authorities as being detrimental to the morals of those who read them (Hajdu 94–95).

Some closer antecedents may be found in Swiss cartoonist Rodolphe Töpffer's *The Adventures of Mr. Obadiah Oldbuck*, originally published in various languages in Europe, but also published as a newspaper supplement in the United States in 1842 (Duncan and Smith 23), and in *The Fortunes of Ferdinand Flipper*, published by the Brother Jonathan Office in the 1850s. Both books present narratives with sequential images and include captions (but no word balloons) under each image. Another closer relative were gag cartoons, which proliferated during the 1880s. Gag cartoons generally combined a verbal joke, often in the form of a conversation between two people, and a visual image. Unlike the interplay between image and text common in most comic books, the image in the gag cartoon did little more than illustrate the joke (Harvey 28). As Robert Harvey notes, "[M]ost cartoons of the earliest vintage are essentially verbal witticisms that are funny without their accompanying illustrations" (29).

The next step in the evolution of the comic book was fueled by a bitter rivalry between two newspaper magnates—William Randolph Hearst and Joseph Pulitzer. Near the end of the nineteenth century, competition among newspapers was increasing—over thirty newspapers were being published in New York and the competition to sell papers was often fierce (Hajdu 9). Pulitzer, seeking an advantage over his rivals, began including a four-page Sunday color supplement in his *New York World*. One of the main attractions of these bright pages was Richard Felton Outcault's *Hogan's Alley*, better known by its main character, The Yellow Kid. Outcault's series was set in the disheveled back alleys of New York's immigrant population and followed the often violent antics of its juvenile community. The raucous humor of *Hogan's Alley* was at once popular and the cause of concern to Pulitzer's competitors. The Yellow Kid became the first major comic strip character in the United States.

Hearst, however, was not to be outdone. He, too, purchased a color press and soon announced that his *New York Journal* would be publishing "eight pages of iridescent polychromous effulgence that makes the rainbow look like a piece of lead pipe" (Waugh 6). In a bold maneuver, Hearst bought out much of Pulitzer's staff, including Outcault, who brought The Yellow Kid with him. In response, Pulitzer simply hired another artist to continue *Hogan's Alley* in the *World*. While at the *Journal*, Outcault continued to innovate. Many of his early drawings of The Yellow Kid were single panels busy with characters and action. In some later pieces, Outcault incorporated a sequence of images without clear gutters. For example, in the October 31, 1897, *Journal*, Outcault presents six sequential images of The Yellow Kid with each image presenting a quick succession of events. The Yellow Kid, attempting to hide from a neighborhood girl, backs into a wooden fence with a hole in it, not realizing that a dog is on the other side. When the neighborhood girl finds him, the dog behind the fence has bitten into The Yellow Kid's hindquarters and tears out a large hole in the Kid's nightshirt. As he pulls away, he realizes his embarrassing predicament and excuses himself to find new clothes. Each image in the brief narrative is subtly separated to form a sequence, the pattern known today as sequential art and essential to comics narrative.

Outcault's inventive use of image and sequence was not the only innovation being developed in comics. Over the next decades, many of the familiar conventions of comics, such as word balloons, gutters, panels of varying sizes, and techniques of lines depicting movement became more standardized and commonplace. While many of the conventions of comics were taking root, the ingenuity of comic creators expanded. Winsor McCay's, *Little Nemo in Slumberland*, James Swinnerton's, *Little Jimmy*, Bud Fisher's *Mutt and Jeff*, George Harriman's *Krazy Kat*, and many others began to demonstrate the creative potential of the medium.

Although many of the most successful comic strips were clever and innovative, early strips had no pretentions to being considered art, let alone high art. For newspaper publishers, the comics served a commercial and highly utilitarian purpose—to increase the sales of their newspapers. For comic artists, comics were a means for displaying creativity, social commentary, or just silliness. Comic readers also played a role in the production of comic strips as their tastes greatly influenced which comic strips survived and which ones did not. The newspapers were swift to maintain popular strips and just as swift to end ones that were not. And, as a popular medium, early comic strips often reflected the hardships of the downtrodden and the lower classes, who, in the large cities where the newspapers were published, were often immigrants with limited English skills. Many of these strips displayed "skepticism toward authority" and "spoke to and of the swelling immigrant populations in New York and other cities" (Hajdu 11). As David Hadju explains, "The comics offered their audience a parodic look at itself, rendered in the vernacular of caricature and nonsense language. The mockery in comics was familial—intimate, knowing, affectionate, and merciless" (11). The dual effects of these comic strips were to give voice to the lower classes and to make their struggles, indignities, and injustices known to the upper classes.

Proto-comics

As with many other successful innovations, progress toward the comic book was rather fitful. In 1911, the promotional manager of the *Chicago American*, Calvin Harris, ordered 10,000 copies of a six-inch high by eighteen-inch wide book compiling previously printed *Mutt and Jeff* comic strips. Readers of the *American* who clipped and mailed in six successive coupons from the paper, along with a small fee, would be sent a copy of the book. To the surprise of Harris and his employers, over 45,000 orders flooded the *American*'s office (Waugh 335–36). From 1919 to 1934, Cupples & Leon sold 9½-inch square black and white reprints of comic strips (Duncan & Smith 27). In 1922, Embee Distributing Company published *Comic Monthly* on cheaper paper and sold each copy for ten cents on newsstands. The run ended after its twelfth book (Duncan & Smith 27). In 1933, Eastern Color Printing Company published what is generally considered the first comic book—*Funnies on Parade*. The smaller, four-color reprint of various comic strips was used as a give-away by Procter & Gamble. The next year, Maxwell Charles Gaines placed ten-cent stickers on *Famous Funnies* and had them set out on newsstands. They sold out quickly and the comic book industry was born (Lente & Dunlavey 27–28).

The Original "Comics"

In 1935, the eccentric Major Malcolm Wheeler-Nicholson began printing *New Fun* with previously unpublished material. He collected previously rejected comic strips and published them in black and white in a thirty-six-page tabloid format (Hajdu 19). The varying quality of the works and the reluctance of newsstands to carry the comic book caused Wheeler-Nicholson's *New Fun* to struggle. Between 1936 and 1939, three major factors contributed to the emergence of the comic magazine as an established product of American popular publishing; these included 1) the increase of the number of themed magazines, 2) the increase of the number of publishers, and 3) the appearance of Superman, the first superhero of the Golden Age (Gabilliet 14). In late 1936 and early 1937, the first themed comic books were published by Comics Magazine Company, Ultem, and DC (*Detective Picture Stories* #1, *Star Ranger* #1, and *Detective Comics* #1, respectively). These titles broke with the standard content of comics, offering readers western-themed, detective, and crime narratives. *Detective Comics*, which still exists today, "was to embody the rise of the publishing outfit founded by Wheeler-Nicholson's magazines" (Gabilliet 15). In the face of his rising debts, Wheeler-Nicholson partnered with his primary creditor, Harry Donenfeld, and Jack S. Liebowitz, in order to form DC, or "Detective Comics, Inc." (16). By 1938, Wheeler-Nicholson had sold his company and his interests to his creditors, which included Detective Comics (Duncan & Smith 31).

That same year, the most significant comic book in the industry's history was published: *Action Comics* #1. For six years, two old high school friends, Jerry Siegel and Joe Shuster, had shopped their character Superman as a newspaper strip and as a comic book character and received no less than seventeen rejection letters (Van Lente & Dunlavey 31; Duncan & Smith 32). Eventually, editor Vincent Sullivan of National Allied Publications accepted Superman for the newly created series to the bewilderment of his employer, Harry Donenfield. Donenfield, upon seeing Superman lifting a car above his head on the cover of the first issue, roundly criticized the absurd image. Superman wouldn't appear on the cover of *Action Comics* again until issue seven. After discovering that children were asking newsstand operators for Superman by name, Donenfield had a change of heart. From issue nine forward, Superman's name or likeness appeared on every cover since. Within two years, the series was selling five-hundred thousand copies a month (Hajdu 31).

The Superman character touched a chord with many readers. Siegel and Shuster had created a hero that was fresh, yet familiar. Superman spoke to the desire for strength and autonomy in a time when few had either. In 1938, the Great Depression gripped the nation and the world; the unemployment rate in the United States was at nineteen percent, and despair and insecurity were widespread.

Superman appeared as a savior, a man who embodied the inward fantasies of young and old alike. Not a few critics have seen elements in the Superman narrative that suggest his being a Christ-like or some other messianic figure, and not a few have sought to problematize this interpretation (Babka; Fingeroth; Garrett; Hajdu; Lewis; Schenck; Weinstein, et al.). However Superman is to be read, as a Christ-figure, a Moses-figure, or something else, the character arrived when his readers were ready to accept him.

The success of Superman led to a massive expansion of the comic book industry over the next few years. In 1939, *Detective Comics* #27 introduced the first adventures of Batman (Gabilliet 19). In the same year, eight new publishers appeared, including Martin Goodman's Timely Comics, which would become the future Marvel Comics (17). As Charles Hatfield notes in his discussion of the origins of Marvel, "the company's history is a maze: known among collectors as Timely, then Atlas [. . .] began in 1939 with a single comic book" (*Hand of Fire* 81). Goodman, in concert with Funnies Incorporated, ordered a new comic book entitled *Marvel Comics*, whose first issue included the original Human Torch, Jim Hammond (Benton 30). DC introduced The Flash (Jay Garrick) in the 1940 *Flash Comics* #1 (Benton 13); Marvel launched *Captain America Comics* #1 in 1941 (Gabilliet 22); and in 1942, DC introduced Wonder Woman in *All-Star Comics* #8 (Benton 191). As Jean-Paul Gabilliet notes, during this time period:

> costumed crime fighters had become the first character types designed primarily for comic books thanks to their graphic and visual potential. In comic-strip form, the stories starring these protagonists made for a much more intense reading experience [. . . .] Superheroes, then, were the first characters to be identified with the comic magazine (19).

New and established publishers—Dell, Fawcett, Lev Gleason, Harvey, EC, Ziff-Davis, and others—joined the frenzy trying to tap into this new market. Hadju notes that:

Comics were in their gold-rush period, a frenzied era of speculation, experimentation, easy rewards, and a kind of aesthetic lawlessness, through the lack of clear, established standards and the limited accountability within the trade. The people creating and publishing comic books were competing by improvising, trying practically anything, rejecting almost nothing, in a freewheeling spirit of innovation entwined with opportunism born, for many, of desperation. (34)

Such boon periods and growth within popular culture would not, however, come without fringe concerns that would become wide-scale debate.

Even before the public's fascination with superheroes began to fade shortly after World War II, other genres of comics were coming to the fore. In 1942, Charles Biro and Bob Wood introduced a comic series that was reminiscent of the gangster films and true crime pulps that had already been popular for a couple of decades in their comic book *Crime Does Not Pay*. (Hajdu 59–60). What distinguished this comic from other crime comics was its gratuitous sensationalizing of violent crimes and its focus "almost solely on lawbreakers and their crimes, rather than crime-fighters and law enforcement" (Hajdu 63–64). The covers enticed with scenes of extreme violence: the cover of issue twenty-four shows a man holding a woman's head against a flaming gas burner; the cover of issue twenty-five shows a man in a phone booth being riddled with bullets; the cover of issue twenty-six shows a beaten man with tattered clothes being thrown from a moving car. And so on. The stories themselves glorified the violence, while at the same time striking a moralistic tone—the comics would decry a life of crime and always end with the perpetrators either being killed or arrested or sent to the electric chair or gallows.

Though the crime comics genre advanced slowly, it soon became dominant. Other crime comics appeared after World War II, with each one trying to "out-gore and out-sex" the other (Van Lente & Dunlavey 66). As the depiction of violence and gore increased, so did public criticism. Biro met this criticism head on, claiming that because the stories were true, which they weren't, that they were a deterrent to crime. However, as pressure continued to mount, Biro made concessions, while defending his product. Starting with issue sixty, the phrase "Dedicated to the eradication of crime!" was added to each cover. The inside front cover of issue sixty-three contained a message from Biro purportedly sharing with readers the "self-imposed censorship" Lev Gleason Publications expected its creators to follow. The message listed twelve standards, among them were the following: "[N]o attempt to emphasize sex appeal will be permitted for publication"; "[c]riminals will not be made attractive either in physical appearance or character"; "[c]riminals must not be shown to enjoy a criminal act." All three of these standards are violated in this very same comic.

Another genre that soon gained prominence was romance. In 1947, Joe Simon and Jack Kirby created *Young Romance*, a comic aimed at an older female readership by telling stories grounded in the real world. Joe Simon noted, "[W]e knew a lot of comic book readers were high school age and, as a result, they wanted to read about people a few years older, so that's how we approached *Young Romance*. We never talked down, and we were very realistic and adult" (Hajdu 159). By 1950, twenty percent of comics being sold were romance titles (Duncan & Smith 37). Ironically, the majority of writers and artists of romance comics were men. Most stories reflected the traditional values of the times and were rather tame as young women were faced with choosing between two men—one a hard-working, decent, if slightly dull man, the other a dangerous, but exciting, man of questionable reputation (Van Lente & Dunlavey 60). Though most of these comics reinforced traditional values, some romance comics challenged conventional boundaries, occasionally depicting teenage girls defying their parents and other authorities without consequence (Hajdu 161–62).

In 1950, EC Comics began to make significant innovations in the comic industry in both product and management. Bill Gaines, who had no interest in his father Max's EC Comics, was forced to take over the struggling company in 1947 when his father died in a boating accident. Max's vision for EC had been to create educational comics, but Bill began to move EC toward what he hoped would be a more profitable product, comics that entertained. At first Bill Gaines followed the trends, imitating comic series that were successful. That direction began to change when, after a discussion with artist Al Feldstein, Gaines decided to pursue making horror comics. In 1950, EC Comics introduced *The Crypt of Terror* (later renamed *Tales from the Crypt*) and *The Vault of Horror* along with *Weird Science*, *Weird Fantasy*, and *Two-Fisted Tales*, which presented realistic war stories. The stories that Gaines and Feldstein created often chaffed against societal norms: "Working allegorically through genre stories, they sought to engender sympathy for misfits, underdogs, and exiles of every breed—human, animal, fish, alien, living, dead, undead, and combinations thereof" (Hajdu 180). Family life was often depicted negatively, as was marriage (Hajdu 179). The message, it would seem, was that the world and its inhabitants could rarely be trusted.

Where EC excelled was in its treatment of its artists, who were paid above the going rates. Gaines also encouraged his artists to develop their own styles, unlike most other publishers who would require artists to conform to an in-house style. He also allowed writers to sign their names to their works (Hajdu 184–85). The result of these business practices were motivated artists and a high quality product that appealed to an older reader. These practices also resulted in many of the best comic book artists working for EC—Johnny Craig, Reed Crandall, Jack Davis, Will Elder, George Evans, Frank Frazetta, Graham Ingels, Bernard Krigstein, Harvey Kurtzman, Jack Kamen, Joe Orlando, John Severin, Marie Severin, Al Williamson, Basil Wolverton, Wally Woods, and others. With such a high quality product, EC's future seemed assured, but the industry was soon to experience a near death blow.

Controversy

A growing concern about the potential harmful effects of comic books was given credibility by the work of Fredric Wertham, a then highly respected and well-known psychiatrist. Comic books had often been the target of attacks that arose and subsided periodically, but Wertham's campaign against comic books gained significant traction when, after a six-month publicity campaign, he published *Seduction of the Innocent* in 1954. In the book, Wertham connected many forms of juvenile delinquency to children reading comic books. His campaign and many fearful media reports preceded the United States Senate Subcommittee on Juvenile Delinquency's hearings in New York on the effects of comic books on America's youth. While most comic book creators avoided appearing at the hearings, Gaines eagerly sought to be invited to the hearings so he could defend the industry. Gaines, though, underestimated the politics at play. He had not slept the night before as he was preparing his statement for the committee. At the hearing, Gaines' testimony was delayed. After waiting for hours, Gaines was medicating himself to stay awake. In his physical condition and having to face professional politicians, Gaines found himself in trouble. Estes Kefauver, Democratic senator from Tennessee who had presidential aspirations, confronted Gaines with the cover of *Crime SuspenStories* #22 depicting a man holding a woman's decapitated head by the hair in his left hand with a bloodied ax in his right. Kefauver asked Gaines if he thought the image was in good taste. Gaines' reply that he thought the image was in good taste caused most observers to become incredulous.

The resulting furor of the hearings led to the forming of the Comics Magazine Association of America (CMAA), which was granted wide censoring authority over the comic book industry. This group quickly developed and implemented the Comics Code, which identified strict standards comic books had to follow and required the inclusion of the Comics Code Authority stamp on works that met its criteria. The code set narrow standards for how crimes and romances could be depicted: it prohibited seductive clothing, profane dialogue, and negative portrayals of religion, race, marriage, or established authority; it even encouraged comic book writers to avoid bad grammar; the code also went so far as to prohibit certain advertisements (knives, toy guns, fireworks, questionable "toiletry products") and required publishers to "ascertain that all statements made in advertisements conform to the fact and avoid misinterpretation" ("Standards"). The code saved its most stringent rules for horror comics, going so far as to prohibit the use of the words "horror" and "terror" in comic book titles and to proscribe the creation of comics "dealing with [. . .] walking dead, torture, vampires, and vampirism, ghouls, cannibalism and werewolfism" ("Standards"). Essentially, the CMAA banned EC from publishing the majority of its comics. The code was rigorously, if arbitrarily, enforced. Printers refused to print comics without the seal. Distributors refused to distribute comics without the seal. Newsstands refused to sell comics without the seal (Hajdu 310). By 1956, EC stopped publishing comics altogether.

The Return and Rise of the Superhero

With comic books now being sanitized and with television becoming a more affordable option, comic book sales began a steady decline (Duncan & Smith 40). Artists found less work available and were offered less money for the work they could find (Duncan & Smith 41). Many companies stopped publishing comics in the 1950s: EC, Eastern Color, Fawcett, Fiction House, Fox Feature Syndicate, Lev Gleason Publications, Quality Comics, St. John, and Standard either closed their doors or were sold to other publishers. One company, DC Comics, was able to survive. In the 1950s, DC was one of the larger comic book companies; it was publishing a variety of comic book genres and still had a few of its superhero comics selling sufficiently well to maintain their publication (42–43). It was during this time period that DC's "three pillars" (Superman, Batman, and Wonder Woman) achieved iconic status in the realm of the superhero genre because of their "exceptional popularity" (Gabilliet 51). The Comics Code may have inadvertently helped the superhero genre to strengthen its footing. As Randy Duncan and Matthew Smith have argued, "The sanitized violence and moral purity of superhero comic books might not have been as titillating as the sexy and gory of the early fifties, but they were a good fit with the standards of the new Comics Code" (45).

Shortly after the code was enacted, longtime DC editor Julius "Julie" Schwartz began updating and reintroducing a number of its superhero characters, who had not seen print for a number of years. In 1956, *Showcase* #4 reintroduced the Flash with a new costume and a new identity (Duncan & Smith 45); this event marked the beginning of the "Silver Age" of comic books (Gabilliet 51).

This new Flash seemed more sophisticated and a better fit with contemporary sensibilities and began to sell well (Van Lente & Dunlavey 97). After this success, Schwartz had the Green Lantern reintroduced as new character Hal Jordan in *Showcase* #22 in 1959, followed by a reworked Justice Society of America, which was updated to the Justice League of America in 1960. Reinventing familiar superheroes helped DC maintain its position in the comic book industry.

The most significant advance in the superhero genre was not to come from DC, however, but from the struggling comic book publisher Marvel. Stan Lee, working for Martin Goodman, was tasked with creating his own superhero group. Lee and collaborator Jack Kirby created the Fantastic Four. Unlike other superheroes, the Fantastic Four was set in the real world. They didn't live in Gotham, Central City, or Metropolis, but rather in New York City. They also displayed human failings. The members of the group irritated one another, bickered, and had real world fears, concerns, and insecurities. *The Fantastic Four* quickly garnered readers. With this success, Marvel quickly created more heroes with more human frailties: Spider-Man, the Hulk, Iron Man, Daredevil, and countless others. This inclusion of realism was to be a characteristic of Marvel Comics and led to its rapid growth within the industry. Throughout the 1960s, superheroes once again ruled the comic book universe.

Underground Comix

Up to this point in the history of comics, the primary motivation for comic creation had been commercial. Whether it was to sell more newspapers or simply to sell a stand-alone product, the creative process of comics was beholden to financial concerns. If comics did not sell, they would disappear from the market. Comics followed and reflected popular trends, and though the furor surrounding horror and crime comics had been loud and destructive to the industry, the challenges to mainstream ideology had been slight. A significant fracturing in comics was soon to take place where ideological concerns, self-expression, and defiance of authority were to take precedence over commercial viability.

These new comics were underground comix. In the early 1960s, many college-aged young people began making and distributing their own comics "in college humor magazines and countercultural newspapers" (Duncan & Smith 52). A number of these early artists (Frank Stack, Gilbert Shelton, Jack Jackson, and others) rose to prominence later in the decade. The first major milepost in underground comix came when Robert Crumb published *Zap* #1 in 1968. Charles Hatfield states that "Zap became the catalyst for a whole new field of comix publishing because Crumb took back the comic book and redefined what it could do" (*Alternative Comics* 8). Soon to follow were other series and works: *The Fabulous Furry Freak Brothers* by Gilbert Shelton, *Bijou Funnies* by Jay Lynch, *Binky Brown Meets the Holy Virgin Mary* by Justin Green. Inventive, offensive, and certainly not for children, underground comix were a thumb in the eye of the dominant culture. With wanton display of sexual fantasies, graphic violence, drug use, and savage satire, the underground's main goal was to mock and offend the dominant power structures of the culture.

But undergrounds were more than just insolence and taboo breaking. Underground comix demonstrated that the medium itself did not have to be limited to children's fare, and though many underground comix seemed to be little more than angry rants against authority, others demonstrated that comix could address broader cultural issues and even develop new forms within the medium that were highly personal, while speaking to the human condition. In 1972, a group of women artists published *Wimmen's Comix* #1. The first issue contained stories dealing with a woman's self-loathing, an illegal abortion, sexual harassment in the workplace, a condescending male patriarchy, a young lesbian's first experience at a gay bar, and other stories confronting contemporary issues. Also in 1972, Justin Green's *Binky Brown Meets the Holy Virgin Mary* introduced deeply confessional autobiography to comix, a form that has become dominant in literary comics (Witek 227).

The 1970s proved to be a challenging decade for the large publishers. During this time period, the market was shared by six mainstream publishers: Archie, Charlton, DC, Gold Key, Harvey, and Marvel, of which DC and Marvel were the largest (Gabilliet 72–73). On a much smaller scale than the taboo-breaking narratives of the emerging underground comix, mainstream comic books also began to explore political issues and to "call into question the dominant ideology that had always been the implicit frame of reference for comics" (Gabilliet 74–75). Significantly, DC overhauled Green Lantern to package him alongside Green Arrow and Marvel redirected *The Amazing Spider-Man* to tackle issues such as intolerance and drug addiction, respectively (Gabilliet 75).

The Emergence of the Alternatives and the Recovery Era

With the end of the Vietnam War, the unifying event for the counterculture and comix, and with obscenity laws being enforced against many undergrounds, the underground comix movement began to fracture (Duncan & Smith 57). Growing out of underground comix were alternative comics, which added greater narrative sophistication, artistic complexity, and thematic concerns to the medium. Hatfield states that:

> Though driven by the example of underground comix, many alternative comics cultivated a more considered approach to the art form, less dependent on the outrageous gouging of taboos (though that continued too, of course) and more open to the possibility of extended and ambitious narratives. (*Alternative Comics* x)

From the mid-1970s through today, alternative comics have come of age and have even influenced the maturing of mainstream comics. Works like Harvey Pekar's *American Splendor*, Art Spiegelman's *Raw*, R. Crumb's *Weirdo*, Dave Sim's *Cerebus*, Los Hernandez brothers' *Love and Rockets*, Alison Bechdel's *Dykes to Watch Out For* have pushed comics toward a greater maturity. Alternative comics have been marked by their "rejection of mainstream formulas," their development of "autobiography, reportage, and historical fiction," their willingness to embrace international art styles, and their penetrating frankness in dealing with personal and political themes (Hatfield, *Alternative Comics* x).

Since the 1970s, new publishers and creators, prizing greater creative freedom than in the past, rejected the norms instituted by the CMAA in the 1950s, as well as all affiliation with the CCA. The first examples of this at Marvel were the escalations in the representation of violence in Frank Miller's final issues of *Daredevil*, and Alan Moore's neo-gothic work on *Saga of the Swamp Thing* at DC (Gabilliet 90). In the 1980s, DC went a step further and embraced the frankness of the 70s with two books that would come to define the larger period of history to follow: Miller's *Batman: The Dark Knight Returns* and Alan Moore and Dave Gibbons' *Watchmen*, both released serially. The dark and gritty reinterpretations of older characters resonated with the comics readership at large and energized the industry to reconsider otherwise staid constructions of their characters.

Along with alternative comics, a number of independent comic publishers arose. These independents attempted to break into the comics market and targeted regular readers of Marvel and DC (Duncan & Smith 65). Independents appealed to established creators as these startups were not beholden to the Comics Code Authority, since their books were marketed exclusively to comic book specialty shops. Independents also "often paid royalties and allowed creators to retain ownership of their intellectual properties" (Duncan & Smith 66). After initial success, a downturn in the comics market in the 1990s led many independents to close their doors, but others, such as Image Comics and Dark Horse Comics have become mainstays in the comic industry. Influenced by both alternative and independent comics, DC and Marvel created separate imprints for creator-owned titles: Vertigo (1993) and Icon (2004), respectively.

Recovery continued with a reimagination of the packaging and marketing of the product as well. During the 1990s, comics began to emerge in the book market with the 'invention' of the graphic novel, or the long-form comic, which encompassed three different forms: collections of newspaper comic strips (*Peanuts* and *Garfield*); collections of comics that were previously published as comic books (*Batman: The Dark Knight Returns* and *Watchmen*, as they are so frequently considered, fit this model perfectly); and books that contained new complete stories from alternative press outlets, which had been previously serialized, such as Art Spiegelman's Pulitzer Prize Winning *Maus* and Daniel Clowes' *Ghost World* (Gabilliet 98–100). As these books took off in popularity, longer works of original content also labeled as graphic novels (itself an increasing contentious if not nebulous term) arose and populated bookstore shelves and online purveyors of comics.

Over the last several decades, the medium of comics has matured, along with its readers. In 1947, Coulton Waugh predicted, "How this tremendous use of comic books will be developed remains to be ticked out on history's teletype, but that it will, seems so certain that when you pick up one of these ugly little books you may be sure you are looking at the crude ancestor of something great" (347). Seven-plus decades later, the literary richness and visual complexity of the form is apparent—Chris Ware, Alan Moore, Art Spiegelman, Gene Luen Yang, and countless others have created works of lasting significance. Comics as a popular medium will remain, even as its artistic and literary borders continue to expand.

Works Cited

Babka, Susie Paulik. "Arius, Superman, and the *Tertium Quid*: When Popular Culture Meets Christology." *Irish Theological Quarterly*. 73 (2008): 113–132.

Benton, Mike. *Superhero Comics of the Golden Age: The Illustrated History*. Dallas: Taylor Publishing Company, 1992.

Biro, Charles & Bob Wood, eds. *Crime Does Not Pay*. New York: Lev Gleason Publications. 63 (May 1948).

Duncan, Randy & Matthew J. Smith. *The Power of Comics: History, Form, and Culture*. New York: Continuum, 2009.

Fingeroth, Danny. *Disguised as Clark Kent: Jews, Comics, and the Creation of the Superhero*. New York: Continuum, 2007.

_____. *The Fortunes of Ferdinand Flipper*. New York: The Brother Jonathan Office, n.d. Web. 01 Mar. 2014.

Gabilliet, Jean-Paul. *Of Comics and Men: A Cultural History of American Comic Books*. Trans. Beaty, Bart & Nick Nguyen. Jackson: UP of Mississippi, 2005.

Garrett, Greg. *Holy Superheroes! Exploring the Sacred in Comics, Graphic Novels, and Film*. Louisville, KY: Westminster John Knox Press, 2008.

Hajdu, David. *The Ten-cent Plague: The Great Comic-book Scare and How It Changed America*. New York: Farrar, Straus & Giroux, 2008.

Hatfield, Charles. *Alternative Comics: An Emerging Literature*. Jackson: UP of Mississippi, 2005.

_____. *Hand of Fire: The Comics Art of Jack Kirby*. Jackson: UP of Mississippi, 2012.

Harvey, Robert C. "How Comics Came to Be." *A Comics Studies Reader*. Ed. Jeet Heer & Kent Worcester. Jackson: UP of Mississippi, 2009. 25–45.

Lewis, A. David. "Superman Graveside." *Graven Images: Religion in Comic Books and Graphic Novels*. Ed. A. David Lewis & Christine Hoff Kraemer. New York: Continuum, 2010. 166–87.

Schenck, Ken. "Superman: A Popular Culture Messiah." *The Gospel According to Superheroes*. Ed. B. J. Oropeza. New York: Peter Lang Publishers, 2005. 33–48.

"Standards of the Comics Code Authority for Editorial Matter as Originally Adopted." *The ComicsBooks.com: The History of Comic Books*. TheComicsBooks.com. n.d. Web. 6 Mar. 2014.

Van Lente, Fred, & Ryan Dunlavey. *The Comic Book History of Comics*. San Diego: IDW, 2012.

Waugh, Coulton. *The Comics*. 1947. Jackson: UP of Mississippi, 1991.

Weinstein, Simcha. *Up, Up, and Oy Vey!* Baltimore: Leviathan, 2006.

Witek, Joseph. "Justin Green: Autobiography Meets Comics." *Graphic Subjects: Critical Essays on Autobiography and Graphic Novels*. Ed. Michael A. Chaney. Madison: U of Wisconsin P, 2011. 227–30.

Hiding the Forbidden Fruit: Comics Censorship in the United States_____

Kim Munson

For as long as comics have been widely available in the United States, critics ranging from Congressmen to clergymen have cast them in the role of the snake in the Garden of Eden; certainly, this has been the case since 1954, when Fredric Wertham's *Seduction of the Innocent* accused comics of enticing children and gullible adults with bright colors and familiar characters and then corrupting their innocence with lurid depictions of sex and violence. After decades of legal battles, arguments about First Amendment freedoms, the repression of mature content, and conflicting psychological studies regarding their impact, all the critical community has[by way of consensus in regards to the question of whether comics are harmful is that it depends upon the person and the context. Are comics that show nudity or graphic violence harmful to children? And at what point does childhood begin or, arguably, end *en route* to a maturity capable of handling such salacious inquiry? This chapter will sample some of the perspectives that have swayed public opinion, influenced the content depicted in comics, and, in some cases, drastically changed the lives of those in the comics community and beyond.

Criticism of "Low Class" Comics in the 1900s

The earliest complaints regarding newspaper comic strips in the United States were rooted more in criticism of their appeal to a lower class taste than about sex or violence, but, in that critique, one can see the outline of every comics censorship argument that followed. In the early 1900s, newspapers were the most prominent (and, in many places, the only) form of mass media available. Joseph Pulitzer, publisher of the newspaper *The New York World,* sought a way to differentiate himself from his competition and find new readership. To attract working class people, who were often immigrants and either illiterate or unable to read English, he printed *The World's* first Sunday comics supplement on November 18, 1894 (Harvey 8). Printed in color on four seventeen-by-twenty-three inch pages, the supplement's first hit was a strip called *Hogan's Alley* by Richard Felton Outcault, which starred The Yellow Kid, a bald little boy in an oversized yellow nightshirt. The Kid was barefoot, inarticulate, and focused on the simple pleasures in life. He spoke broken English to his friends, who, themselves, were broad stereotypes of New York immigrants. The few adult authority figures that appeared were outsmarted and abused by the Kid and his pals. The strip mirrored the dreams of New York's working class, dubious of authority and yearning to be free.

William Randolph Hearst, publisher of *The New York Journal*, stole Outcault away, and the creation of other popular strips for Hearst soon followed, such as the *Katzenjammer Kids* and *Happy Hooligan*. The beleaguered working class finally had something of their own that was created for and spoke to them. Historian David Hadju, author of *The Ten Cent Plague: The Great Comic Book Scare and How it Changed America,* explains:

> Unlike movements in the fine arts that crossed class lines to evoke the lives of working people, newspaper comics were proletarian in a contained, inclusive way. They did not draw upon alleys like Hogan's as a resource for refined expression, as Toulouse-Lautrec had employed the Moulin Rouge, nor did they use Hooligan's clashes with the law for pedagogy, to expose the powerful to the plight of the underclass, as John Steinbeck would utilize Cannery Row. The comics offered their audience a parodic look at itself, rendered in the vernacular of caricature and nonsense language. The mockery in comics was familial—intimate, knowing, affectionate, and merciless. (11)

Loving derision, as such, generally translated into favorable audience reaction and financial returns for the papers.

Granted, the Sunday "Funnies" were not loved by everyone. By 1906, articles critical of the strips began to appear in magazines. Seen through the lens of the art and literature available to upper class citizens, the Sunday comics were accused of being raucous and savage by comparison, opening up a brutal and unsophisticated world to impressionable children. This point of view, that the Sunday Funnies were tawdry and badly drawn, that they exalted violence, lawlessness, and undercut literacy, is exemplified by the challenge to parents that appeared in the 1909 *Ladies' Home Journal* article "A Crime Against American Children":

> Are we parents criminally negligent of our children, or is it that we have not put our minds on the subject of continuing to allow them to be injured by the inane and vulgar "comic" supplement of the Sunday newspaper? One thing is certain: we are permitting to go on under our very noses and in our own homes an extraordinary stupidity, and an influence for repulsive and often depraving vulgarity so colossal that it is rapidly taking on the dimensions of nothing short of a national crime against our children. (Hajdu 12)

For the most part, newspapers ignored this criticism, and the comics pages absorbed it and, if they were listening at all, responded by creating more refined strips, such as George Herriman's *Krazy Kat* and Winsor McCay's *Little Nemo in Slumberland*. The generation of children who grew up reading the Sunday supplements started creating comics of their own, looking to pulp magazines, like *Dime Detective* and *Amazing Stories* for inspiration. Many classic detective and adventure strips grew out of this brew, such as *Dick Tracy* (Chester Gould, which premiered in 1931); *Terry and the Pirates* (Milton Caniff, 1934); *Flash Gordon* (Alex Raymond, 1934); *Prince Valiant* (Hal Foster, 1937); and *The Spirit* (Will Eisner, 1940). (Walker 320, 370, 360, 373, 378) These heroic epics, beautifully drawn, resonated with adolescent boys and working class men who, historically, were seen as the core readership at the time. The strips reflected the assimilation of these former immigrants into the mainstream of American life and their adoption of the American Dream.

Juvenile Delinquency and the Post-War Comics Scare
Strips of the action-adventure variety continued to be popular into the 1930s, both in the newspapers and as collections reprinted in

comic books. Comic books featuring original material began to appear around 1935, and in 1938, *Action Comics* premiered Jerry Siegel and Joe Shuster's landmark character, Superman, an event that arguably vaulted the superhero genre into the stratosphere and was quickly followed by Captain Marvel, Batman, and other heroes. Publishers kept looking for new ways to entertain their audience of men and boys, and a proliferation of crime and detective titles ensued. These books were often lurid, with depictions of violent crime and scantily clad women, featuring uncomplicated plots aimed at the same working class readers who once enjoyed the Sunday Funnies with similar aplomb.

Criticism of comics also continued, with articles disparaging comics appearing in major newspapers and in mass circulation magazines like *The Atlantic Monthly*. Alongside the previous complaints of lawlessness and violence, one literary critic, Sterling North, wrote in the May 8, 1940 edition of *The Chicago Daily News* that comics were so badly drawn, written, and printed that they would strain young eyes and ruin their perception of color. The National Organization for Decent Literature, a Catholic organization formed in 1939, provided concerned churchgoers with a list of forbidden comic books.

Still, there were many leaders who were unconvinced by these arguments. Childrearing expert Josette Frank wrote in her popular 1939 handbook for parents, *What Books for Children?* that comics gave children an indirect outlet for emotional expression, saying: "However unacceptable they may be to adults, the comic strips continue to appeal to children; and for valid reasons" (Hajdu 60). She goes on to explain that by reading comics, children are able to experience the "pleasure of transgressing," but their guilt is immediately cleared away by the culprit in the tale receiving punishment for their actions and that children often find wicked and violent actions funny. Frank explains, "How far such stories meet a deep psychic need of childhood we can only surmise," noting "that they do fill such a need seems evident" (Hajdu 61). While there may have been vehement criticism of comics in some circles, there was no hard evidence that comics were harmful to anyone, and, at that time, there was no movement toward large-scale censorship.

Comics publishers redeemed themselves somewhat during the World War II era, as they wrote stories of their superheroes supporting the war effort. Popular heroes, like Superman, Batman, Wonder Woman, Captain America, and the Sub-Mariner, helped to foil Nazi plots and sell war bonds. They encouraged their young readers to take positive action, like collecting scrap metal for weapons manufacturing. By the end of the war, the comics industry was booming with some 25,000,000 comic books sold a month. Unfortunately for the publishers, this boom did not last: their war-time efforts came up short as the post-war era brought renewed and intensified scrutiny of the comics industry, accusations that were accepted with such public fervor that it almost destroyed the industry.

In general, Americans were concerned about the direction of the country in the post-war era, as they refined their world within new outlines of consumer consumption and experienced new worries about the post-nuclear age and the political Cold War. They had seen how effectively the Nazis used mass media to manipulate their citizens, and they were suspicious of anything that seemed to question or attack what they saw as traditional American values imparted by parents, teachers, and religion. The war had disrupted families. Mothers left the home and entered the workforce as fathers fought overseas, leaving children with an unprecedented amount of free time without parental oversight. Teens began to develop their own interests and culture, and concerned adults began to worry about these disturbing changes, which they called juvenile delinquency.

Branford W. Wright, author of *Comic Book Nation: the Transformation of Youth Culture in America,* explains:

> Much of what concerned adults termed juvenile delinquency was simply adolescents asserting their independence and discovering themselves as individuals within their peer group [. . . .] Statistics did not support the widespread fears about rising juvenile crime, but the press, professional "experts," civic groups, and government agencies all heightened public anxiety about it nevertheless [. . . .] Comic books were an easy target for those who attributed juvenile delinquency to products of youth culture. The most visible, least censored, and most

popular expression of youth entertainment, comic books were also the most bewildering and alien medium to adult sensibilities. (88)

Critics equated the coincidental proliferation of crime, jungle, and other lurid comics with the perceived rise in juvenile delinquency. As the controversy grew, all types of comics came under attack as the comic book industry became labeled as a subversive entity out to corrupt the impressionable minds of the nation's youth.

Not everyone agreed with this view. Echoing some of the observations of Josette Frank, the influential Dr. Benjamin Spock sought to reassure parents about comics in the first edition of *The Common Sense Book of Baby and Child Care,* noting that children between the ages of six and ten believed that they knew the difference between right and wrong and enjoyed seeing right triumph. He advised moderation and encouraged parents to regulate their children's comics reading instead of banning it outright, feeling that the comics allowed them to "indulge their aggressive impulses without acting on them" (Wright 89). Other articles around this time concurred, saying that young people were aware of the modern world and, with the proper parental guidance, knew reality from fiction. A New York folklorist named Gershon Legman contributed a particularly unique viewpoint to the critical dialogue about comics. *In Love and Death: A Study in Censorship*, a hundred-page book self-published in 1949, he blamed censorship itself for the perversion of American culture. Legman argued that since obscenity laws hindered the open discussion of sex and demonized its depiction, violence became a titillating substitute (Wright 91). He questioned this odd double standard and said that the problem with comics was actually a symptom of the American public's repression of sex and subsequent addiction to violence (Wright 92). That said, he did not approve of comics and felt that superhero comics particularly had fascist overtones. Aside from a review in *The New Republic*, his argument seemed to fall on deaf ears. America did not seem to be in the mood for his brand of introspection.

Unfortunately for comics readers and publishers, instead of introspection, hysteria over comics had begun to take root.

According to local newspaper accounts, between 1945 and 1948, there were public burnings of comic books organized by parochial schools in Binghamton, New York; Auburn, New York; and Chicago (Hajdu 114–127). A trio of juvenile crimes supposedly inspired by comics were especially troubling: a young boy accidently hanged himself; three young boys tied up a friend and tortured him with lit matches; and in 1948, two boys (aged six and eleven) stole a small plane and flew it across Oklahoma, telling police that they learned how to do it from a comic book.

In 1947, a spokesman for the American Bar Association stated that youth crime was growing, and that these crimes were not the only danger that may arise from comics emphasizing violent crime. He maintained that even if no crime were evident in a particular location, these books weakened the "moral codes and ethical concepts" of American youth (Wright 90). He concluded by saying that "with almost every child and adolescent bombarded many times daily with the jargon of the criminal and horrors and depraved method of his activity, we should rejoice that we have as much normal and rational child behavior as we do" (90). Everyone from the Fraternal Order of Police to J. Edgar Hoover, Director of the FBI, warned of the evils of comics. The movement against comics was building to a head, and in 1948, it found a leader in the aforementioned Dr. Fredric Wertham, the psychologist whose publication of *Seduction of the Innocent* would launch a puritanical censorship campaign, leading to the Comics Code Authority, an agreement to self-censor by the comics publishers that would change the course of comics for decades.

Seduction of the Innocent and the Comics Code Authority

Dr. Fredric Wertham (1895–1981) was born in Bavaria and immigrated to the US in 1922 after finishing his medical training in Europe. In 1932, he became the senior psychiatrist at Bellevue Hospital in New York City, moving on to direct the Psychiatric Clinic at Queens Hospital Center. He established the Lefargue Clinic for low income individuals in Harlem in 1946, and it was there that he began to study the effects of comics reading upon children. He believed he had found a causal link between comics and the experiences of the juvenile offenders he treated after hearing repeated admissions from his patients that comics, especially the violent and lurid ones, were their favorite form of entertainment. *Publishers Weekly* estimated that 540,000,000 comic books were printed in 1946, and despite the critics, comic reading by children was still mostly unregulated and unsupervised (Wright 88).

By 1948, Wertham had become known as the leading authority on the topic of comics and juvenile delinquency. In March of that year, he got his first opportunity to share his theories with a national audience when *Collier's* magazine published "Horror in the Nursery" a substantial article by Judith Crist that extensively quoted Wertham and his assistants. In the same month, Wertham's presentation to the Association for the Advancement of Psychotherapy, entitled *The Psychopathology of Comic Books,* received generous coverage from *Time* magazine. In May, *The Saturday Review of Literature* published his second article "The Comics . . . Very Funny," which was also reprinted in *Reader's Digest*. In these articles, Wertham accused comics of eroding the moral fiber of children and told stories of crimes committed by his young patients that he insisted could only be inspired by comic books. He spoke of the sexual threat of comics, that women in comics were sexually exploited, violently assaulted, and unrealistically drawn. He argued that the exaggerated physical attributes of these women would give young girls an inferiority complex, possibly even resulting in a fear of sex or frigidity. Attention getting panels from the worst of the crime comics were reprinted out of context to bolster his claims.

By July of 1948, cities across the United States had begun to limit sales of comics, and comics publishers responded by forming the Association of Comics Magazine Publishers (ACMP). Hoping to head off an outright ban of comics, the members of the ACMP offered to comply with a self-regulatory code of standards, but Wertham felt that the publishers did not go far enough, and he continued to attack both comics and the new code. By 1953, a few months after the creation of the US Senate Subcommittee to Investigate

Juvenile Delinquency, the *Ladies' Home Journal* published several excerpts of Wertham's forthcoming book, *Seduction of the Innocent*, in their November issue. *Seduction,* written for a wide audience of laypeople, renewed and expanded upon Wertham's previous accusations against comics and comics publishers.

When the subcommittee's hearings on the influence of comic books began on April 21, 1954, Wertham was scheduled to testify on the first day. He told the committee that they were making a mistake by limiting their inquiry to violent crime and horror comics because violence was found in all comic book genres and that there was no question comics had a negative effect on children; the only question was how far reaching that effect would be. Ultimately, the most widely reported testimony of the hearings was not by Wertham, but by EC Comics publisher William Gaines, who attempted to defend a gruesome cover drawing of a woman's severed head by saying that he thought it was in good taste *for a horror comic*. In the end, the subcommittee decided to leave the regulation of comics content to the publishers, a finding Wertham felt was inadequate and a disservice to the American public.

Other experts were critical of Wertham and his research methodology. As Wright points out:

> The flaws in his arguments were obvious. It was hardly surprising that juvenile delinquents read comic books, since upwards of 90 percent of all children and adolescents read them. Wertham devoted intense clinical study to the worst juvenile behavior, but he could not account for the millions of young people who read comic books and demonstrated perfectly normal behavior and attitudes. (96)

While his sweeping claim that all children were negatively influenced by comics could be ignored, Wertham's claim that certain disturbed children could be inspired to attempt copy-cat crimes by particularly violent comics was harder to dismiss. In response to his critics, Wertham accused experts defending comics as paid shills and apologists, spreading propaganda for the industry.

The publishers, who had already formed the AMCP, had had mixed results in their previous attempts at self-regulation, with member publishers disagreeing on the definition of the standards for the content and balking at the expense of reviewing the artwork. After the 1954 hearings, they tried again, this time calling their new set of standards the Comics Code, to be administered by an industry group of experts called the Comics Code Authority. In creating the Code, they combined the film industry's Hayes Code, the AMCP's previous Code, and other in-house standards already adopted by the publishers resulted in the establishment of forty-one specific regulations.

The bulk of the Code dealt specifically with crime and horror comics, with horror comics being almost regulated out of existence. Interest in crime comics had already peaked by the time the Code was adopted, and publishers were seeing growing sales in horror and terror titles. They hoped that by sacrificing the lucrative horror books, the public would see that they were taking self-regulation seriously. Crime comics would still survive, but they had to follow the strict rules of the Code. Amy Kiste Nyberg, author of *Seal of Approval: the History of the Comics Code* explains:

> Without ever admitting that depiction of crime led young readers to become juvenile delinquents, the code nonetheless placed an emphasis on portraying crime in a negative light, on creating respect for established authority, on depicting commission of crime in such a way that young readers would not be tempted to imitate what they read, and on making sure that the excess violence was purged. (112)

The Code also attempted to placate conservative critics by banning profanity and obscenity, even warning against the use of slang that could promote use of bad grammar. "The Code spelled out ways in which comic book content would also uphold the moral values of society," Nyberg notes, "There was never to be any disrespect for established authority and social institutions. Good always triumphed over evil, and if evil had to be shown, it was only in order to deliver a moral message. Content would foster respect for parents and for honorable behavior" (113). Books that passed the review of the Comics Code Authority would be allowed to be published with the CCA's "Seal of Approval" on their covers.

Compliance with the CCA Code rapidly caused dramatic changes in the comics industry. Publishers were left mainly with, to borrow a rating from the movie industry, 'G-rated' romance, teen, and funny animal comics that were only suitable for children. Many comics publishers went out of business or stopped publishing comics all together, and creators/artists lost their jobs as the content changed and companies folded. Between 1954 and 1956, the number of comic titles published annually dropped from about 650 to 300, and eighteen publishers disappeared, with no new ones entering the field (Wright 179). The Code was revised twice, in 1971 and 1989, to adapt to America's changing moral views and because the distribution model had changed to a direct model that was not dependent on newsstand sales. This change in distribution lessened the impact of the Code since publishers could now bypass the traditional magazine distribution system. Although mainstream publishers, like DC and Marvel, cooperated with the CCA voluntarily, the ability to sell comics in specialty stores meant that comics could be distributed to retailers without the CCA's seal of approval, opening the way for more adult stories and a new wave of independent publishers.

The Comic Book Legal Defense Fund and Obscenity

Underground Comix appeared in the mid-1960s, reflecting the interests and values of the US counterculture. Rebelling against the sanitized stories offered by CCA-approved comics, the undergrounds showcased uncensored sex, use of illegal drugs, and satirical political commentary. They were distributed through an independent network of head shops, specialty shops, and college bookstores unconcerned with the supposed subversive content of these books.

By 1971, Marvel Comics also began to push the envelope, publishing a three-issue story arc in which Spider-Man finds out that his roommate is addicted to drugs. Conceived as an anti-drug story, Marvel initially requested permission for approval of the story line from the Comics Code Authority, but it denied the request. After going ahead and publishing the story anyway without the seal, Marvel reassured the CCA that they would adhere to the code in the future. This disagreement was one factor that led to the first revision of the code later that year. In the midst of this self-regulation of comics content, a key legal development occurred which would have a significant impact on the underground comics movement.

In their landmark 1973 decision, *Miller v California*, the US Supreme Court ended a decades-long effort to define obscenity by establishing a three-prong test: 1) a work would be found obscene if the average person, applying contemporary community standards, would find that the work, taken as a whole, appeals to the prurient interest; 2) that the work depicts or describes, in a patently offensive way, sexual conduct specifically defined by the applicable state law; and 3) that the work, taken as a whole, lacks serious literary, artistic, political, or scientific value (Greenberg 150). When this standard was established in 1973, sales of underground comix were already in decline as the counterculture movement came to an end, and self-censorship, due to the passage of *Miller*, was one of the final nails in the coffin. Contemporary community standards varied drastically from one region of the US to the other, and most of the national publishers of underground comix could not see a way to proceed with the content they were known for without inviting a lawsuit in certain parts of the country. As comics publishers gradually adapted or broke away from the rules of the Comics Code, the *Miller* verdict became one of the new tools of censorship.

These First Amendment battles have continued to the present day with even higher stakes than before, observes law professor and attorney Marc Greenberg. In his article "Comics, Courts and Controversy," Greenberg describes the events that led to the creation of the Comic Book Legal Defense Fund (CBLDF):

In December 1986, a Friendly Franks comics store in Lansing, Illinois, was raided by police. Six officers entered the store and seized seven books including *Omaha the Cat Dancer*, *Weirdo*, and *Heavy Metal*, which they suspected of obscenity. They arrested Michael Correa, the store's manager, and closed the store for five days. A few weeks later, they added *Elektra: Assassin*, *Ms. Tree*, *Bodessey*, *Elfquest*, and *Love & Rockets*. In addition to the charges of obscenity, Sargent Jack Hoestra, the arresting officer, told the *Gary Post Tribune* that he noticed a "satanic influence" in many of the comics sold at Friendly Franks, and then continued, saying "Oh yes, there was absolutely a lot of satanic influence in the comics there . . . If you know what you're looking for you can see the satanic influence all over." (137)

Frank Magiaracina, the owner of the Friendly Franks chain, called Denis Kitchen, owner of Kitchen Sink Press and publisher of *Omaha the Cat Dancer* to tell him the news. Kitchen was aghast at the lack of merit in the case and felt obligated to help Correa and Magiaracina. At a comics convention in St. Paul, Minnesota, he brainstormed with his friends and colleagues, and decided to create and sell a special limited edition portfolio to raise money for their legal fees. Kitchen was able to get fourteen artists to contribute artwork and a printer that would print the work at cost. Through the sale of the portfolio, Kitchen was able to raise twenty thousand dollars, which he deposited in a bank account he named the Comic Book Legal Defense Fund (CBLDF). Correa was tried and convicted of intent to disseminate obscene material before the Fund could help him mount a defense. Kitchen used CBLDF funds to hire Burton Joseph, a prominent attorney that specialized in First Amendment cases, and they won a reversal of the case on appeal, overturning Correa's conviction.

Seeing that he still had some money left and assuming that there would be similar cases in the future, Kitchen established the CBLDF as a non-profit organization in 1990. Since then, the Fund has aided in the defense of comic artists, retailers, and comics readers accused of obscenity and related charges. They have had many victories, but some of their losses have had life-changing consequences for the accused. For example, in Florida in 1994, despite the efforts of the Fund, comic artist Mike Diana was convicted of obscenity and was fined, jailed, and ordered not to draw during his three-year probation period. This was enforced by police who were allowed to search his home unannounced at any time. In Oklahoma in 1997, the co-owners of Planet Comics, Michael Kennedy and John Hunter, were charged with felony trafficking of obscenity and experienced two years of such intense harassment (bricks thrown through the glass door of their store, eviction, divorce, home searches by police) that they finally accepted a plea deal and closed their store forever. And last, but by no means least, in Iowa in 2006, manga fan Chris Handley was charged with owning "obscene visual representations of minors engaged in sexual conduct" and was sentenced to six months in prison, five years of probation, and had to forfeit his entire manga collection (thousands of books, of which only a tiny percentage contained sexual content). In this particular case, an adult was tried and convicted for reading and collecting comics in his own home merely because the books contained drawings of people of indiscriminate age having sexual contact. It was no longer the case that just the comics publishing industry had come under attack and was expected to self-regulate: now the focus had shifted onto distributors, individual creator/artists, and readers alike. These types of cases still occur to this day. As Charles Brownstein, the Executive Director of the CBLDF, told *Print* magazine's Michael Dooley:

> Today we're seeing unprecedented cultural appreciation of comics. But more instances of book bans and challenges happen every year, such as this year's attempted ban of *Persepolis* in Chicago. We're also seeing readers being targeted with criminal prosecutions for the content of the comics they read. Comics are at the heart of 21st century popular culture, but their power, derived from the static image and its ability to speak volumes to audiences, continues to make them prime targets for censorship. (59)

Is there a solution? . . . Is there a problem?

In the end, the industry and public at large both are left with the same fundamental questions from a hundred years back: Can comics that depict violence or sexuality have a negative effect on children? Most field studies have not found a link between viewing these materials and violent behavior. Marc Greenberg argues that "[c]orrelational studies, which focus on the relationship between two or more facts or events in an effort to determine causality, are often criticized for making an unsupported leap from conduct that may be linked, but is not evidence of causation" (181). As an example, he notes that The American Academy of Pediatrics, a long-time critic of the influence of television, has had to acknowledge that despite what it estimates as teenagers' exposure to an 'estimated 14,000 sexual references and innuendos every year on television' [that] 'there is no clear documentation' that the relationship between television viewing and sexual activity of any kind 'is causal'. (Greenberg 181)

In fact, others have found that there might be psychic benefits to the forbidden fruit offered by comics; Wright concludes:

> As recent outbreaks of violence at Columbine and other high schools have so horribly illustrated, young people continue to face a confusing, lonely, and sometimes frightening world that so often seems to spin out of control. For many adolescence can be an age of intense pain and isolation, when emotional demons must be exorcised either through fantasy imitating life or by real action imitating fantasy. Should the former alternative be exhausted or denied, then some may choose the latter, possibly with tragic consequences. (285)

In the end, it seems that there is no black-and-white answer to the questions raised by the urge to censor comics, and compassion and communication to all those involved, from creators, to publishers, to the readers, themselves, might be the only fair and reasonable response.

Works Cited

Dooley, Michael. "An Uncensored Look at Banned Comics." 68.1 (February, 2014): 48–59.

Greenberg, Marc H. "Comics, Courts and Controversy: A Case Study of the Comic Book Legal Defense Fund." *Loyola Los Angeles Entertainment Law Review* 32.2 (2011–2012): 121–186.

Hajdu, David. *The Ten-Cent Plague: the Great Comic-Book Scare and How it Changed America.* New York: Picador, 2008.

Harvey, Robert C. *Children of the Yellow Kid: The Evolution of the American Comic Strip.* Seattle: Frye Art Museum, 1998.

Nyberg, Amy Kiste. *Seal of Approval: the History of the Comics Code.* Jackson: U of Mississippi P, 1998.

Walker, Brian. *The Comics: The Complete Collection*. New York: Abrams, 2008.

Wright, Bradford W. *Comic Book Nation: the Transformation of Youth Culture in America*. Baltimore: John Hopkins, 2001.

US Comics, Moral Capital, and Social Change: 1954–2014_____

Matt Bryant Cheney

From the mid-twentieth to the early twenty-first century, the development of the comic book as a cultural force in the United States has taken place as the country experienced perhaps the quickest-moving period of social change in its relatively short history. These changes are well-known and their efficacy constantly debated: the political enfranchisement of African-Americans from widespread legalized segregation to the election of Barack Obama as the nation's first biracial President, the closing (however glacial) of the education and earnings gap between women and men, the technological revolution from the room-sized military computer to the iPhone, the widespread development and proliferation of nuclear weapons following World War II and the Cold War, the transition from primarily nation-based warfare to those carried out against paranational militant terrorist groups, etc. With the recent overturn of the Defense of Marriage Act and the parade of states that have legalized homosexual union, the moral capital of the United States is shifting in the direction of the LGBT community. Demographically, an increase in racial and ethnic diversity shows that now nearly, or perhaps even over, fifty percent of babies born in the United are from families of color (Cohn). The list goes on.

By opening here with a discussion of the influence of social change *on* comics and, conversely, their participation in US social change, this chapter does not seek to make what those in the social sciences might call a confusion between correlation and causation. By listing all of these changes, this chapter does not mean to propose that comics somehow helped facilitate all of this change in the United States cultural imagination, although a few specific examples will show where this is absolutely the case. In fact, sales figures for comics have, in some instances, been alarmingly low during times of substantial social or political change, and, often, the comics offering the most robust social commentary in the United States have not sold well at all. In other cases, however, some were bestsellers (Two examples: Denny O'Neil & Neil Adams' *Green Lantern/Green Arrow* in the 1970s and Bryan K. Vaughn & Fiona Staples' *Saga* in the last three years). Rather, this chapter will draw attention to these concurrent phenomena by arguing that comics have both been shaped by *and* helped to shape our understanding of US social change over the last sixty years. With a topic such as this, it would be tempting to attempt a sort of annotated list of all comics containing any kind of social commentary or, even, politically-driven stories aimed at social change. However, this chapter is more interested in an attempt to theorize *how* a few comics have dispatched a moral capital to engage with these social issues and, historically, used these social issues to add a then much-needed credibility to an artistic medium and industry that had often found itself arguing for critical respect to justify its very existence.

Of course, perhaps the most pervasive debate in comics scholarship involves the exact cultural space that comics occupy and the extent to which it is necessary to argue for their canon status as cultural objects. Bradford Wright, for example, argues in *Comic Book Nation* that such an endeavor, "however, distracts from the fact that the vast majority of comic books produced over the years has amounted to junk culture cranked out by anonymous creators who had little more than a paycheck on their minds," and, further, "to classify comic books as 'junk,' however, is not to put them down or imply that they have nothing to say. On the contrary, their perennial lowbrow status has allowed them to develop and thrive outside the critical, aesthetic, and commercial criteria of more 'mature' media" (xiv). Wright claims (and takes as a key assumption in his entire study) that comics should be read primarily as having been written for young people, while numerous other scholars would take Wright to task on that point, the youth orientation of many comics historically points to a certain moral responsibility that the readership placed on comics that was, of course, most emblemized in the mid-1950s by Fredric Wertham's *Seduction of the Innocent* and the establishment of the Comics Code Authority. Comics, perhaps more than other recent narrative mediums, have shouldered a moral burden that has forced writers and artists to find other means of cultural legitimation in order to justify their existence and prevent another crisis in the industry, such as the CCA, which resulted in a loss in circulation from roughly 3,200 individual publications to 1,500 in the United States between 1950 and 1959 (Gabilliet 47). In other words, comics utilize a form of cultural capital infused with moral concerns in the populist medium in order to gain artistic and social prominence.

Of Moral Capital and Comics

Before getting into the comics, a few key premises—namely what is "moral capital" and to what extent is it connected with American social movements—demand definition. More than other genres, such as poetry or the novel, comics, itself a medium, developed almost entirely outside the sphere of aesthetic judgment within the academy and thus found itself more subject to economic considerations, particularly sales figures. Thus, a discussion of cultural capital and comics has more to do with questions of public relevancy that, more or less, might point to conditions that result in a book finding an audience. Since Fredric Wertham connected American comics with their status as moral or didactic art objects in 1954, their cultural capital has been irrevocably caught-up in what political theorist John Kane and others have called moral capital. Kane writes that:

> things valuable or pleasurable in themselves—people, knowledge, skills, social relationships—can also be resources that enable the achievement of other social, political or economic ends. The presumption is that people, corporations, and societies that develop these forms of capital possess investable resources capable of providing tangible returns [. . . .] Capital, in other words, is wealth in action. Moral capital is moral prestige—whether of an individual, an organization, or a cause—in useful service. (7)

Kane, here, is more concerned with the accumulation of moral capital that politicians and leaders utilize in furthering their agendas and wielding political power. One can see a connection on the level of cultural value with what happened to the comics industry in the wake of *Seduction of the Innocent* and the Comics Code Authority based on Wertham's exhaustive psychological research. While the social commentary inherent in comics often leads toward underscoring political injustice, the socially symbolic content of these books also aesthetically refigures the moral premises that underlie these political concerns.

In 1957, three years after the publication of *Seduction of the Innocent* and the establishment of the Comics Code Authority, many comics publishers (most emblemized by the fall of EC Comics) had gone bankrupt as the remaining creators turned again to the tame, unwaveringly-just superheroes who worked alongside the law enforcement and the US government to simply, well, take down bad guys. That same year, an independent comic, *Martin Luther King and The Montgomery Story,* was produced outside the purview of the CCA that, along with its corresponding social movement, complicated the assumptions of the code at its heart, which is embodied by its first five rules:

1. Crimes shall never be presented in such a way as to create sympathy for the criminal, to promote distrust of the forces of law and justice, or to inspire others with a desire to imitate criminals.
2. No comics shall explicitly present the unique details and methods of a crime.
3. Policemen, judges, government officials, and respected institutions shall never be presented in such a way as to create disrespect for established authority.
4. If crime is depicted it shall be as a sordid and unpleasant activity.
5. Criminals shall not be presented so as to be rendered glamorous or to occupy a position which creates the desire for emulation. ("Comics Code")

Even the most graphic, violent, and salacious of the pre-code comics publishers could have challenged the code in as profound a way as an independently produced comic from 1957 that never had the opportunity to do so. *Martin Luther King and The Montgomery Story*, a sixteen-page magazine, was produced by the Fellowship for Reconciliation (FOR), the New York anti-war organization that was directly involved with nonviolence training in the South, which helped spark the various sit-ins and marches that would take place for at least the next ten years following the Montgomery Bus Boycott in 1955. The book tells the story of Jones, an African-American man in Montgomery, Alabama, who vacillates between advocating violent or nonviolent responses to Jim Crow laws. Jones encounters the teachings of Martin Luther King, Jr. (who had just been appointed leader of the Montgomery Improvement Association) and after an account of the basic series of events that ultimately lead to the desegregation of buses in Montgomery, our protagonist claims that he will never need to keep a gun anymore: "I've thrown my gun away—it had gotten much too heavy for me ever to lift again!" (10).

Following the first five rules from the Comics Code, it might be instructive to imagine how *The Montgomery Story* might have been judged had it been submitted for CCA approval. First, disorderly conduct and failure to obey police direction are depicted as not only positive but crucial and favorable courses of action. Particularly in the case of Jones, he is depicted quite sympathetically and ultimately shown to be morally-justified in his collusion with the Montgomery Boycott. Second, instructions are presented at the end of the publication in a section titled "How the Montgomery Method Works" that is meant to inspire readers to replicate these actions (*Martin Luther King* 13). Third, the nature of the Montgomery Bus Boycott itself was an attempt to discredit laws that had been established to maintain order, and the book clearly depicts law enforcement officers issuing ludicrous traffic tickets and abusing African Americans. Fourth, protesters are shown to be determined, hopeful, and even happy individuals who find a sense of community and purpose with one another. And, finally, see items one through four. Additionally, on the back cover of the publication, one sees Dr. King implying that God is in jail waiting for protestors: "You'll find God waiting there for you, holding you and supporting you, giving you a victory far beyond what you had hoped." Needless to say, this has potential to "create the desire for emulation" (16).

Andrew Aydin has investigated the historical circumstances of the comic's writing and learned that, in addition to the collaboration between FOR Communications Director Alfred Hassler and unemployed former comics writer Benton J. Resnik, Dr. King himself was involved in the final edits for which the Civil Rights leader made very specific suggestions and clarification of certain events in the story, such as the first individual to be arrested in Montgomery. While King is featured prominently on the cover (with a celestial beam of light shining down on him as he looks over a bus scene in Montgomery) and discussed extensively, the decision had only been made later to feature him on the cover after his rise to national prominence in the wake of the bus boycott (Aydin 10).

Rather than work through a comics industry distributor, the decision was made, in addition to making a few small newsstand solicitations, to use the book as a more direct teaching tool to those who might get involved in the movement. Frankly, the book never pretends to be anything other than what it is, what FOR Director of Communication Richard Deats said was, "intended to convey to semiliterate persons the story of nonviolence and its effectiveness as seen in the Montgomery movement. The medium of the highly popular comic book was believed to be the best way to reach masses of exploited African-Americans." (Aydin 15) Perhaps without realizing it, FOR published one of the first underground comic books in the US, and the necessity for its status as such proves just as pervasive as the anti-censorship, often shock-inducing bend of the underground comix movement that would arise in the late 1960s.

The Montgomery Story is not necessarily easy evidence that comics were pushing for social change quite early, but rather to complicate the narrative of comics history that focuses on publishers geared toward profit motive and industry standards. *The Montgomery Story* came from a fairly simple desire to help people become involved in the movement rather than to tell the movement's story to outsiders. The fact that such a socially-engaged comic story would have had no chance of being published under the purview of the Comics Code Authority points simultaneously to the truly stifling reach of the industry watchdog *and* the lack of moral capital possessed by the Civil Rights Movement in its fledgling years. The story of *The Montgomery Story*, however, points to a very different situation than that currently facing larger publishers more interested in reaching a popular audience through the most prevalent tradition in American Comics, the superhero comic.

Holding Out for a Socially-Conscious Superhero

Following the release of Marvel Comic's *Fantastic Four* #1 in 1961, many have noted the beginning of the 'Marvel Age' of comics, more often referred to as the Silver Age of comics or what Jean-Paul Gabilliet has called the "Age of Innovation," wherein superheroes (most notably, Spider-Man) began to exhibit more frustration with their powers and, even, self-doubt in their ability to do good. Instead of the unwavering judgments of DC's powerhouse heroes Superman and Batman, the characters created by Stan Lee, Jack Kirby, Steve Ditko, et al., as Jared Gardner writes, "were impulsive, often irrational, and wracked with the fears and frustrations endemic to adolescence and the atomic age" (112). One such superhero team was the X-Men, whose 1963 origins are particularly of interest in considering comics' engagement with social change.

Arguably, 1963 was perhaps the most defining year for the Civil Rights Movement, the events of which built the momentum that ultimately led to the passage of two marquee pieces of legislation, the Civil Rights Act of 1964, which legislatively deemed all Jim Crow laws illegal, and the Voting Rights Act of 1965, which extended the reach of the 1964 Act to more specific attempts to suppress black voters. Prior to the release of *X-Men* #1, widely publicized demonstrations occurred in Birmingham that spring where protestors (led by King and the Southern Christian Leadership Conference) were famously attacked by police dogs and fire hoses under the order of Public Safety Commissioner Eugene "Bull" Connor. Governor George Wallace of Alabama had protested the enrollment of African American students to the University of Alabama by standing in the doorway until President Kennedy ordered the National Guard to escort students to their classes on June 11th. Civil Rights leader Medgar Evers was murdered on June

12th, and the now iconic March on Washington occurred on August 28th, which included King's "I Have a Dream" speech (Williams vii). President Kennedy would be assassinated in Dallas, Texas, on November 22nd. As seen with the tricky matrix of reasons that the Civil Rights Movement could not be depicted in comics, Lee and Kirby sought to write a comic that would address racial conflict in a way that could also carry the very-necessary Comics Code Seal.

How, specifically, do the X-Men correspond with the Civil Rights debates of the early 1960s? In a 2000 interview with *The Guardian*, Stan Lee offers a bit more insight into the creation of the X-Men that confirm the comic's obvious connection with Civil Rights:

> The big problem was figuring out how they got their superpowers. I couldn't have everybody bitten by a radioactive spider or zapped with gamma rays, and it occurred to me that if I just said that they were mutants, it would make it easy. Then it occurred to me that instead of them just being heroes that everybody admired, what if I made other people fear and suspect and actually hate them because they were different? I loved that idea; it not only made them different, but it was a good metaphor for what was happening with the civil rights movement in the country at that time. (Lee)

Certainly, the key here with connecting the notion of mutants with race lies chiefly in the fact that mutants are born with their powers, rather than acquiring them through some accident, such as the spider bite that turns Peter Parker into Spider-Man. For Lee, whose character creations have always underscored the more pragmatic accounts of the *how* and *what* of superhero powers, this move toward ostensible racial coding alters the superhero origin towards being *inherited* rather than *acquired* notions of human difference, a fact that would extend quite easily to questions of ethnicity and, several decades later, sexuality. Note, for example, that the X-Men find themselves necessarily segregated from society in a school, which, as an institution, was still the most prevalent site of segregation debates following the Brown v. Board of Education rulings in the mid-1950s. However, the fact that they are all white teenagers also corresponds to the widespread fear of juvenile delinquency that had helped fuel anti-comics fervor: instead of using their powers to exact criminal behavior, the X-Men are constantly under the direct supervision of Professor Charles Xavier, a responsible adult who constantly checks their attitudes and maintains team discipline by chastising members for being late to meetings (Lee & Kirby). By these code-switching maneuvers, the *X-Men* were actually able to garner moral capital from multiple ideological angles: for those sympathetic to the struggle for Civil Rights, these characters provided an appreciated narrative that subtly addresses problems of inherited human difference. For those concerned about the perceived degradation of youth morality that led to the establishment of the CCA seven years earlier, they saw teenagers being trained to be responsible citizens. In so doing, as Bradford Wright argues, "Marvel managed to strike an antiestablishment pose without appearing political" (219).

Over the years, and especially since the reboot of 1975 with *Giant-Size X-Men* #1 headed by Chris Claremont, Len Wein, and artist Dave Cockrum, the X-Men have become a sort of epicenter for the exploration of human diversity, multiculturalism, and discrimination in mainstream comics. The rebooted 1975 team alone, for example, features for the first time the characters of Colossus (Russian Piotr Nikolaievitch Rasputin), Storm (African Ororo Munroe), Thunderbird (Apache John Proudstar), and Nightcrawler (German/Gypsy Kurt Wagner) (Wein). Themes of systematic bigotry and discrimination were further emphasized into the 1980s through the depiction of forced segregation and, even, extermination of mutants through the establishment of the US Mutant Control Agency and the Mutant Control Act (or Mutant Registration Act) in the Marvel Universe showing the US government attempting to register mutants as second-class citizens in order to better control them, a move reflecting the registration of Jews during the Holocaust and black South Africans during Apartheid (*Uncanny X-Men* #181). In *Uncanny X-Men* #150, writer Chris Claremont revealed that the X-Men's first and most-persistent adversary, Magneto, had been a survivor of Auschwitz during the Holocaust, an event in his life that fueled his hatred of non-mutant humans (38). The Holocaust motif has continued to run through the various X-Men storylines since the early 1980s, including the increased revelation of government experiments having been done on mutants, such as Wolverine, who gained his claws and adamantium skeleton following government investigation of his regeneration powers (*Marvel Comics Presents* #72-84). The 1980s X-Men stories, produced during the rising awareness of the AIDS epidemic in the gay community, also saw the rise of the first openly gay superhero in mainstream comics, Northstar (*Alpha Flight* #106), who in 2012 married longtime partner Kyle Jinadu in *Astonishing X-Men* #51. All of this points to the consistent acquisition and maintenance of moral capital in X-Men stories that have allowed the series, far and above the innovative character development and fairly consistent presence of above-grade writing, to maintain widespread appreciation from audiences both strongly associated with the comics fan community *and* in pop culture more broadly. The X-Men have carried forward Lee and Kirby's initial vision of addressing bigotry through superhero comics and, in so doing, thrived in the post-code comics landscape.

Yet, while the evolution of the X-Men began with an example of what a comics publisher needed to do in order to discuss bigotry while under the purview of the CCA, O'Neil and Adams' *Green Lantern/Green Arrow* series depicts what becomes possible with the initial erosion of the code's influence in the early 1970s. Simply put, while Stan Lee had first dared to publish a comic without the Comics Code Authority Seal, *Spider-Man* #96, O'Neil and Adams' run on the combined DC title has often been cited, by *Comic Book Men* star Walt Flanagan for example, as the moment comics "gained a conscience" and for good reason ("Clash at the Stash"). It is telling that the very first post-code mainstream comics were necessitated by the urge of comics editors and writers that they were not fulfilling a moral obligation to talk about real, political concerns and that a move to such a format would reinvigorate the title. As other chapters in this volume account, Green Lantern and Green Arrow encounter a wide array of social concerns including all of the following: African American civil rights, affordable housing, gang violence, the plight of American Indians, cults, overpopulation, water pollution, deforestation, and the exploitation of coal miners. In encountering these issues, Green Lantern and Green Arrow are traveling with one of the Guardians of OA, the council who oversees the work of all Green Lanterns throughout the galaxy, in an attempt to investigate Hal Jordan's intentions to focus more on domestic concerns following Green Lantern's assistance (at the urging of his anarchist partner Green Arrow) in the arrest of a New York slum lord in *Green Lantern* #76. The now iconic issue features one of the most famous panels in comics history, wherein an elderly man admonishes the white Green Lantern: "I been readin' about you . . . how you work for the **blue skins** . . . and how on a planet someplace you helped out the **orange skins** . . . / . . . and you done considerable for the **purple skins!** Only there's **skins** you never bothered with—! / The **black** skins! I want to know . . . **how come?!** / Answer me **that**, Mr. **Green Lantern**!" (O'Neil & Adams 13).

In some cases, it seems that O'Neil was worried about getting it all in, combining multiple social concerns into one storyline. For example, in *Green Lantern* #78, titled "A Kind of Loving, A Way of Death," Lantern and Arrow, following an opening gang fight scene, find themselves traveling to a town on an American Indian reservation, where the same motorcycle gang uses racial slurs against the American Indian bartender (his tribe is never specified), whose story of systematic discrimination particularly interests the Guardians of OA. Following a barroom brawl that dispatches the motorcycle gang, Lantern and Arrow find that Black Canary has been brainwashed by a pseudo-Native American cult leader named Joshua, who Green Lantern accidentally kills in the end with a power punch from his ring. Some aspects of these combined issue-stories could be seen as quite problematic, especially the passive use of "redman" and "pale face" in the Native American-themed tales, but one must remember that it was only in 1975 that the decision was made to lighten the code and allow for more nuanced exploration of *any* injustice that implies a mishandling on the part of US authorities ("Comics Code"). Regardless of the series often sensationalist heavy-handedness and occasional insensitivity toward people of color, superheroes were at least now given the opportunity to acknowledge that street criminals and super-villains were not the only evil plaguing the world. In other words, the Comics Code Authority had lost a significant amount of its moral capital in avoiding these issues until the mid-1970s.

After eleven issues and several other crossover storylines with DC's *The Flash*, the story of Green Lantern's investigation into the *real* problems facing America ends in *Green Lantern* #88, in which John Stewart, an African-American architect from Detroit steeped in the rhetoric of the Black Power Movement, becomes Hal Jordan's alternate as the Green Lantern of Earth by order of the Guardians. In many ways, the issue is the most successful of the O'Neil/Adams run because it is the natural culmination of the Green Lantern and Green Arrow partnership by acknowledging that even after traveling across the country and learning about numerous issues of poverty, discrimination, and injustice, there are still perspectives of these issues that Jordan cannot realize: those of the oppressed. In writing Stewart into the larger *Green Lantern* narrative, O'Neil indirectly acknowledges white privilege in a way never before successfully handled in other black superhero narratives, such as Marvel's Black Panther or Luke Cage. The effect on Hal Jordan, I think, exemplifies a process of social attunement where the subject is able to tap into these concerns more effectively moving forward, and, in depicting the Green Lantern's attunement to the ills of society far beyond that of super-villains and interstellar conflict, O'Neil and Adams injected much-needed moral capital into the comics medium that would help carry it through the next decade.

Comics Find Moral and Cultural Capital Simultaneously

James English argues of cultural prizes "that they are the single best instrument for negotiating cultural and economic, cultural and social, or cultural and political capital—which is to say that they are the most effective institutional agents of *capital intraconversion*" (10). By "intraconversion," English here refers to the transition of one form of capital into another, and following that, the history of comics and social change are implicitly tied with the status of comic books as legitimate cultural objects, one can link the awarding of prizes to comics (especially those of wide-reaching prestige) to their moral capital. The awarding of the Pulitzer Prize to Art Spiegelman's *MAUS* in 1991 (after a long serialization throughout the 1980s) offered comics' first real integration of moral and cultural capital, making possible the autobiographical/journalistic method that Adams and O'Neil were hoping for in the 70s, but could not access within the genre of superhero comics. Beyond its oft-discussed innovations in comic depictions of memory and narrative complexity, Spiegelman's timing with *MAUS* could not have been better having found wide release in the midst of the highly-publicized construction of the United States Holocaust Memorial Museum in Washington, DC following the work of the President's Council on the Holocaust headed by Elie Wiesel and set in motion by President Jimmy Carter thirteen years earlier (United States Holocaust Memorial Museum). *MAUS'* success, beyond legitimizing comics in a way never before achieved, opened up new opportunities for comics writers to engage with the social issues that had before been quite difficult to deal with *both* during the code era and immediately after in the 1980s when much of the innovation was in pressing the boundaries of violence and subject matter in the superhero genre and reconnecting comics with their darker roots in the pulp genre. While *MAUS* did not deal explicitly with social change in the sense of political movements, Spiegelman introduced a mode that made a more dynamic depiction of US social change possible, or at least offered an example of engagement with history from a more intentionally subjective angle. Graphic novels dealing with African American history have, in particular, benefited from this groundwork.

While accounts of the Civil Rights Movement were few and far between in comics, biographical and autobiographical accounts of the movement akin to *MAUS*, in addition to other significant events in African American history, have begun to emerge in the last decade. On the end of historical accounts, Kyle Turner's *Nat Turner* (2008) stands as the most significant graphic novel to date that deals with American chattel slavery. More in line with the subjective mode identified in Spiegelman's work are two more personalized graphic novels published just in the last year, both drawn by Nate

Powell: *March: Book One* (a collaboration of Congressman John Lewis, Andrew Aydin, and Powell) and *The Silence of Our Friends* (by Mark Long, Jim Demonakos, and Powell). These books have found varying levels of success and critical acclaim, but in terms of politically-engaged comics, there has never been a more perfect example than John Lewis' *March* series, in which the Congressman and former SNCC member credits *Martin Luther King and The Montgomery Story* with helping catalyze his involvement with the Civil Rights Movement in the first place. Some sixty years later, Lewis is able to tell the story of his experiences in a more personal way than was afforded to the FOR and Dr. King in crafting their comic. Now that both the memory of the Civil Rights Movement *and* autobiographical comics have accumulated enough moral capital to reverse the cultural conditions of graphic narrative in the 1950s, writers can revisit the movement with a more subjective, nuanced angle that warrants the assignment of a label many have found helpful over the years in distinguishing more intentionally aesthetic novels with an autobiographical bend: creative nonfiction.

* * *

Where does this leave the relationship between comics, moral capital, and social change today? While comics as a genre have been historically quite behind in celebrating women writers and, of course, in offering depictions of non-sexualized female characters, Hilary Chute has argued, "Some of today's most riveting feminist cultural production is in the form of accessible yet edgy graphic narratives" (2). While Chute spends the bulk of her study working with more independent comics and graphic novels, it is also worth mentioning the quite intentional development in serialized comics of female-centered narratives, including Kelly Sue DeConnick's *Captain Marvel*, Sana Amanat's *Ms. Marvel*, and DC's New 52 reboots of *Batwoman* (depicting Kate Kane as a lesbian), *Batgirl*, and *Harley Quinn*. However, while the readership continues to find much social worth in the superhero and otherwise "genre" comics being released by DC and Marvel, it seems that this really is the moment for the creator-owned publisher, Image Comics.

In more recent years, especially following the rise in popularity of Robert Kirkman's *The Walking Dead*, Image Comics has also contributed to the more culturally and morally legitimated mode of comics writing that consistently competes with the big two producers for readership. While some attempts at making comics more socially relevant have fallen into the trap of tokenism and (at worst) outright pandering, Image seems to have allowed a creative space for comics that engage on a different aesthetic stratosphere than most titles offered by their much-larger rivals. Vaughn and Staples' *Saga,* for example, has garnered praise for its un-sentimentalized depiction of women, exemplified perhaps most vividly the opening scene from the first issue, which features Landfallian heroine Alana giving birth to Hazel, the narrator, and yelling at her star-crossed Wreathian lover Marko, "Am I shitting? It feels like I'm shitting!" (Vaughn 5). While the heroics of the first three volumes would lead one to believe that Marko and Alana will be together forever, their daughter, the narrator Hazel, drops a bomb on readers in the final page of #19 stating, just above an image of the entire family in embrace, "This is the story of how my parents split up" (24). Somewhat reminiscent of O'Neil and Adams, in the first twenty issues of *Saga* alone, Vaughn and Staples have incorporated stories dealing with the economic exploitation of service workers, immigration, gay marriage, human trafficking, deforestation, and forced removal. In other words, outside the purview of corporate comics, *Saga* has utilized the necessary demands of moral capital as a comics story to engage with social change and, perhaps, in so doing escalated its value as an art form.

The difference, though, lies in the multiplicity of comics readership that has evolved into, what Jeffrey A. Brown has called the "creator vs. corporate" problem in comics fandom. It is the condition where comics have morphed from a more or less populist medium where readers often all read the same titles and follow the same storylines into a less centralized mode that has grown to include readers ranging from the most avid comic shop customer to occasional readers of web comics to literary scholars who came to graphic narratives rather late (25). Needless to say, quite a lot of work still needs to be done, and an exploration of moral commitments in these books only scratches the surface in understanding the vast, often stigmatic, and artistically innovative role comics have played in US ideology and social change over the last sixty years.

Works Cited

Aydin, Andrew. "The Comic Book That Changed the World: *Martin Luther King and the Montgomery Story*'s vital role in the Civil Rights Movement." *Creative Loafing* 42:14 (1–7 August 2013). Web. *Altweeklies.com.* 13 July 2014.

Brown, Jeffrey A. "Comic Book Fandom and Cultural Capital." *Journal of Popular Culture* 30:4 (Spring 1997): 13–31. Web. *Wiley Online Library.* 12 June 2014.

Chute, Hillary. *Graphic Women: Life Narrative & Contemporary Comics.* New York: Columbia UP, 2010.

Claremont, Chris. *Uncanny X-Men #150.* Illus. Dave Cockrum. New York: Marvel Comics, 1981. Web. *Marvel Unlimited.* 1 July 2014.

"Clash at the Stash." *Comic Book Men.* Exec. Prod. Kevin Smith. AMC. Web. Netflix. 1 January 2014.

Cohn, D'Vera. "Are Minority Births the Majority Yet?" *FacTank: News in the Numbers.* Pew Research Center, 4 June 2014. Web. 24 June 2014. "The Comics Code Authority (As adapted in 1954)" *Comics Magazine Association of America.*

Comicartville.com. n.d. Web. 15 June 2014.

English, James. *The Economy of Prestige: Prizes, Awards, and the Circulation of Cultural Value.* Cambridge, MA: Harvard UP, 2005.

Gabilliet, Jean-Paul. *Of Comics and Men: A Cultural History of American Comic Books.* Trans. Bart Beaty & Nick Nguyen. Jackson: UP of Mississippi, 2010.

Gardner, Jared. *Projections: Comics and the History of Twenty-First-Century Storytelling.* Stanford, CA: Stanford UP, 2012.

Kane, John. *The Politics of Moral Capital.* Cambridge: Cambridge UP, 2001.

King Jr., Martin Luther. "Letter From Birmingham City Jail." *A Testament of Hope: The Essential Writings and Speeches of Martin Luther King Jr.* Ed. James W. Washington. New York: HarperCollins, 1986.

Lee, Stan, & Jack Kirby. *The X-Men: Marvel Masterworks*. Vol. 1. Ed. Cory Sedlmeier. New York: Marvel, 2009.

Lee, Stan. Interview by Bob Strauss. *The Guardian*. Guardian News and Media Limited, 2000. Web. 1 June 2014.

Lewis, John, & Andrew Aydin. *March: Book One*. Illus. Nate Powell. Marietta, GA: Top Shelf Productions, 2013.

Martin Luther King and The Montgomery Story. New York: Fellowship of Reconciliation, 1957.

United States Holocaust Memorial Museum. "History." *USHMM.ORG*. 20 June 2014. Web. 2 July 2014.

Vaughn, Brian K. *Saga*. Vol. 1. Illus. Fiona Staples. Berkeley, CA: Image, 2012.

Wein, Len. *Giant-Size X-Men #1* (1975). Illus. Dave Cockrum. *The Uncanny X-Men: Marvel Masterworks*. Vol. 1. Ed. Cory Sedlmeier. New York: Marvel, 2009.

Williams, Juan. *Eyes on the Prize: America's Civil Rights Years—1954–1965*. New York: Penguin, 2002.

Wright, Bradford. *Comic Book Nation: The Transformation of Youth Culture in America*. Baltimore, MD: Johns Hopkins UP, 2001.

The Rhetorical Construction and Negotiation of Cultural Difference in American Nonfiction Comics

Daniel Lawson

> In contemporary capitalist societies as in most other social formations, there are inequalities in the distribution of power and other goods [. . . .] In order to sustain these structures of domination, the dominant groups attempt to represent the world in forms that reflect their own interests, the interests of their power. (Hodge and Kress 3)

When the contemporary American sees repeated images of undifferentiated women in beauty ads, images of African Americans portrayed as gangsters or criminals, images of successful entrepreneurs as white, well-dressed, middle-class men, or images of American Southerners as backwards and rural primitives, he or she is looking at representations that serve the interests of the powerful. In other words, representation (whether visual or verbal) is often ideological—it constructs a way of knowing that seems commonsensical, but at the same time legitimates unequal social relations. These images circulate throughout society, making the dominant social group's beliefs about what exists, what is good, what is possible seem objective—natural, even. Thus, in studying these images, it is possible to examine how meaning is made and to account for its social effects—in short, how preferred readings of images make inequality seem normal. These preferred readings are so widespread that even when authors and audiences are not trying to reproduce them, they can still subtly rearticulate that discourse. Comics, like any other pop culture medium, are not exempt from ideology. Comics creators can often unwittingly act as points of articulation in dominant discourses. Moreover, as explained by scholars, such as Chris Murray, Don Thompson, William Savage, et al., comics have even, at times, been used as overt propaganda. And though comics' Other has drifted away from the Japanese and Germans of World War II, it has found a more contemporary Other: Arabs and/or Muslims (Murray 142).

Murray in particular offers an insightful formulation of the interaction of United States propaganda and pop culture during World War II that he labels *pop*aganda: "Popular culture [also] borrowed from official discourse and propaganda. With the boundary between propaganda/official discourse and popular culture thoroughly breached it becomes misleading and meaningless to distinguish between them as separate categories" (142). During World War II, comic books were exemplary as pop culture artifacts that served as media for domestic propaganda. And though Murray claims that "[t]he emphasis on play, the pleasure to be derived from the defeat of the enemy seems childish to modern eyes, as does the emotive and robustly patriotic rhetoric of much *pop*aganda," (142) *pop*aganda still circulates in comics—sometimes via officially sanctioned "nonfiction" titles.

While the practice of rhetorically constructing difference along gender, sexual, racial/ethnic, and cultural lines in superhero comics has been fairly well-documented, not as much attention has been paid to the practice in nonfiction comics genres. This is an important distinction to make, because as a collection of genres intended to report something ostensibly true about the world, the construction of difference in nonfiction has perhaps even more troubling implications and repercussions. Moreover, much of the comics scholarship that studies Othering focuses primarily on the narrative matter rather than how the medium itself is involved. That is, these accounts focus on how difference is created in the stories themselves, usually through casting cultural Others as villains or racist sidekicks in fairly canned and clichéd narratives. And although such examinations are necessary (for indeed, a great deal of cultural Othering occurs in narrative), such an approach elides the role the medium itself plays in navigating cultural difference.

But what does the medium of comics have to offer writers and artists in this milieu? Given the continuing prevalence of

Islamophobia and anti-Arab racism in the United States (only amplified in the wake of 9/11), the examples in this discussion will be grounded primarily (though not exclusively) in contemporary examples from American nonfiction comics. This chapter focuses on the formal properties of comics and examines three means by which writers and artists rhetorically construct, negotiate, or subvert cultural difference in comics. First, the essay will examine the affordances of panel-level signification, wherein the style and drawings themselves can be used in fostering or countering Othering discourses. Next to be examined will be how the sequencing of these panels can inform and be informed by Othering discourses. Finally, there will be an analysis of how comics artists and writers assert the authenticity or immediacy of the comics experience and, thereby, its objectivity.

A Matter of Style: Othering and Coding at the Level of the Panel

Othering is the practice by which a dominant social group portrays subordinate social groups (this may be along racial, cultural, socio/economic, religious, or gender lines) as inferior, strange, or alien. Such a portrayal helps the dominant group define itself as intrinsically superior and acts as an alibi for its dominance as legitimate. Given that comic books are a visual medium, perhaps the most apparent means of Othering in them beyond the narrative is through coding at the level of the panel—that is, through using artistic style to convey implicit attitudes about cultural Others. As Roland Barthes argues, there is no drawing without style: the artist cannot reproduce every feature of what is represented and thus has to make decisions about what the drawing is intended to convey (43). Consequently, when attempting to interpret the rhetorical work of a visual medium in a given piece of discourse, one must evaluate what features have been (re)produced and which may have been occluded. For instance, comics scholars such as Murray, Don Thompson, as well as Randy Duncan and Matthew Smith have pointed out the use of style in crafting negative portrayals of Japanese and Germans during war time. As Thompson observes of World War II era comics, "The

Japanese all wore glasses and had buck teeth (or, often fangs) and claw-like fingernails. Their skins were usually yellow, often greenish-yellow" (112). Such depictions immediately communicate their subjects' inhumanity. Unfortunately, similar practices have persisted in contemporary comics (both fiction and ostensibly non-fiction) as well.

For contemporary examples of the portrayal of cultural Others (especially regarding Arabs and Muslims), the graphic adaptation of the 9/11 Report (subsequently referred to here as *9/11 R:GA*) is an especially fertile site. Written and drawn by Sid Jacobson and Ernie Colon, the *9/11 R:GA* was created with the sanction of the 9/11 Commission. In fact, commission members, Thomas Kean and Lee Hamilton wrote the Foreword of the piece and commissioned it in hopes to reach a broader audience than either the original report or its abridged summary did. In it, the artists take what they deem the most important features of the five-hundred-sixty-seven page report and condense it to one-hundred-seventeen pages of image-heavy text. Many of the ways in which Jacobson and Colon render in the text are at the level of those images.

Some such means include graphic techniques, like perspective, shading, coloration, and text bubbles. Much like a film director, comics artists can control the qualities of a given panel. Perspective, for instance, can influence how readers perceive the subject portrayed in the panel. A shot constructed from far away and high above the subject can make him or her seem weak or isolated. Eye-level shots are generally used to establish identification with the subject, and Dutch angle shots (wherein the camera is tilted to make the horizontal plane diagonal) are used to foster confusion or alarm. Shading and coloration can be used to indicate "good guys" and "bad guys"; American comic book heroes are typically colored in primary colors whereas villains are rendered in secondary colors. It can also facilitate the mood of a scene, relying on cool colors (in hues of blue and green) for calm, sadness, depression, or darkness, or hot colors (in hues of red or yellow) to indicate anger, rage, or excitement. Finally, color can also be used to facilitate the illusion of lighting, which can in turn signify shadows and the general starkness of a scene. Evil characters are often drawn as cloaked in shadows.

Consider, for example, a depiction of the Hamburg Group in the *9/11 R:GA*. In it, three of the four members of the Hamburg Group, "key players in the 9/11 conspiracy," are shown in what the reader must assume (based on the surrounding text) to be an example of them interacting with "life in the West" (Jacobson & Colon 57). The perspective on the panel is somewhat lower than eye-level, and the three Hamburg Group members are at the foreground, looming menacingly over the viewer. The only speech bubble in the panel consists of one Anglo man saying to another, "You notice they speak only in Arabic and keep to themselves." Though the speech bubble could be interpreted to indicate the xenophobia the men encountered in the West, the surrounding context and its placement on the page seem to signal something else: after panels and text indicating their membership in the 9/11 conspiracy, their status as "aspiring jihadists," and their "anti-U.S. Fervor," the Arab men cloak their terrorist intentions in a language no one around them understands, and they do not assimilate—they "keep to themselves" (Jacobson & Colon 57). Worse, given that these men were indeed key players in the attack, the Westerners depicted in the panel were right to be suspicious of them. By this logic, any group of insular non-native speakers could be potential terrorists. Two of the characters are inexplicably colored blue, not only visually designating them as outsiders but quite literally foreshadowing the events to come by having them entering shadows as they leave the Westerners behind them. The images of the terrorists themselves further this notion. All three are drawn in the style of comic book villains: heavy brows, squinting eyes, high foreheads, and expressions that convey (in order, from left to right) contempt, secretiveness, and mental incapacity. And although these individuals *were*, in fact, key players in the conspiracy leading to 9/11, they are drawn no differently than any other Arab or Muslim in the book.

Of course, comics have a long tradition of relying on stereotypes to visually convey information about characters to the reader. Comics artist and scholar Will Eisner explains:

Comic book art deals with recognizable reproductions of human conduct. Its drawings are a mirror reflection, and depend on the reader's stored memory of experience to visualize an idea or process quickly. This makes necessary the simplification of images into repeatable symbols. Ergo, stereotypes . . . In comics, stereotypes are drawn from commonly accepted physical characteristics associated with an occupation. These become icons and are used as part of the language in graphic storytelling. (*Graphic Storytelling* 11–12)

Eisner uses depictions of stereotypes to demonstrate how physical characteristics can help a reader determine the profession of a given character. These characteristics help transmit meaning quickly and allow the artist to package a number of significations into one signifier. Stereotypes are, however, dangerous in the way they essentialize certain characteristics in subjects. In particular, Eisner's discussion of using animal features is useful here. Eisner explains the use of animal characteristics in the representation of people as a way to capitalize "on a residue of human primordial experience to personify actors quickly" (*Graphic Storytelling* 14). While his formulation may be a bit simplistic because different cultures regard a given animal differently, it still indicates the intention and interpretation of stereotypes inherent in crafting these resemblances, particularly for American audiences of contemporary comics.

To return to the *9/11 R:GA*, many of the techniques Eisner outlines for stereotyping make an appearance in the depictions of Arabs and Muslims in the book. Almost all—and not solely those identified as terrorists—of the Arab men depicted in the book have high foreheads and widow's peaks, heavy and arched eyebrows, down-turned mouths, and eyes that do not hail the reader directly. When one of these characters' gaze is directed at the reader, it is as if through the corner of the eyes. Comparing these portrayals to those which Eisner uses as examples, most resemble those caricatures of foxes and snakes, animals associated in the West with evil and trickery (*Graphic Storytelling* 14). By contrast, Westerners (particularly white Westerners) are portrayed in the style of comic book heroes: lantern jawed, proportionate, upright, and resolute. Popular fictional comics such as Frank Miller's *Holy Terror* employ similar tactics, often visually (and narratively) conflating Arabs and Muslims with terrorists and vice versa.

Props and symbols can also be used as stereotypes to quickly convey attitudes and information to readers. Duncan and Smith, for instance, explain how in World War II era comics, "Arrogant Germans wearing monocles leered as they branded their captives with a red-hot swastika" (250). The swastika then served not only as a symbol for the Nazis in general, but also as an instrument of torture, implicitly linking the two. In the case of the *9/11 R:GA*, the scimitar functions as such a prop. The scimitar has long served as a locus for Western anxieties and imaginations of Eastern barbarism. So much has it been so thoroughly associated with the cultural and religious Other that when describing stereotypes and objects, Eisner claims its depiction can be used to signify "Bad Knife" (*Graphic Storytelling* 15). The weapon makes numerous appearances in the *9/11 R:GA*, though no mention of scimitars is made in the original report.

And while panel-level signification can be used to reinforce negative stereotypes and reify cultural difference, comics authors have used it to negotiate that difference as well. For example, Ted Rall is a comics artist, writer, journalist, and columnist who has reported on issues in the Middle East. Rall relies upon what McCloud refers to as "abstraction" and "simplification" in his portrayal of characters; he states, "When we abstract an image through cartooning, we're not so much eliminating details as we are focusing on specific details" (30). What is interesting in Rall's case is that he generally avoids negative stereotypes in his signifiers, opting instead for only the barest of line drawings to help the reader understand who is speaking. If a character is wearing, for instance, a turban, it is not synonymous with evil, as it is in say, the *9/11 R:GA* or *Holy Terror*. And if artists, such as Rall, use abstraction in their portrayal of cultural Others, *Palestine* author Joe Sacco uses a different ploy: detailed caricatures that resist any easy cultural signifiers.

Sacco's aesthetic draws upon comics artists, such as R. Crumb, and movies, such as Sergio Leone's westerns, both of which emphasized the ugliness and grittiness of visual detail. And though Sacco's subjects in comics, such as *Palestine* or *Safe Area Gorazde*, are often drawn strangely, little of the strangeness is attributable to cultural difference; indeed, Sacco draws himself in the comics as uglier than any of the subjects. Sacco uses detail to "objectify" his subjects—to give them reality and weight. As these subjects are typically Arabs and Muslims suffering from various forms of colonialism, oppression, or more overt forms of violence, their detailed renderings make their suffering and humanity more prominent on the page. In McCloud's words about Japanese comics art styles, "while most characters were designed simply, to assist in reader-identification—other characters were drawn more realistically in order to objectify them, emphasizing their 'otherness' from the reader" (44). And though this dynamic is certainly in play in Sacco's work, Sacco grounds that Otherness in his own perspective. That is, rather than asserting that he is merely drawing what is there, he explains his own unease in encountering and negotiating difference. In short, his style is not intended to dehumanize his subjects, but rather to present his own initial reactions and attempts to understand Otherness.

The Space Between Panels: Othering through Closure

Although comic books are a graphic medium, graphic representation is not unique to comics. Indeed, any of the methods outlined above can be (and have been) used in other graphic media—propaganda, advertisements, posters, movies, and more. What distinguishes comics from these other graphic media, then, is its reliance on the sequencing of images through space (rather than through time, as they are in, say, film). As a result, Othering practices are not limited to the level of the panel. If each panel acts as a discrete frozen moment in the narrative in time and space, the collection of these panels allows the reader to make meaning by juxtaposing them—to speculate on how what is depicted in the panels moves through time and space. The reader fills in the narrative gaps through what comics scholar Scott McCloud calls closure. As McCloud explains, "If visual iconography is the vocabulary of comics, closure is its grammar [. . .] in a very real sense, comics is closure!" (67). In short, the reader sees a panel, surmises what occurs in that panel, and then based on the panels that come before and after it, revises that meaning. Eisner calls this participation in the creation of meaning the "tacit cooperation" between reader and artist (*Comics and Sequential Art* 41). In short, the reader is implicated in the discourse because he or she imagines what occurs between panels based on what he or she sees to be the most probable action. On the one hand, this can make Othering discourses somewhat difficult, given the tenuousness of the artist's control over what the reader might imagine. On the other hand, this tenuousness enables comics artists to foster difference in more subtle ways than what is available at the level of the individual panel.

One such way is through privileging the verbal text in the work, offering the pictures to act as an illustration for what is described in the text rather than allowing the panels themselves to drive the narrative. As such, much of the agency the reader enjoys in meaning-making in comics decreases. As Gunther Kress describes about the medial logic of verbal text, most of the agency lies with the speaker/writer. Listeners (and, to a lesser extent, readers) are, as Kress puts it, "dependent—at least in their initial hearing and reading—on sequence and on sequential uncovering [. . . .] If the hearer or the reader wishes to reorder what has just been said or what has been written, the recording has to be done on the basis of and against the author's prior ordering" (13). In such a configuration, the audience's agency can thus only be framed in the binary terms of passivity or resistance and works against the tacit cooperation between reader and artist usually inherent in comics. The pictures merely act as more immediate signifiers that are subordinate to the textual message. When those pictures engage in the sort of coding described in the previous section, when coupled with seemingly neutral text (such as that found in the *9/11 R:GA*), they are implicitly naturalized—they simply show what is being said. If there is a difference, the reader thus fills in those gaps.

This practice can lead to what comics critic Douglas Wolk has described as "innocuous speculation" in pieces like the 9/11 Report. He writes, for example:

A description of the Northern Alliance in Afghanistan mentions that Ahmed Shah Massoud's soldiers "were charged with massacres". . . . That panel looks dynamic in a way that no other images in the pages around it do; it also represents a kind of fantasy that has no place in a book like this, because a medium as subjective as comics heads into very dangerous territory when it conflates documented fact with speculation for artistic effect. ("'Maus' it's Not")

Thus, in the closure between images, between text and image, and between fact and speculation, there are a great many opportunities for the rhetorical construction of difference.

Similar techniques are used throughout the book by drawing upon tropes from spy and crime comics genres. Tropes are figures that invite readers to draw upon well-established genre canards to fill in the gaps between what is presented on that page and the cultural milieus that inform them. For example, in westerns, "good guys" often wear white hats and "bad guys," black. Like Eisner's description of stereotypes, such narrative and visual tropes help the reader not only process intentions quickly, but also the mode in which they are to be processed. In the case of the *9/11 R:GA*, the book is peppered with depictions of intelligence agents in dramatic action poses kicking down doors, spies speaking over their shoulders to sinister-looking Arabs pretending to read the paper, and FBI agents delivering vital, but doomed, intelligence to shadowy superiors. In each instance, Arabs are typically cast in the role of criminal, crazed terrorist, or jihad-waging zealot. Accordingly, clichés and characterizations that what would seem out of place in the actual report are implicitly conveyed in the adaptation with relative normalcy: such caricatures hardly seem incongruous with a medium that is usually associated (in America) with superheroes and action. The use of recurring stereotypes then helps to reinforce dominant depictions of Arabs and Muslims as menacing and violence-prone outsiders. That is, the repeated negative images are also wed to the tropes of spy- and action-comics genres. And as genre scholars have demonstrated, genre is not simply a text, but rather what is done with those texts. Genres structure the world through recurring rhetorical situations, enabling readers to anticipate and respond to them. Thus, the genre knowledge readers bring to bear on those texts—good guys, bad guys, and dramatic action—help them make sense of those texts. Readers draw on simplistic genres to fill in the gaps between what is said in the report and what is shown in the art.

Closure also enables readers to make deductions about certain symbols, depending on how they are presented and repeated, through visual metonymy—through a depicted object making reference to a greater whole. To return to the example of the scimitar in the *9/11 R:GA*—the several instances of the scimitar appearing in different context would be troubling enough individually, but their metonymic linking has even more sinister connotations. The first, and perhaps the most subtle uses of the signifier is—strangely enough—in the early portions of the book depicting the hijacking of the planes. Though the graphic adaptation begins with a depiction of the hijacking, the knives depicted are not identified as box-cutters until very late in the timeline reconstructing the events on pages twenty to twenty-five. Even then, they are never explicitly identified other than with an image of a box-cutter by the text "Likely Takeover." Up to this point, the weapons the terrorists use look little like angular box cutters rather than curved, long knives. The curved knife thus links the hijackers metonymically to the other (invented) scenes and individuals depicted in the book that feature scimitars. Most of these instances are not in the context of terror per se, but instead in other conflicts in the Arab world. The implicit visual argument is that the hijackers were of an ilk with those who were also depicted employing the curved knife in the book—they are all metonymically linked to Islam.

Seeing Is Believing: Realism and Erasure

For the first two approaches (panels and sequence) to work at all, the case must be made that what is rendered on the page is how things truly are. What is the "truth" or "authenticity" of an image? Is it true that "seeing is believing," or is the image just as arbitrary a signifier as the word? In other words, there has to be an assumption of some sort of natural relationship between the image and what it portrays. Racist caricatures are only effective if the reader assumes them to be true. As Theo Van Leeuwen and Carey Jewitt describe, pictures encourage the notion of presence—that is, of being thrust into a specific time and place with what is depicted. Of course, the image is just an arbitrary signifier, and in fact, some comics scholars suggest that the very form of comics itself is a parody of the notion that any sort of representation can adequately convey the essence of the subject.

Still, claims of "seeing is believing" persist in comics, especially in nonfiction comics or genres set in 'the real world'. For example, as Duncan and Smith point out, the creators of Marvel's series *The 'Nam* promised to present a realistic experience of the Vietnam War (246). However, as Annette Matton points out, "the book really follows the tradition of earlier war comics in supporting the established ideology" (155). In short, claims of unmediated realism often act as an alibi for dominant ideology, masking the work of coding and closure in fostering Othering discourses. Given the medium's inherent parodic qualities regarding the truthfulness of its signifiers, writers and artists who operate within it must thus account for those qualities.

One such way is through arguments for the medium's "accessibility" or "authenticity." Sacco himself has asserted the immediacy of the comics medium: "And, one of the effects of things about comics is you're dropping a reader right into a situation, you know. Prose writers, of course, can be very evocative, and I appreciate what they do, but I find there is nothing like thrusting someone right there. And, that's what I think a cartoonist can do" ("Presenation"). His use of argument thus alludes to the sense in which Jay Bolter and Richard Grusin use the term *immediacy*. That is, as a form of representation that works to "make the viewer forget the presence of the medium . . . and believe he is in the presence of the object" (272–273). Sacco's extra-textual arguments for authenticity, combined with the gritty detail of his renderings, intend to convince the reader that he or she is experiencing the situations Sacco depicts as Sacco experienced them.

A similar argument is made by the co-chairs of the 9/11 Commission who wrote the Foreword to the graphic adaptation.

Lines such as "one of the most important and tragic events in our nation's history needed to be accessible to all" and "We commend [the artists] for their close adherence to the findings, recommendations, spirit, and tone of the original" indicate some implicit claims that are developed further in the actual adaptation (Jacobson & Colon ix–x). The first of these claims is that text/language is a filtering agent capable of obscuring or rendering inaccessible "truth," which is then external to language. In addition to the lines above, this assumption is also conveyed in the certainty with which the Chairs assert that there is only one version of the event and what preceded it: "*the story of 9/11*" (Jacobson & Colon ix, emphasis mine). The assertion of text-as-filtering-agent connotes the second implicit claim, that of the existence of a transcendent signifier, and that it is visual. In other words, according to the Commission, by stripping away language and allowing pictures to demonstrate the facts (It is implied that seeing is, after all, believing), they have somehow authorized an edition that will be easier ("all ages") to apprehend than its prose-based parent. Admittedly, the graphic adaptation does not require as much reading per se as the original. However, there was already a summarized version of *The 9/11 Commission Report*, published and readily available. One then has to assume that it is specifically the comics form that makes this edition more accessible. Whereas Sacco, however, grounds his presentation in his own admittedly biased perspective, the *9/11 R:GA* gives no such caveat. Rather, its creators assert that it is merely showing things as they are.

Within the comics themselves, visually, artists may use a photorealistic style for much of the work, in order to lend it a realistic ethos while subtly coding Others. They may even photo reference well-known people, places, or events—reproducing the photographs and incorporating those likenesses into the comics panels. This helps ground other interpretations in the work in the 'real world' and lends those interpretations a similarly realistic ethos. Such a practice is what media scholars Bolter and Grusin refer to as *erasure*, the attempt to erase the artists' presence in order to foster the illusion of unmediated reality. Both the *9/11 R:GA* as well as Jacobson and Colon's follow-up work, *After 9/11: America's War on Terror* contain very detailed photo referenced images of well-known political figures intermingled with highly stylized depictions of violence and Muslim Others. Such a presentation works to naturalize accounts of Arab and Muslim violence: if one knows the "truth" of the photograph drawn upon in one panel, how can one dispute the "truth" of a scimitar-wielding maniac in the next?

Many comics creators, however, make it a point to call attention to the work of mediation, even in what are considered more realistic images or accounts. For example, by the end the chapter in Palestine called "Getting the Story," Sacco tries to get a sense of what happened in a shooting incident in Hebron. Over the course of navigating Sacco's interviews, his own perceptions of what he is being told, and the conflicting accounts therein, the reader gets a sense of complicated narratives that converge in this occurrence. At the very end of the section, Sacco reproduces the *Jerusalem Post*'s report, a terse and very reductive piece that often contradicts what Sacco's cartoons painstakingly create. It gives an abstracted, disembodied account that privileges one version as objective whereas Sacco's ethnographic approach (which negotiates several subjectivities, including his own) gives the reader a fuller, more nuanced, and seemingly more authentic rendering. In *In the Shadow of No Towers*, Art Spiegelman inserts obviously digitally altered images of the falling World Trade Center Towers amidst cartoons and caricatures of political figures.

One such double-page spread includes a panel of Spiegelman depicting himself as his Maus persona, while flanked between armed and dueling caricatures of Osama bin Laden as a rat and George W. Bush as a chimp. Below the panel, a caption reads, "Equally terrorized by Al-Qaeda and by his own government [...] Our hero looks over some ancient comics pages instead of working. He dozes off and relives his ringside seat to that day's disaster yet again, trying to figure out what he actually saw." Below it are digital, hand drawn, and cartoonish representations of the WTC towers intermingled. As Grusin argues, "Spiegelman's book clearly exemplifies the double logic of remediation, insisting simultaneously on the unmediated authenticity of his immediate experience and on the inseparability of his experience from the materiality of its hypermediation" (26). In short, Spiegelman's account resists any easy urge to affix a transcendental signifier to official accounts of that day.

New Perspectives and Final Thoughts

Thankfully, there has been a great deal of pushback in recent years against Othering discourses in popular comics, including anti-Arab racist and Islamophobic discourses. Even as a blatantly Islamophobic (though critically derided) work, like *Holy Terror*, continues to sell in American markets, other works have introduced other perspectives. For example, nonfiction comics from outside of America, such as Marjane Satrapi's *Persepolis* and Didier LeFevre and Emmanuel Guibert's *The Photographer: Into War-Torn Afghanistan with Doctors Without Borders*, have enjoyed both critical and commercial success with American mainstream audiences. These comics (and in the case of *Persepolis*, a movie adaptation) do a great deal to complicate simplistic notions of Islam and the Arab world.

Similarly, superhero comics from abroad featuring Muslim protagonists, such as *The 99* and *Buraaq* have also started seeping into American markets as well. American superhero comics themselves have begun to incorporate Arab and Muslim protagonists, such as Green Lantern Corps member Simon Baz and the new Ms. Marvel, Kamala Khan. These characters normalize the appearance of Arab and Muslim characters in comics in roles beyond villain, side-kick, or exotic Other. Still, rhetorically countering Othering discourses requires more than mere inclusion. For example, Baz, though a protagonist, is not necessarily a featured character so much as part of an ensemble (as many minority characters have been). And although Ms. Marvel is Marvel's first Muslim character to headline her own comic book, the character suffers from being something of what John Jennings and Damian Duffy have labeled a "hand me down hero." That is, she is a minority character who, similar to characters like Jim Rhodes or John Stewart has taken on the previous superhero identity of a white character—in this case, Carol Danvers, who upgraded from "Ms." to "Captain." Still, comics discourse regarding cultural Others has come a long way from the "childishness" of World War

II *pop*aganda described by Chris Murray. *Pop*aganda still circulates, however, and informs how we conceive of, create, and come to understand difference when reading the comics page.

Works Cited

Barthes, Roland. *Image-Music-Text*. New York: Hill and Wang, 1977.

Duncan, Randy & Matthew Smith. *The Power of Comics: History, Form & Culture*. New York: Continuum Press, 2009.

Eisner, Will. *Graphic Storytelling and Visual Narrative: Principles and Practices from the Legendary Cartoonist*. New York: W.W. Norton and Company, 2008.

_____ . *Comics and Sequential Art: Principles and Practices from the Legendary Cartoonist*. New York: W.W. Norton and Company, 2008.

Grusin, Richard. *Premediation: Affect and Mediality After 9/11*. New York: Palgrave Macmillan, 2010.

Hodge, Robert, & Guther Kress. *Social Semiotics*. Cambridge, UK: Polity Press, 1988.

Jacobson, Sid, & Ernie Colon. *The 9/11 Report: A Graphic Adaptation*. New York: Hill & Wang, 2006.

_____ . *After 9/11: America's War on Terror (2001–)*. New York: Hill and Wang, 2008.

Jennings, John, & Damian Duffy. "Finding Other Heroes." *Other Heroes: African American* Comic *Book Creators, Characters and Archetypes*. Eds. John Jennings & Damian Duffy, 162–166. Raleigh, NC: lulu. com, 2007.

Kress, Gunther. "Gains and Losses: New Forms of Texts, Knowledge, and Learning." *Computers and Composition*. 22 (2005): 5–22.

Matton, Annette. "From Realism to Superheroes in Marvel's *The 'Nam*." *Comics & Ideology*. Eds. Matthew McAllister, Edward H. Sewell, and Ian Gordon. New York: Peter Lang, 2001. 151–176.

McCloud, Scott. *Understanding Comics: The Invisible Art*. New York: HarperPerennial, 1993.

Murray, Chris. *Comics and Culture: Analytical and Theoretical Approaches to Comics*. Eds. Magnussen, Anne & Hans-Christian Christiansen. Copenhagen: Museum Tusculanum Press, 2000. 141–156.

Sacco, Joe. *Palestine*. Seattle: Fantagraphics Books, 2001.

_____. "Presentation from the 2002 UF Comics Conference." *ImageTexT: Interdisciplinary Comics Studies* 1.1 (2004). Web. 14 November 2010.

_____. *Safe Area Gorazde: The War in Eastern Bosnia 1992–1995*. Seattle: Fantagraphics Books, 2002.

Savage, William W., Jr. *Commies, Cowboys, and Jungle Queens: Comic Books and America, 1945–1954*. Hanover, NH: Wesleyan UP, 1990.

Thompson, Don. "OK. Axis, Here We Come!" *All in Color for a Dime*. Ed. Lupoff, Dick & Don Thompson. New York: Ace Books, 1970. 110–129.

Van Leeuwen, Theo, & Carey Jewitt. *Handbook of Visual Analysis*. London: Sage, 2001.

Wolk, Douglas. "'Maus' It's Not." *Salon.com*. 8 Sep. 8 2006. Web. 21 July 2014.

CRITICAL
READINGS

Negotiating Popular Genres in Comic Books: an Impossible Mission. Against All Odds. Yet, Somehow, the Chapter Is Saved!_____

Joseph Michael Sommers

At the outset, it might be wise to clear space to account for a fundamental misunderstanding: comics, in all types, forms, adaptations, and modalities are not a genre; they are a medium that contains countless genres. In his seminal 1993 volume, *Understanding Comics: The Invisible Art,* Scott McCloud wrote:

> The world of comics is a **huge** and **varied** one. Our definition must encompass all these types—while not being so broad as to include anything which is not comics. "**Comics**" is the word worth defining. As it refers to the medium *itself,* not a specific **object** as "comic book" or "comic strip" do. (4)

Further, he visualized the "vessel" of comics as being a pitcher filled with an inky-black liquid containing nothing less than a collaboration of writers, artists, trends, genres, styles, subject matter, and themes, noting that "the artform—the **medium**—known as a comics is a vessel which can hold any **number** of ideas and images [with the trick being] never to mistake the **message** for the **messenger**" (6). Not unlike I. A. Richards' famous distinction between tenor and vehicle, McCloud's notion is relatively simple: 'comics', not unlike books or films, is merely another form of media; "forms of expression," says Douglas Wolk, "that have few or no rules regarding their content other than the very broad ones imposed on them by their form" (11). All of which states that the idea of "comics," themselves, is a vast cosmos with many, many inhabitants. As such, comic *genres* might be best described as the planetary systems within this universe where particular characters, plots, and storylines develop and play out in the visual medium of sequential art.

Interestingly, as Wolk, et al. argue, this notion of genre is a particularly tricky biscuit to even attempt to discuss, given the fact that genres are by no means mutually exclusive of other genres and, interpretively-speaking, one person's teen romance could be another's teen adventure could be another teen's abject pulp horror serial. Such is the danger of entering Riverdale in *Archie*, particularly in the twenty-first century, where Archie Andrews, Jughead, and company seem to intersect with Robert Kirkman's *The Walking Dead* to give the comics world *Afterlife With Archie*. This is Roberto Aguirre-Sacasa and Francesco Francavilla's rather mature take on Riverdale after the zombie apocalypse. . . . And readers thought high school dating was a dicey proposition beforehand.

With eyes towards negotiating so many overlapping Eulerian circles in the Venn diagram of comic genres, this chapter will establish some ground rules simply to organize the discussion. 1) This essay will discuss comic *books*. Movies, video games, televised serials, so-called "infinite" comics, etc. all easily could fall within the realm of comics, but, to simply bracket the discussion, this essay will concern itself with the stalwart paper press and staples. This will also mitigate discussions of both medial adaptation and what theorist Henry Jenkins has called "transmedia storyteling" or "convergence culture," whereby "the flow and content across multiple media platforms" stretches comic narratives in manners commensurate (2), as example, with what Marvel Comics has done with its collapses of its cinematic universe, 616 continuity, and Ultimates continuities. These discussions are part of the historical present of comics, fascinating, and already captured in other chapters of this book. 2) As Wolk has rightly claims, there exists an axiological discourse within comic studies that so-called "highbrow comics are, somehow, not really comics but something else (preferably with a fancier name)" (12). This is, of course, navel-gazing madness and a classism that this essay has absolutely *no* interest in. The semantics and comic book store politics involved in the distinction between comic books, graphic novels, picture books, graphic narratives, illustrated texts et al., while *also* fascinating, is also something better left to a different essay of greater polemical flavor. To simplify this matter, Will

Eisner's simple and perfect definition of "sequential art" will define the parameters of the discussion:

> The format of the comic book presents a montage of both word and image, and the reader is thus required to exercise both visual and verbal interpretive skills. The regimens of art (e.g. perspective, symmetry, brush stroke) and the regimens of literature (e.g. Grammar, plot, syntax) become superimposed upon each other. The reading of the comic book is an act of both aesthetic perception and intellectual pursuit. (8)

Within that construction, different genres easily can announce themselves and be distinguished. 3) The Zombie *Archie* Rule: genre is a funny word; it's the root word of "generic," which this list will try *not* to be . . . but likely will be to some degree. (It is not all-inclusive nor tries or could be; however, it *is* alphabetically arranged.) There will be overlaps and ambiguities between the ideas presented here: comics, such as Jeff Smith's ingenious *Bone*, could easily classify, given a particular audience, under "adventure comics," "fantasy comics," "humor comics," "comics for children," etc. as Smith's genius and transcendence defies simple classification and stratification. While examples will be specifically chosen to demarcate popular genres within the medium of comics (with distinction given to periodic classifications), one reader's toe-*mah*-toe is easily another's toe-*may*-toe. Such is the joy of interpretation and resolution to agree to disagree on matters of classification.

However, for the record: a tomato is a berry. Neither a vegetable nor a fruit.

Abstract Comics

Abstract comics are a somewhat tenuous consideration of the medium, as who is one to discern what is 'abstract' as opposed to what might otherwise be seen as 'concrete'? The easiest, or least contentious, definition would likely concern something that uses the traditional methodological and narratological standards of sequential art and storytelling with a visual aesthetic determinate of 'abstraction'. As this volume is particularly concerned primarily with American comics, this genre becomes somewhat more tenuous as non-American comic makers, such as graphic novelist and cartoonist Henrik Rehr (who actually now resides in America) or Quebec artist and cartoonist Benoît Joly, tend to populate this category with greater frequency.

However, while writing that with one set of keystrokes, one can easily cite the work of cartoonist R. Crumb, whose ubiquitously known 1960s–70s comic *Fritz the Cat* has become somewhat infamously remembered for its mature scenes depicting sexual hedonism, if not outright countercultural moral decay. By Crumb's own admission, his work reflected a drug culture he himself was surrounded and immersed within, psychedelic and surrealistic flourishes that one might imagine would occur when you mix one part Walt Kelly's concept of anthropomorphism and a heavy pinch of LSD.

Counterpoised, perhaps, against someone like Gary Panter, who tends to be classified more as an underground comics creator veering into a more balanced expressionism (His work might be best and most widely-known in an entirely different medium: Panter was the set designer for the 1980s children's television serial *Pee Wee's Playhouse.*), one can find a somewhat tedious compromise whereby abstract comics could easily be classified as 'aesthetically odd'. And, bringing that unseemly rubric to bear, it becomes even more tenuous by way of construction when one figures that these comics and comics magazines (such as *RAW* in the 1980s) gave rise to the first published work of Art Spiegelman's *Maus*. *Maus*, being one of the most venerated American comics (having won the Pulitzer Prize), seems to cut a stern line between the likes of Crumb and Panter, as Spigelman's use of anthropomorphized mice, cats, and dogs allowed him a filter to tell a painful and endearing biographical narrative of his parents tale of escape from the Nazi Holocaust. As such, perhaps it is fitting that no concrete definition can be attributed to comics defined, generically or periodically, as abstract.

Adult Comics

By definition, the genre of adult comics seemingly would entertain an audience: adults. Then again, whosoever, by terms of comic studies, would figure into an age bracket of 'adulthood'? However, adult comics euphemistically belies other portents; adult comics are, generally, categorized as sexually-explicit comic books and assorted erotica that, in other areas of the world, might be known as *hentai* (heteronormatively-male-centric manga pornography) or *seijin manga* (similarly constructed and sexed to women). Replete with a history as old, if not older, than comics from the so-called Golden Age of Comics, Tijuana Bibles (as noted, possibly most famously, in Alan Moore's seminal, no pun intended, *Watchmen*) and other such books designed with the notions and attributes set forth to elicit sexual release through depiction of periodically-consistent taboos, fetishes, or societal immortalities are as prevalent as any other so-called pornographies.

There is no marked consistency to their definition or genre; the Tijuana Bible might be little more than a crudely-drawn and assembled eight-page fascicle, printed with no further express purpose than to give the reader sexual release and sold to the consumer under the counter of a tobacconist or house of burlesque in the appropriate time period. Likewise, other adult books could be marvels of construction and aesthetic beauty on point with the work of known mid-twentieth century burlesque photographer and filmmaker Irving Klaw (who, himself, had published work of burlesque *fumetti*, or photo comics, occasionally featuring one of the more famous pin-ups in American history, Bettie Page, as well as illustrated fetish work from notable comic makers, such as Eugene Bilbrew and Eric Stanton).

Two points of immediate interest reside in this historical construction of adult comics: 1) While outright fetishism and sexual innuendo became the calling card of shunting this genre of comics strictly into the world of the alternative/underground set, few seemed to have similar distaste with the idea when packaged with a comic more easily couched in a different genre, such as the superhero comic. Wonder Woman, a Golden Age mainstay to the day, frequently found herself in situations of bondage and fetishistic entreat commensurate with less lurid adult comics, but completely consistent with the genre itself. William Moulston Marston, the

Harvard educated psychologist and co-creator of *Wonder Woman*, imbued her characterization with populist trends of submission, physical bondage, restraint, and sublimated eroticism specifically to touch upon the Zeitgeist of what he perceived to be a growing movement in popular culture oncoming since the 1930s. Given her perseverance throughout time and space, it would appear he was on to something. Finally, 2) comics from this period more attuned to the gory, grotesque, or pulp (*Weird Tales, Tales from the Crypt,* etc.) are the more outwardly considered books that led to the creation of the Comics Code Authority, that offspring of Fredric Wertham's infamous mischaracterization of childhood media, *Seduction of the Innocent,* and the Senate Subcommittee Hearings on Juvenile Delinquency that arose as a result of that publication. These hearings blanketly characterized comics of all sorts and varieties (age restrictions and content be damned) as *for* children, thus equating adult comics, essentially-speaking, as a form of children's pornography. And, with the foundation of the CCA in 1954, this genre of book was driven ever further underground.

Alternative Comics

Much discussion, primarily due to alphabetization, has already been given towards this nebulous entity known as alternative comics (once known in certain periods and quarters as Underground Comics(-x) . . . which might as well be even more simply characterized as "Comics Not Published By DC or Marvel," or, less snarkily, "Small Press Comics"). Periodically, these comics and comic book publishers arose from the ashes of the Underground Comix movement as early as 1970 with Last Gasp comics and its founder Ron Turner himself being a vestige of the underground era. Other such American notables in this genre include Fantagraphics, Jeff Mason's Alternative Comics, and Top Shelf Productions.

This genre is more a hodge-podge by its own construct as, by definition, it can contain all or any of the other genres on this list as long as the product arising from these publishing houses is not affiliated with a so-called mainstream publishing house. As such, originally self-published material, such as *Love and Rockets* by

Gilbert, Jamie, and Mario Hernandez, a comic the brothers had put out themselves beginning in 1981, was acquired and is now published by Fantagraphics. *Love and Rockets* can sit aside a comic such as Kevin Eastman and Peter Laird's anthropomorphized superhero title *Teenage Mutant Ninja Turtles* from Mirage Studios in 1984, which can be couched in the same class and discussion as the work of Daniel Clowes (*Ghost World*), Chris Ware (*Building Stories, Jimmy Corrigan: the Smartest Kid on Earth*), Craig Thompson (*Blankets, Habibi*), or even Image Comics and its original core of superhero hero artists/ creators: Todd McFarlane, Jim Valentino, Rob Liefeld, Jim Lee, Marc Silvestri, Whilce Portacio, and Erik Larson, all of whom made some of the most mainstream superhero comic books of the 1990s. As such, perhaps the better classification of alternative comics might be "creator-owned comics" distinguishing the concept from both manner of art, narration, style, audience, etc. and rightly placing the focus back directly into the manner of ownership; in such creator-owned comics, the creator retains rights and ownership of the things created as opposed to work-for-hire artists and writers who craft properties that become owned and controlled by the company (as is the case with DC and Marvel).

Autobiographical Comics

Another in the category of 'the name says it all', autobiographical comics point to a trend in the comics industry originating, again, out of the underground comics movement, of comic writer/illustrators who take the hard look at themselves as grist for the mill of their comic construction. As varied and variable as the lives chronicled, autobiographical comics go as far back in time to noteworthy strips, such as Harvey Pekar's *American Splendor*, chronicling his life as a file clerk in Cleveland, Ohio, but begin to take hold in American circles when Spiegelman's *Maus*—itself as much an autobiographical chronicle, since it is a memoir of his parents' experience—wins the Pulitzer Prize at its point of completion in 1992. (It had been published, all but the last chapter, in its near entirety in *Raw* since 1980.) Since then, comic writers/illustrators as wide and varied as Alison Bechdel (*Fun Home, Are You My Mother?*) David B.

(*Epileptic*), the aforementioned Craig Thompson (*Blankets*), etc. have all offered looks into their own lives to the comic reader. Whether the functionality of these books operates as a sort of empathic bond with pictures for the reader or outright voyeurism is a point of contention that likely could be made in every single case. The point remains that some of the most insightful and critically-acclaimed work from all these generic forms seems to arise with the same simple narratives that are found in fictional narratives not featuring art.

Children's and Young Adult Comics
One of the more fascinating entries in this digest of genres might be comics designed for the child and young adult reader. This would be the case stemming from the point of the inception of the CCA that comics, as a medium, are primarily *all* designed for this age bracket (a notion that is an overgeneralization of the idea that there is no difference between the child reader and the adolescent, or young adult, reader). CYA comics are most often characterized along the lines of the collapse of the word "comic" with "humor," which fails as even a basic designator from psychoanalytic studies of literature forward. However, there is truth to the notion that many of the comics designated for the CYA reader are, in fact, funny—giving rise to the antiquated terminology of comics as "funny books." In fact, however, the rise of this genre of comics comes from a classic standpoint of American consumerism; the glut of this type of comic arises, not coincidentally, with the recognition of the CYA reader's buying power in Post-World War II 1940s. As comic publishers recognized the younger reader as one who might be inclined to make an impulse purchase at the checkout counter or newsstand, the publisher supplied them with period-specific and approved material to purchase.

One of the seminal producers of such comics is the ubiquitously-known Archie Comics, publisher of the title of the same name in addition to others surrounding the protagonists of Riverdale, such as *Betty and Veronica*, *Jughead*, etc. The books are as formulaic and derived from the exploits of teenagers traversing the minefield of high school life in the 1940s onward might suggest; dating, automobiles, fast food, dealing with those obnoxious adults (teachers, parents, bosses), etc. permeate the humor in these books building an immediate response with the YAC reader whether from a position of empathy with the adolescent reader or envy with the child reader awaiting access to this mysterious world of fast cars and girls. The power and reception of these books were monumental in the publishing industry as they unequivocally depowered superhero books' control over the publishing world and, arguably, ended the Golden Age of Comics en route to the Silver Age of Comics which were popularized by . . . young adults and teens (see *Spider-Man*, Sue and Jonny Storm from *The Fantastic Four*, etc.) who were filled with doubts and self-loathing that could be empathized with by both adults and young adults alike.

Comics specifically attuned to children, now and then, are, while by no means a rarity, certainly something that often runs into direct conflict with its sequentially artistic sibling: the picture book. It is by no means to say that these comics do not exist, particularly when one considers the Sunday Funnies in most American newspapers. Recently, however, these books tend towards being spin-offs and adaptations of popular cartoon programming and merchandizing such as: *Sonic the Hedgehog*, *Scooby Doo*, *Looney Tunes*, and any of a myriad host of products put forth by Disney. As such, it is not with any note of dismissal that further address is not given to comics specifically attuned to the youngest of the audiences. It is more to the point that they are a greater minority than others genres yet to be catalogued.

Crime Comics

Like many of the generic categories presented here, crime comics, short of your occasional Frank Miller *Sin City*, Ed Brubaker *Criminal*, or even Brian Azzarello (*100 Bullets*, *Batman: Year One*) noir comic, are extremely popular comics of a bygone era. Hitting their zenith in the 1940s and 50s, these highly moralistic and graphically violent books were the toast of the pre-Wertham era of comics. However, due to their highly gritty depictions of things such as gunplay, drug use, actualized/realistic murder, etc., they quickly became targeted by the CCA as not separating reality from the comic sphere enough to make parents and parents' groups comfortable. This notion is all the more interesting as one of the most popular of the genre, Chester Gould's *Dick Tracy*, used grotesques of gangsters and hyperbole to sublimate the violence in a manner that might befit a younger reader. Possibly more ironic still was the fact that these comics did not celebrate violence; rather, they tended to proselytize the notion of staying within moral and legal boundaries enforceable by the juridical laws of the land. Part of that message, however, often resulted in the horrific punishment of those criminals who broke with the enforced hierarchy by police who would not tolerate it. As such, conservative pundits transformed such violence as being not only in poor taste but as possibly enticing to the young mind. In an effort to staunch the bleed from the poor reception of such books from the CCA, publishers bowdlerized and effectively neutered the content of these books to palatable levels, simultaneously all-but-murdering reader interest in the genre in an ironic twist.

Fantasy Comics

Not unlike crime comics in periodization or reception, fantasy comics were a 1940s–50s phenomenon that actually survived far better than the aforementioned genre due, largely, to the plurality of subgenres hidden under that umbrella term. Fantasy comics can stretch into a vast number of subgenres, including (and certainly not limited to) pulp comics, horror comics, speculative fiction (aka: science fiction), magic, mysteries, mythologies, and even superhero comics, when one considers the work of creators, such as Jack Kirby whose *Thor*, for example, was originally an incarnation held within the pages of *Journey Into Mystery* and became a Silver Age mainstay in popular superhero comics, such as *The Avengers*. Another example is Stan Lee and Steve Ditko's *Dr. Strange*, who debuted in *Strange Tales* and has appeared in various incarnations of his own title to *The Defenders* and *The Midnight Sons*.

At its heart, fantasy comics seem to distinguish themselves from other genres by possessing some sort of arcane secrecy that is granted

---

to the reader and, therein, leads to their unbridled success and appeal to comic readers. This was likely why Wertham's attacks seemed to target them: *clearly* these books that discussed topics that were 'forbidden' (such as was in *Forbidden Worlds*) or mysterious (*House of Mystery*) were disclosing information that was likely subversive or troubling to the minds of American youth. Such dubious contexts were, of course, utter hogwash as the books contained little more subversive or threatening than anything otherwise published in the non-visual format by the likes of H. P. Lovecraft or J. R. R. Tolkien. Likewise, what did *Tales from the Crypt* offer the youthful reader that was so much more heinous than reading classic accounts in works, such as Robert Louis Stevenson's *Strange Case of Dr Jekyll and Mr Hyde*, Bram Stoker's *Dracula,* or Mary Shelley's *Frankenstein*? Many of these titles actually became comics in their own right before 1954 and found themselves thrown upon a Procrustean bed of now being too frightful in their visualization and comic adaption; whereby, prior, they were considered relatively modern classics.

Many of these historical fantasy titles were published through EC comics and its publisher William Gaines, who inherited *Educational Comics* (also known as *Entertaining Comics*, when the former was acquired by DC Comics) from his late father Maxwell Gaines in 1947. By 1949, William Gaines was publishing titles with a considerably more horrific bent, whether that be the aforementioned *Tales from the Crypt* or *The Vault of Horror* or even comics expressing a non-patriotic examination of the horrors of war in *Frontline Comic*. Science fiction comics, such as *Weird Science* and *Weird Fantasy* also populated the line allowing EC to virtually run the gamut of fantasy, science, and horror. Deep within that production, though, were stories pulled directly from folk and fairy tales by the Brothers Grimm; classic fictions from authors such as Ray Bradbury; and the seeds of a small satirical book that branched off and became known today as *Mad Magazine*. *Mad* actually became the bellwether title for EC's future as Gaines' sole publication to survive the CCA and their cull of inappropriate comics titles.

The story of Fantasy comics, however, does not end poorly after the mid-century in America. Major comics distributors, like

Marvel and DC, continued to put out CCA-approved Fantasy books after 1954. For example, sword-and-sorcery books became a boom industry in the 1970s after Marvel produced Roy Thomas' *Conan the Barbarian* in 1970. Kirby continued on with his work in various places, crafting a series of works for DC called "The Fourth World" in the early 70s and bringing forth creations such as *The New Gods, Mister Miracle*, and *The Forever People*. Darkseid, a creation arising from that pantheon of comics, gave Jim Starlin the impetus to create a similar character for Marvel he named Thanos who was inserted into a growing stable of cosmic heroes and comics who had foundations in older Silver Age titles such as *The Fantastic Four*. Even further in the contemporary age, DC unfurled a line of comics it dubbed as its Vertigo imprint in the early 1990s, where edgier comics could hold their own under a major publisher. Comics, such as *Hellblazer, The Sage of the Swamp Thing, The Sandman, Doom Patrol, Shade: The Changing Man, V for Vendetta, Transmetropolitan*, et al., arose with significantly more mature themes and fantastic content that did not fit in the mainstream DC Universe up until its restructuring with their "New 52" and the Vertigo line's ultimate cancellation in 2013. In that time period, most all major comics publishers have since retired the old Comics Code Authority, and, by 2001, even Marvel stopped displaying the CCA flag on their covers, thus allowing the ever all-encompassing field of fantasy comics to continue to bloom and prosper at a rate unseen since its genesis.

Romance Comics

Of the types of comics on this list that might retain the blanket terminology of "pulp," this genre remains without comment; romance comics, or perhaps better, "Romantic Love Comics," can transcend genres as aptly as alternative comics, since the distinct features and markets of this set tend towards plot lines dealing with archetypal romantic concerns: love (unrequited and fulfilled), marriage, jealousy, betrayal, etc. If televised soap operas came packaged in booklet form, this would likely be the result.

Arising in the post-World War II moment, and likely typified by Jack Kirby and Joe Simon's *Young Romance*, these books were remarkably popular in the decline of Superhero comics, as they tell risqué stories and have Harlequin-style plot lines. Titles such as *My Romance, My Life*, and *Young Love* frequently outsold competing products and newsstand fare with their more "adult" storylines, focusing on the battlefield of the post-war household and targeting an entirely new demographic of comics readers: young women. The stories were markedly formulaic, advocating for a normalizing behavior for young women that involved finding a good man and a good place within the domestic setting of the home, essentially punting the World Wars' identity of a stronger, more independent woman. Of course, like the other pulp comics found in this chapter, 1954's implementation of the Comics Code virtually decimated the content in these books through self-censorship and bland storytelling. And what hadn't been irreparably marred by that point in history was deemed as anachronous and antiquated in thought by the time of the Women's Right's Movement in the 60s and 70s, when this type of title's audience of young girls and young women simply didn't seem to find congruity with their comic counterparts.

Superhero Comics

It's fitting, perhaps, that this chapter ends on what likely amounts to the largest and most popular genre of comics: the superhero. Rising up from the 1930s and traversing the hills and valleys of the twentieth century in terms of popularity to come out at the top of the heap by the 1980s, where the genre has never since relinquished control, superhero comics are likely considered the backbone of popular comprehensions of the medium with ubiquitous figures, such as Superman, Batman, and Wonder Woman, rising out of the Golden Age (and surviving to this day) and passing the torch to characters such as Spider-Man, The X-Men, and the Fantastic Four in Silver Age . . . and so on and so forth into the present moment, where the concept of superheroism has literally been turned on its ear by the poststructural reflection of a concept steeped in the social and cultural mores of the period times the genre has traversed.

Generically, superhero comics almost have to be broken down periodically, as comics arising in the so-called Golden Age, a period *very* roughly defined as arising with the arrival of Superman in *Action Comics* in 1938 and, likely, ending near or around the transmogrification of *DC All Star Comics* into *All-Star Western* in 1951. Defining what makes these comics "super" by way of their heroes is difficult, by comparison to, say, the Silver Age, whereby technological advances, such as the splitting of the atom and, therein, the deployment of the atomic bomb give rise to heroes with backstory vested in science and science fiction, particularly in Marvel Comics, but there are certainly some attributes that seem to universally apply: 1) These heroes possess abilities or capacities that separate them from normal heroes, whether that be Batman's riches and intellect or Superman's laundry list of physical attributes that give him virtually nigh omnipotence. 2) They are separated from the normative citizenry by their abilities (oft requiring a secret identity so that they can have some semblance of a life amongst humanity). Sometimes that separation came by the way of a domino mask or a pair of glasses (Alan Scott's Green Lantern and Superman, respectively), and sometimes the hero simply retreated back to his or her own home away from the prying eyes of the public, such as Namor and Wonder Woman. (Diana, of course, also occasionally kept a public persona as well.) 3) Tights. Sometimes capes. And frequent reversals of the pants/underwear binary. 4) They fought, inexplicably and without prejudice on the side of justice. *American* justice. Perhaps no better figure emulates and retains this concept more than Steve Rogers, Captain America, who regularly fought with troops on the side of the Allied forces, occasionally punching Adolf Hitler square in the face. These heroes were not always endorsed by America, mind you; Namor originated as an enemy of America, one who fought alongside it and, thereby, gained some trust. Batman operated best, perhaps, when barely within any of Gotham's laws and was seen as a vigilante. Others, Superman, Wonder Woman, and Cap, most notably wore America's colors in their suits and, as a result, received political endorsement and cachet as such.

By the time of the Silver Age's birth—roughly equated with the rise of the Barry Allen version of the Flash in 1956 and the Marvel revolution of the early sixties bringing in figures such as The

Fantastic Four, The Amazing Spider-Man, The Incredible Hulk, The X-Men, et al.—these comics and superheroes were, in many cases, the children of the Wertham hearings: scientifically and science fictionally-inclined, self-doubting, and in many ways flawed. These characters became tied up and imbricated with the sociocultural politics of the counterculture. Many of the lesser figures of the Golden Age did not survive; others did (Superman, Wonder Woman, Batman), but took a backseat to these new arrivals, and others still became transformed à la the Flash or the second Green Lantern, Hal Jordan, (Alan Scott and many others were shunted into a different reality known as Earth Two to account for the dual histories) in DC, and Captain America found himself frozen in a block of ice since the end of World War II, only to be thawed out and joined together with a series of more recently constructed heroes as a member of Marvel's *Avengers*. In many ways, this Silver Age of Comics seems to have brought about a new innocence within the characterization of these superheroes, all of which seems to explain the death and demise of the era in 1973 when Spider-Man failed to save the life of his girlfriend, Gwen Stacy, when she plummeted to her death at the hands of the Green Goblin.

Possibly the less said about the so-called Bronze Age, the better; the age of superheroic rust, as Kyle Eveleth notes in another chapter, might be more applicable. Running from, roughly, the team-up of Green Lantern and Green Arrow in 1971 to the monumental books of the mid-eighties, Alan Moore's *Watchmen* and Frank Miller's *The Dark Knight Returns*, the era became somewhat known for its more socially-conscious messages and a return to dark, pre-Wertham plotlines involving drug use, environmental degradation, and more than the occasional death. Gwen Stacy's untimely death seems to be the pivotal moment between the Silver Age's decline and the Bronze Age's rise; however, others will easily cite Denny O'Neil's characterization of Green Arrow's sidekick Speedy as a drug user as another touchstone moment of the era. By this point, comic plotlines and character constructs seem to be considerably less concerned with narrative storytelling anywhere near as much as dealing with socially-relevant issues, such as Iron Man's alcoholism in the infamous "Demon in a Bottle" story arc or the rise of minority superheroes, such as Luke Cage, Shang Chi, John Stewart, Vixen, or Black Lightning. These books were met by a considerably more mixed reception than the prior generations and began to cause the rise in team-up books in which multiple superheroes were paired in an effort to give the reader more hero for their book. (*Power Man and Iron Fist* or *The Brave and the Bold* are obvious incarnations as such from Marvel Comics and DC, respectively.) Interestingly, the public's disinterest in many of these titles led to a counterrevolution *against* traditional superheroes and a rise of new anti-heroic heroes in this era, such as Ghost Rider, Deathlok, and sword-and-sorcery titles, such as *Conan the Barbarian* and *Savage Sword of Conan*.

By this point, the genre seemed to be at odds with itself after so many years of adaptation, modification, and, possibly, supersaturation of the product. Not to be unexpected then, another counterrevolution arose: the Modern Age of Superhero Comics, which some would argue still goes on to this day. Triggered by the Moore and Miller books mentioned earlier, the best terms to describe these books might be: dark, psychological, and deconstructive. The seeds for this generation of books were likely planted far earlier, in 1982, with Moore's own revival and deconstruction of *Marvelman/Miracleman*, where a Silver Age character, Michael Moran, was retconned and reintroduced to the public in a manner that both reinvigorated the construct, but dramatically altered the content by forcing the character to adapt to the modern age after a period of obsolescence. Part of that reinvigoration was to reconsider the idea of the superhero as someone with considerable public endorsement and recast that hero along more vigilante/anti-heroic lines. Taking a cue from Miller and Moore, comics began to look at these demagogic characters and cast the non-superpowered public as still being in awe of them . . . but also being quite afraid of them as well. These characters, such as the X-Men and X-Force, could do just as much damage as they could good, and they were likely things that needed to be more closely scrutinized before they discovered that with great power came great responsibility . . . but maybe great power could mitigate great responsibility as who could stop me?

(See Magneto or Marvel's "Civil War" storyline where superheroes are actually forced to register with the government to the extent that they actually went to war with each other over their rights to privacy and secret identities.)

Stakes escalated in superhero storylines. Soon it was not enough to destroy a building, or a town, or even a world, but characters like Chris Claremont's Dark Phoenix would have to snuff out entire galaxies and civilizations to keep consumers interested and impressed. And to raise the stakes sometimes meant killing characters that were once deemed unkillable leading to massive cross-comic books story arcs, like "The Death of Superman" where the title character himself was *actually* killed by a newly introduced character, Doomsday . . . for a short period of time. And, as comics writer Max Landis once adroitly put it, with the death and return from death of Superman, DC literally found a way to do something relatively unheard of on a wide scale of superhero books: they killed death, itself. Such might be a wary, but accurate, final statement of the modern age of comics: in an era where death is utterly irrelevant, there does not seem to be a topic or a taboo that cannot be broached in capes-and-cowls books. Whether that is a grand moment of possibility or the breaking point of unfinalizability, where anything can be . . . so it *is* will likely only be known by those who record the end of this era with whatever supplants it next.

Works Cited

"Comics Symposium." *Children's Literature Association Quarterly* 37.4 (Winter 2012).

Eisner, Will. *Comics & Sequential Art*. Paramus, NJ: Poorhouse, 1990.

Jenkins, Henry. *Convergence Culture: Where Old and New Media Collide*. New York: New York UP, 2008.

McCloud, Scott. *Understanding Comics: The Invisible Art*. New York: HarperPerennial, 1993.

Pawuk, Michael. *Graphic Novels: A Genre Guide to Comic Books, Manga, and More*. Westport, CT: Libraries Unlimited, 2007.

Wolk, Douglas. *Reading Comics: How Graphic Novels Work and What They Mean*. Cambridge, MA: Da Capo, 2007.

The Improbability of Assignment: Arriving at a Golden Age of Comic Books_____

Joseph Darowski

When referencing the comic book industry, the term Golden Age is used fairly commonly by fans, retailers, and publishers to describe an early era, perhaps the earliest era, of comic book history. However, this term has not been adopted by all, and, even when it is used, its meaning is not necessarily concrete. Because of this ambiguity, it is important to establish the meaning of the term, even while acknowledging that there are other opinions and counterarguments for veritably any and all aspects of its construction and usage. For the purpose of this chapter, it will be argued that the Golden Age of Comic Books represents a period roughly between 1938 and 1955. Specifically, the opening set of brackets marks the first appearance of Superman in DC Comics *Action Comics* #1 (1938); Jerry Siegel and Joe Shuster's seminal construction of what is still recognized as *the* American superhero is generally considered by all as the Golden Age's beginning. Somewhat more contentiously, perhaps among a constellation of other events, the first appearance of the reimagined Flash (Barry Allen) as crafted by Robert Kanigher, John Broome, and Carmine Infantino in *Showcase #4* (Oct. 1956) is considered the beginning of the Silver Age of Comics and, consequently, the close of the Golden Age.

Demarcating the history of the comic book industry by the launch of *Action Comics* and the relaunch of *The Flash* highlights the preeminence of the superhero in these comic books. On the one hand, this is natural, as the superhero genre of the medium has been the driving economic force of the industry for several decades. On the other hand, this construction ignores a vast and rich history of the comic book industry, an industry that has found success with myriad other products beyond superhero narratives and their accompanying books. In using those two specific comic books to bookend the Golden Age, this chapter does recognize the importance of the superhero genre, likewise it also attempts to demonstrate that a key aspect of the Golden Age of Comic Books was the manner in which the industry continued to flourish even as interest in superheroes waned approaching the latter half of the Golden Age.

The Problemicity of *Golden* Ages: a Medial Analogy

The history of the comic book industry has been divided into generally accepted eras, beginning with the, as one might expect, the Golden Age. However, *generally* is a far cry from universally, and the concept of Golden, Silver, Bronze . . . some actually include an Iron period, and Modern Ages are contested by professionals, scholars, and fans alike for reasons that vary as much as the dates and issues surrounding the periods' demarcation. In particular, the eras that follow the Silver Age are subject to even more contentious debate. Even amongst those who use the term Golden Age, the details surrounding the era are not firmly established.

Before even trying to establish the key aspects of the Golden Age of Comic Books, it may be useful to consider the term itself: The Golden Age. The very term accentuates a set of unspoken markers and assumptions: The height of culture and society. Or an era distinguished by unusually high quality. Or the first in a successive series of ages. Or a bar of accomplishment by which subsequent eras might be measured. Golden Age is the sort of label that gets tossed around in multiple contexts determinate by usage and medium, and, because of that, its meaning can be quite ambiguous. However, certain things are relatively clear: The origin of the term is tied to Greek mythology. Hesiod identified five ages of humankind beginning with the Golden Age and descending through the Silver, Bronze, Heroic, and Iron Ages. But, as with any term that has been used for centuries and crossed languages, its meaning was appropriated, altered, expanded, and obscured by those evoking it for various anecdotal purposes. The comic book industry is not alone in experiencing disagreement over the conception of its Golden Age. A consideration of different mediums and genres brings to light the common usage of Golden Age to define an era, but also the frequent disagreement about what constitutes the Golden Age of that entertainment form.

Like its Greek origins, a Golden Age could be the first in a series of eras of a particular medium. For example, in American television, the 1950s is often considered its Golden Age because that was the era when the medium became popularly-established (King). However, several critics have begun referring to a more modern era of television when *The Sopranos* (1999–2007)*, Mad Men* (2007–2014), and *The Wire* (2002–2008) aired on cable channels as a new Golden Age of Television. Andy Greenwald explains that a new Golden Age of television began with the premiere of *The Sopranos*:

> During the roughly 10-year period that followed, the small screen went from being cinema's idiot brother to the last auteur-driven mass medium. What was once seen as a cul-de-sac of hacky cops and laugh tracks became a thrillingly limitless canvas for storytellers and creators. The Golden Age brought us the taut urbanity of *The Wire*, the soulful rusticity of *Friday Night Lights*, and the manic insanity of *Arrested Development*. It put polar bears in the tropics and profanity in the Old West. (n.p.)

If, as Greenwald posits, a medium can have two Golden Ages, what relevancy does the term carry without any critical consensus?

In the realm of Hollywood cinema and filmmaking, the term Golden Age is most often used to refer to the aural arrival of sound in films likely with the release of *The Jazz Singer* (1927) starring Al Jolson. It was a period recognized as having unsurpassed growth in the medium, and it was an era when many of the styles of storytelling and the art of editing recognized today were being established. But Hollywood had been making films for decades when this Golden Age began making it as a somewhat contentious allegory to comics or other less established mediums.

By way of, perhaps, a stronger comparison, science fiction literature has two different eras that are commonly referred to as the Golden Age. It had become standard practice among science fiction fans in the 1950s and 1960s to call the era from 1938–1946 the Golden Age of Science Fiction following the so-called Pulp Era (and preceding the aptly-titled New Wave). More recently, though, reassessment of the genre by some, such as Mike Ashley, has led to the conclusion that 1950–1954 was the more likely the genre's Golden Age because of the rise of the "flood of new and re-emerging writers" and a wider recognition of the science fiction genre by an established community and readership ("Golden Age of Science Fiction").

As shown through the previous examples, identifying a Golden Age for any medium or genre can be a problematic, if not outright dicey, proposition at best. In comic books, the Golden Age refers to a specific era of comic books, when many of the operating procedures were established, when conventions about the size and content of comic books were being normalized, and when the superhero genre was indelibly linked with the comic book medium. But, even with that definition, there is still some debate.

What Is Generally Considered as the Golden Age of Comic Books?

No matter what set of dates, periods, or critical interpretations are accepted, one fact seems relatively certain: the delineation of the comic book industry into "ages" is simply an arbitrary act, retroactively attempting to overlay some sort of order onto an immensely complex and multifaceted business. No system is going to be perfect, and that is why so many varying systems have been developed. These issues are not unique to popular culture products. When debating the demarcation of Victorian Literature and Modern Literature in the English literary canon, Josh Rahn argues that "Literary periods are never the discrete, self-contained realms which the anthologies so suggest. Rather, a literary period more closely resembles a rope that is frayed at both ends. Many threads make up the rope and work together to form the whole artistic and cultural milieu" (n.p.). This metaphor of a frayed rope is certainly applicable to the beginning and ending of the Golden Age. Different historians have identified disparate strands as the most important factor in defining the beginning and end of the era.

As an example, in 1933, Maxwell Gaines took several pre-existing newspaper comic strips and decided to see if he could get the public to pay for material they could have already purchased in the newspapers (Wright 3). This new product, *Funnies on Parade*, was the first modern comic book in America, and, theoretically, it could be seen to have begun the Golden Age of Comic Books a full five years predating the release of *Action Comics* #1.

Maybe.

Five years later, Jerry Siegel composed the following: "As a distant planet was destroyed by old age, a scientist placed his infant son within a hastily devised space-ship, launching it toward Earth!" And, with those words, the first text in the first Superman comic book story ever published, the Golden Age of Comic Books *arguably* began in 1938. So, which is it going to be: 1933 or 1938? It all depends on whom you ask and what they consider as their mitigating factors. For example: the most common definition of the era spans a fifteen- to twenty-year time period that covers the late-1930s to mid-1950s. Due to the relativity of the matter, some historians and fans simply avoid using the term Golden Age at all. In *The Power of Comics*, Randy Duncan and Matthew J. Smith refer to the years most typically associated with the Golden Age as two distinct eras, "The Era of Proliferation" and "The Era of Diversification" (23). Robert Beerbohm prefers to refer to the period that is commonly called the Golden Age as "The First Heroic Age" and the "Atomic Romance Age." While Golden Age, as part of a general nomenclature, may be the most common term, there is simply no consensus in how the history of the comic book industry should be divided at its onset.

In fact, the first known usage of the term Golden Age arrived not in critical discourse, but in an early comic book fanzine called *Comic Art*. In *Comic Art* #1 (Spring 1961), Dick Lupoff writes that comics "came in the thirties, their golden age was in the forties. They declined in the fifties with only one late-blooming flower, the EC line, really coming forth in that decade" (5). How that term took a journey from a self-published fanzine to an industry standard is somewhat unclear. What is known is that the adoption of the term by price guides, especially considering how the concept of comic books as an accepted medium became established largely through commercial ends, helped to cement its usage within the circle of comic book fans. Presently, publishers, retailers, and fans are likely to use the term Golden Age to refer to comics that were published between the late 1930s and the mid-1950s. The academic community resigns, largely, to concur.

Both DC Comics and Marvel Comics, the largest publishers of superhero comic books in America, have referred to the Golden Age in their official publications even across numerous retcons and reorganizations of their own storied histories. DC Comics has published *Superman: The Golden Age Omnibus*, which collects and reprints early *Superman* comic books from between 1938 and 1940. Marvel Comics has released the *Golden Age Captain America Omnibus*, likewise, which reprints Captain America comic books from the 1940s. Both publishers, likewise, will use the term Golden Age in marketing and reference materials. Marvel's online database identifies the Golden Age "as lasting from 1938 until the mid-1950s" (*Marvel Comics Database*). DC's online database similarly explains that the Golden Age is "a period beginning in 1938 and ended in the mid '50s" (*DC Comics Database*).

While problematic, perhaps, in terms of denoting a specific era by way of dates or even periodization, the term has become remarkably useful for identifying different versions of popular characters who, as other chapters in this collection show, have undergone significant metamorphosis by way of age. For example, the company now known as DC Comics published the adventures of many different costumed heroes in the 1940s. But most, with the exception of Superman, Batman, and Wonder Woman, ceased publication in the latter portion of the Golden Age. Heroes such as the Flash (Jay Garrick) or Green Lantern (Alan Scott) had their adventures told in comic book form in the 1940s and then, in the early Silver Age, many of those heroes were revived, but with new origin stories, new secret identities, and redesigned costumes. Thus, the Golden Age Flash, Jay Garrick, was created by Gardner Fox and Harry Lampert. This Flash had attained his super-speed powers after he accidentally inhaled "hard water vapors" in a laboratory. This version of the Flash first appeared in 1940 and would appear in various comic books until 1951. In 1956, Kanigher, Broome, and Infantino created a new version of the Flash, who first appeared in

Showcase #4 (Oct. 1956). This Flash had the secret identity of Barry Allen. Allen gained his superpowers when a bolt of lightning hit a case of chemicals in a police lab where Allen was working. In terms of trying to keep these characters separate, DC generally refers to two as: Jay Garrick, the Golden Age Flash, and Barry Allen, the Silver Age Flash. (Recently, in DC's ret-con, *The New 52*, many of these characters have been resigned to different elements of the DC multiverse, with Garrick and Scott now existing in the so-called *Earth 2*.) This reimagining of the Flash is often (but again, not universally) cited as the beginning of the Silver Age of Comic Books. While many comic book superheroes retained the same secret identity and basic origin story across the different ages of comic books, several Golden Age characters that had lost popularity were relaunched in the Silver Age in a manner analogous to what was done with the Flash.

The Golden Age, as such, is a useful term to define a specific era of comics. While it may not be perfect, it successfully serves the purpose of identifying an era so that creators, publishers, and fans have a common ground when discussing the history of the industry. For our general purposes, the clearest definition is that the Golden Age of Comic Books began with the publication of *Action Comics* #1 and ended when the Silver Age began, with the publication of *Showcase* #4.

General Aspects of the Golden Age of Comic Books

There are several important things to recognize even while working from the tenuous notion that the Golden Age began in 1938 with the publishing of *Action Comics* #1. First, *Action Comics* #1 was not the first American comic book, nor was it was not the first comic book with original content. Both of these claims can be encountered occasionally, and they are undeniably and definitively incorrect. Granted, defining the first American comic book is tricky in and of itself. One of the first pieces of sequential art published in America was *The Adventures of Obadiah Oldbuck*, which was a translation of a work by the Swiss cartoonist Rodolphe Töpffer. Published in 1842, *The Adventures of Obadiah Oldbuck* did feature the necessitated combination of words and text in sequential order to tell a story, but was not formatted like the comic books acknowledged today. Similarly, *Journey to the Gold Diggins by Jeremiah Saddlebags* was an early American produced piece of sequential art, but it was not formatted akin to a traditional comic book (Rhoades 3). The same goes for the wide variety of newspaper supplements that were produced from the late 1880s even through to the present day. Generally referred to as comic strips, these share much of the same narratology of comic books but not the format.

The earliest comic books that begin to align with our current understanding of the term were reprints of newspaper comic strips. Max Gaines approached a publishing company, Eastern Color Printing, with an idea he had to reprint newspaper comic strips only to be told that they already reprinted several newspaper strips as promotional tabloid-sized giveaways for clients. As Shirrel Rhoades notes, "Gaines suggested folding the tabloid in half to create a sixty-four-page magazine," thus introducing the primary format comic books have had to this day (10). Gaines' reprint, entitled *Funnies on Parade* was a hit that immediately bred imitators. With titles like *Funnies on Parade*, *Famous Funnies*, and *The Funnies*, the label "comic book" first took root as a description of these new periodicals (Wright 2). While a trip to a modern comic book shop may make that label seem like an overall misnomer, with comic books that focus considerably more on superheroes, fantasy, sci-fi, and horror than comedy, the term "comic book" was considerably more apt in those early days of the industry. The primary genre of these early comic books was indeed comedy, though even before Superman cemented the links between the superhero genre and the comic book industry, other genres began to be explored by the young industry.

Despite the earlier comic books, *Action Comics* #1 was a game changer for the industry. Siegel and Shuster, the co-creators of Superman, took existing elements of popular culture and repackaged them within their landmark creation. Following in the footsteps of the frontiersman and cowboys of dime novels, the adventurers and crime fighters of the pulps, the detectives and cops of radio dramas and the burgeoning cinema, Superman introduced the superhero genre to eager readers in 1938. Oddly enough, he was originally intended to be remarkably similar to the character that would eventually become known as his primary antagonist, Lex Luthor; after several failures with this idea, Siegel and Schuster repackaged him as a heroic protagonist, and the comic book industry would never be the same (Jones 82–84). Indeed, American popular culture would never be the same. As Jim Steranko puts it, "A bold new champion who could leap off the page [. . .] would herald the Golden Age of Comics" (1).

Following in Superman's footsteps, other superheroes began gracing comic book pages. Some, like Batman and Wonder Woman, would continue to be published uninterrupted for decades. Others, like the Green Lantern or Dr. Hypno, would have much briefer runs, but would be revisited frequently. Many were expressly propagandistic and jingoistic, chief among these being Marvel's initial foray into Captain America, a character that was, essentially, a walking American flag. Even before America entered the war, Cap was featured on a comic book cover (*Captain America Comics* #1, March 1941) punching Hitler in the face in a bold and controversial symbolic gesture, shepherded through to publication by the character's creators, Jack Kirby and Joe Simon. Perhaps because of the proudly American theme of many superheroes and their stories, through World War II, superheroes remained one of the most popular genres exploited by comic book publishers. The superhero genre and the comic book industry first became linked in the Golden Ages, and they became inextricably connected in the minds of many. As Douglas Wolk explains:

> There is no way of getting around it: if you are going to look honestly at American comic books, you are going to encounter superheroes. The spandex wall is the public face of the medium, and its monolithic presence is what leads to the conflation of the superhero genre and the comics medium by people who don't know any better. (89)

Wolk, however, clearly writes and argues from a modern perspective. Readers during the Golden Age would have found a wealth of alternatives to the superhero genre, even during the height of this era's fascination with superheroes during the Second World War.

In fact, one of the most important aspects of the Golden Age of the comic book industry is that it survived and thrived even as the superhero genre waned in popularity. Notable genres of the medium, which are commented on in greater depth in other chapters of this volume, include romance comics, western comics, crime comics, and horror comics. EC Comics, (which never did, but might as well have stood for *Evolving* Comics) had published Bible stories when the company was called Educational Comics and humorous animal comics when the company went by Entertaining Comics; EC again shifted its focus in the late 1940s. Owner William Gaines transitioned his titles into the crime genre and away from wholesome, kiddie entertainment. Then, in 1950, the company embraced the horror genre with titles such as *Tales from the Crypt* and *Vault of Horror* (Jones 253–256). EC Comics' success with crime and horror comic books inspired many imitators, much as Superman's success had spawned the first wave of superhero comic books. However, not everyone was pleased with the industry's new direction. Comics were harmless enough when they featured comedic gags and superheroes that defended the social order, but, when they were perceived to treat crime and horror as entertainment, some feared that the industry was a cause of juvenile delinquency.

The Golden Age Ends

The comic book industry had great success in the 1940s with the superhero genre and had redefined itself in the early 1950s. The industry was not associated with any single genre and tested the waters with new products to discover the evolving tastes of readers. However, when readers embraced horror comic books, some cultural critics raised alarm about what influence comic books might wield over readers. Concerns about the content of comic books were highlighted by some, most notably Fredric Wertham in his book *Seduction of the Innocent*. The United States government held hearings to determine if there were links between the material published in comic books and juvenile delinquency, as Wertham had asserted. In a few cities around the country, it has been reported that comic book burnings were held in the name of protecting the children from the corruptive influence of comic books. In light of this notorious press, the comic book industry instituted a self-censorship board that would regulate the content publishers could include if they wished their products to be sold on newsstands or at retail locations. The Comics Code Authority placed severe limitations on the content of comic books, limitations that particularly crippled EC Comics and their line of crime and horror comic books. Partially in response to the new stipulations that comic books always feature good triumphing over evil, DC Comics began to exploit the superhero genre anew. While true crime comics may end with the bad guy escaping justice, the Flash could, and generally did, always chase down an adversary without fail.

As every era ends, a new movement invariably takes its place. For this reason, it makes the most sense to place the end of the Golden Age adjacent to the beginnings of the Silver Age. Similarly to the uncertainty around the beginning of the Golden Age, there is some debate as to what constitutes the beginning of the Silver Age of Comic Books: Was it the formation of the Comics Code Authority, or the relaunch of the Flash, or Marvel Comics establishing their own superhero narrative universe couched in angst-ridden adolescent protagonists and science fiction? In addition to the symmetry it provides with the origins of the Golden Age, it makes sense and is oddly appropriate to begin the Silver Age with the reintroduction of the Flash, which reinvigorated DC Comics' superhero titles because this represents a new chapter for the industry. There was clearly a Golden Age Flash fitting that era's cultural mores, and now there would be a Silver Age Flash doing the same. (Not to mention several future versions arising in later ages, such as Wally West.) Superheroes would be embraced by the industry in a new direction that adhered to the stipulations of the Comics Code. Soon, DC would reintroduce several of their Golden Age heroes and group them together in The Justice League, itself a reimagined Justice Society, a popular team title from the Golden Age.

The success DC Comics experienced with these titles would eventually inspire the company that would become known as Marvel Comics to revisit the superhero genre as well. Soon, Jack Kirby, Steve Ditko, et al., were providing the art and Stan Lee, purportedly, the text for titles such as *The Fantastic Four, The Incredible Hulk, The Avengers, The X-Men*, and, of course, most-notably arising from the pages of *Amazing Fantasy #15, The Amazing Spider-Man.* Spider-Man, possibly embodies the greatest change from the Golden Age to the Silver Age: Rather than being a self-assured and purely noble emblem of the moral establishment, Peter Parker was a self-questioning and snarky adolescent hero who would set the Marvel superhero universe off and running, if not swinging from a gossamer thread of webbing, throughout the skyscrapers of New York City. While DC Comics began the Silver Age with a new iteration of the Flash, Marvel Comics would help cement the preeminence of superheroes in the mainstream comic book industry with their new heroes and corresponding titles. While the Golden Age heroes were largely infallible and concerned with the greater good, Marvel's Silver Age heroes had feet of clay, bickered amongst themselves, and were as concerned with personal problems as with societal ills. The prominence and power held over the marketplace of DC Comics and Marvel Comics and their respective narrative universes continues to this day.

In Memoriam: The Golden Age: 1938–1955
Despite the earlier existing comic books, despite the existence of many other genres of stories told in the comic book industry, it makes sense to tie the beginning of the Golden Age to the first appearance of Superman, as he brings about the dawn of the superheroes. It is also logical to connect the transition into the Silver Age with the reimagined superheroes of DC Comics, beginning with the Flash in 1955, that likely inspired Marvel Comics to embrace a new model of superhero in their line of comic books. While this method does highlight the importance of superheroes to the movements within the comic book industry, it does not exclude the other genres that populate the greater medium of comics. In fact, one of the most

important aspects of the Golden Age is that the industry endured and adapted to the audiences' changing tastes following World War II. The popularity of other genres, including humor, romance, western, war, crime, science fiction, and horror are a key aspect of the Golden Age. The industry was not limited by the superhero genre that so many critics and fans alike associate with the medium. The industry embraced the superheroes at the height of their popularity during the war and followed readers' interests elsewhere, when they had become disenchanted with superhero adventures, whether it be from super-saturation of the genre or legislative concerns over content. In subsequent ages, the relationship between superhero comic books, the industry, and fandom will alter considerably, but the Golden Age is as defined by its transition away from superheroes as it is by the impact of that genre at the beginning of the era. Everything else are matters left open to debate, conjecture, and the arguments hopefully still held today by a righteous fan base in comic book stores and classrooms.

Works Cited

Beerbohm, Robert. "Re: Origin of Golden Age and Silver Age terminology." Comix-Scholar Email Chain. 11 February 2013.

DC Comics Database. "Golden Age." n.d. Web. 30 July 2014.

Duncan, Randy, & Matthew J. Smith. *The Power of Comics: History, Form, & Culture*. New York: Continuum, 2009. "The Golden Age of Science Fiction." *The Encyclopedia of Science Fiction*, 3rd ed. 19 Feb. 2012. Web. 30 Jul. 2014.

Greenwald, Andy. "The Return of *Mad Men* and the End of TV's Golden Age." *Grantland.com*. 27 March 2012. Web. Accessed 24 Feb. 2014.

Jones, Gerard. *Men of Tomorrow: Geeks, Gangsters, and the Birth of the Comic Book*. New York: Basic Books, 2008.

King, Susan. "The Golden Age of Television." *The Los Angeles Times*. 8 Nov. 2009. Web. 24 Feb. 2014.

Lupoff, Dick. "Re-Birth." *Comic Art #1*. Cleveland, OH: Oblivion Press, 1961. PDF scan.

Marvel Comics Database. "The Golden Age of Comic Books." n.d. Web. 30 Jul. 2014.

Rahn, Josh. "Victorian Literature." *The Literature Network*. Morehead State University. 2011. Web. 2 August 2014.

Rhoades, Shirrel. *A Complete History of American Comic Books*. NY: Peter Lange, 2008.

Siegel, Jerry, & Joe Schuster. "Superman, Champion of the Oppressed!" *Superman: The Golden Age Omnibus, Vol. 1*. Ed. Rowena Yow. New York, DC Comics: 2013.

Siegel, Jerry, & Joe Schuster. *Superman: The Golden Age Omnibus, Vol. 1*. Ed. Rowena Yow. New York: DC Comics: 2013.

Simon, Joe, & Jack Kirby. *The Golden Age Captain American Omnibus*. New York: Marvel Comics, 2014.

Steranko, Jim. "Foreword." *Superman: The Golden Age Omnibus, Vol. 1*. Ed. Rowena Yow. New York: DC Comics: 2013.

Wolk, Douglas. *Reading Comics: How Graphic Novels Work and What They Mean*. Cambridge, MA: Da Capo Press, 2007.

Wright, Bradford W. *Comic Book Nation: The Transformation of Youth Culture in America*. Baltimore: Johns Hopkins UP, 2001.

The Silver Age Playbook: Minting the Modern Superhero

Matthew J. Smith

"History is written by the victors," said the former British Prime Minister Winston Churchill. Case in point, the history of the comics medium has often been defined by fans of the superhero genre, a type of comic book storytelling that ultimately outlasted every competing genre, from westerns to horror comics, and has come to dominate the marketplace to this day. However, while the periodic highs and lows of the superhero genre have come to define how we conceptualize the history of the American comic book industry, historians Gerard Jones and Will Jacobs note that "there was no point from the 1940s to the 1970s, when superheroes represented more than 20 percent of the total product of the American comic book industry" (Jenkins 16). Despite the market dominance of alternative storytelling in the forms of crime, romance, horror, and funny animal comics, the superhero did eventually and then extensively come to command most of the comic book marketplace. By virtue of being the genre that not only persisted but ultimately prevailed, superheroes have had the opportunity to define the medium that spawned it retroactively. Hence, we talk of a Golden Age marked by the first appearance of the superhero (Superman in the pages of *Action Comics* #1 cover dated June 1938) and a Silver Age commencing with the rebirth of the superhero (Flash in the pages of *Showcase* #4 cover dated October 1956).

Into the Silver Mines

The notion of naming ages according to metals is derived from ancient Greek mythology. According to the poet Hesiod, the gods originally crafted human-like races out of various metals, including gold, silver, and bronze. Each race passed away, some undone by their own flaws, until the gods ultimately crafted creatures of flesh, who endured thereafter (Hamilton 86). The legacy of a system of metallurgic designations continues to this day, most famously in our system for awarding medals to the first (gold), second (silver), and third (bronze) place finishers in major athletic contests such as the Olympic Games. Thusly, a second period of significance, in this case of the superhero genre, is named the Silver Age. That designation came about because it was applied by a fan, though almost a decade into the age itself. "In *Justice League of America* #42 (February 1966), letter writer Scott Taylor of Westport, Connecticut, wrote, 'If you guys keep bringing back the heroes from the . . . Golden Age, people 20 years from now will be calling this decade the Silver Sixties!'" (Schelly 151). The term was subsequently embraced by a wider swath of the fan community, notably in the fan press and then in collector's circles, including the bible for collecting, the *Official Overstreet Comic Book Price Guide.*

The Golden Age had, of course, been rife with superheroes, institutionalizing such perennial favorites as Superman, Batman, and Wonder Woman, but also introducing numerous others whose comic book titles dominated the newsstands in the lead up to and then throughout World War II. After the war, though, superheroes began to decline in popularity, but the comic book industry responded with an expanding slate of genres to entertain a widening readership base. Funny animals, teen humor, crime, war, horror, western and romance comics garnered increasingly significant shares of the comic book marketplace into the late 1940s and throughout the 1950s, leaving only a handful of superheroes regularly appearing on America's newsstands. But the increasingly mature themes in many of these other genres, most notably the crime and horror comics, spurred an outcry for tighter policing of comics, one a skittish industry responded to in 1954 by creating a self-censoring board, the Comics Code Authority. In order to bear the Authority's seal of approval— and thus the uncritical support of distributors and newsstand vendors—comics had to conform to a rigid set of guidelines that neutered the punch of most mature comics storytelling. The industry was set in search of expanding offerings among those genres that worked well within the restrictions of the Code, and superheroes were one option that various publishers began to reconsider.

Early attempts at reviving the superhero genre did not meet with success. Publisher Martin Goodman had attempted to revive Golden Age stars the Sub-Mariner, Human Torch, and Captain America under his Atlas imprint in late 1953, but they were abandoned once again by October 1955. Likewise, Charlton Comics brought back another Golden Age star, the Blue Beetle, for a series of appearances from late 1954 through 1955, but, once again, simply revisiting once successful characters of yesteryear didn't seem to catch on. Perhaps the audience was eager for new heroes who better fit their times? Prize Comics gave seminal Golden Age creators Joe Simon and Jack Kirby seven issues to try out *Fighting American* between 1954 and 1955, and Magazine Enterprises issued a new hero in *The Avenger* for four issues also in 1955. Even the initial efforts of industry leaders, such as National Periodical Publications (later DC Comics), were unremarkable. National introduced the Martian Manhunter as a feature in the pages of *Detective Comics* #225 (November 1955) to accompany headliner Batman in the monthly magazine. Despite his fantastic origin as an inhabitant of the Red Planet, the Martian Manhunter behaved more like a detective than a superhero, and he appeared in a back-up feature with no discernable impact on sales. Batwoman debuted (in *Detective Comics* #233, May 1956) two months before the Flash, but she caused no discernable bump in sales. All of these attempts may simply not have gelled because the Baby Boomer generation, which was the principle audience, hadn't yet come to the age where they were interested in superheroes (Schelly 151); perhaps they were content with buying funny animal comics until the point at which National attempted a clever synthesis of the old and the new.

Silver Plating

The Silver Age began in the pages of *Showcase* #4, a magazine that National published to try out new concepts before launching them in their own series (Coogan 205). Prior to experimenting with superheroes, *Showcase* had featured firemen, western scouts, and frogmen, none of which enjoyed enough sales to justify an ongoing series of its own. But the reintroduction of the Flash proved to be lightning in a bottle.

The original Flash, who had debuted in the pages of *Flash Comics* #1 in January 1940 had faltered, last appearing in an issue of *All-Star Comics* #57 in February–March 1951. Casting about for ideas of what to feature in the next issue of *Showcase,* members of National's editorial staff argued that the turn-over in readership—which was held to be about a five-year span—meant that the character was probably forgotten by their readership and a new generation of readers might be interested in the novelty of "the fastest man alive" (Schelly 145). Julius Schwartz, who oversaw most of National's science fiction comics, was chosen to edit the issue, and he in turn assigned the lead story to writer Bob Kanigher and art to penciller Carmine Infantino and inker Joe Kubert. The creative team did not simply recast the previous Flash, whose alter-ego was named Jay Garrick, but introduced a new character in the role, a police scientist named Barry Allen. Accordingly, Infantino designed a fresh, sleek costume. The modern spin on the classic concept caught the audience's attention. However, it took some time for sales figures to report the success of the Flash's debut, and the cautious editorial team brought the Flash back for two more trial runs in *Showcase,* the second in issue #8 (May–June 1957) and then a pair of issues, #13 (March–April 1958) and #14 (May-June 1958), before finally rewarding the Flash with his own, ongoing title. Barry Allen may have picked up the numbering left behind by his predecessor's series with *Flash* #105 (February–March 1959), but everything else about the series was moving forward at full speed.

Spurred on by the success of the Flash, Schwartz targeted for revision another Golden Age star from National's stable: the Green Lantern. Originally, Alan Scott, the wielder of a power ring crafted from a magical lantern, Green Lantern had debuted in *All-American Comics* #16 (July 1940) and last appeared in *All-Star Comics* #57 (February 1951). In *Showcase* #22 (September–October 1959), writer John Broome and artist Gil Kane cast a test pilot named Hal Jordan who was recruited to become a member of an intergalactic peace-keeping force, the Green Lantern Corps, wielding a power ring based on space age science rather than magic. Within months of his trial run in *Showcase*, the new Green Lantern was starring in his own title (July–August 1960).

And then Schwartz set his sights even higher, aiming to re-introduce the superhero team. The premiere superhero team, the Justice Society of America, had faded away in 1951 and for this iteration Schwartz changed the name and much of the roster. In a February–March 1960 debut in the pages of *Brave and the Bold* #28, crafted by writer Gardner Fox and artist Mike Sekowsky, the Justice League of America banded together "the mightiest heroes of our time" including heavy hitters Superman, Batman, and Wonder Woman, as well as new stars Flash and Green Lantern and second stringers Martian Manhunter and Aquaman. The Justice League was in its own title by that fall. Schwartz would go on to refurbish other Golden Age stars, including the Atom and Hawkman, rebranding them with new powers, new costumes, and new identities, but most situated more comfortably in the world of science fiction. Additional debuts would continue as the sixties rolled on, including the Metal Men, Teen Titans, Deadman, and Batgirl. The era would also see National revamp the images of characters such as Batman, Wonder Woman, and Green Arrow.

Other publishers were tentative in testing the waters before diving into producing superhero comics once again. Archie Comics was the first competitor to experiment with the superhero revival, debuting *The Adventures of the Fly* and *The Double Life of Private Strong* in late 1959. Charlton Comics also premiered Captain Atom as a feature in *Space Adventures* #33 (March 1960). Neither publishers' efforts caught on in quite the same way as National's had. However, another publisher was positioning itself to take advantage of the resurgence, leaving its own indelible mark on the genre thereafter.

A Silver Voice

As the Silver Age of comics was dawning at National, things could not have been going much worse for publisher Martin Goodman's comics line, most recently operating under the Atlas Comics imprint. In 1957, a botched distribution deal had landed the line with Independent News, a part of the National corporate family. Independent imposed limitations on Goodman and would agree to distribute only eight titles a month. At the time, he had been printing more than 30 titles a month. Goodman and his editor, Stan Lee, narrowed their line down to sixteen bi-monthly titles to alternate into the eight slots and laid off most of their creative staff.

But by 1959, Lee was able to provide freelance work to artists again, and that included welcoming back Jack Kirby to the Goodman stable. Kirby had worked for Goodman during the Golden Age, most famously creating Captain America along with his collaborator, Joe Simon, in 1941. Goodman fired Simon and Kirby when he discovered that they were moonlighting for National and the split had left a bad taste in Kirby's mouth. However, the comic book market had grown leaner by the late 1950s and Kirby, seeking to provide for his family, re-affiliated himself with the company. It was a return that would change comic book superheroes forever.

It was common practice for Goodman to direct Lee to follow whatever trend dominated the market. Whenever one genre came to prominence with other publishers, Goodman would have Lee produce more of the same. So, when it became clear that National's superheroes, most notably its hit *Justice League of America* was a success, Goodman ordered up superheroes. Rather than just boilerplate the same old, tired tropes, Lee opted to try something bold. Frustrated after more than twenty years in the business and considering walking away from it, Lee took the counsel of his wife and decided to write a superhero series that he would want to read. He outlined a team of imperfect heroes who would not only face monstrous menaces but fought among themselves, too. Kirby, having already brought a quartet of adventurers into action in the pages of National's *Challengers of the Unknown,* defined them visually. *Fantastic Four* #1 (November 1961) featured a brilliant scientist, the woman who loved him, his best friend, and her kid brother. But more importantly, Mr. Fantastic, the Invisible Girl, The Thing, and the Human Torch were interesting characters whose foibles and problems were relatable in a way that National's clean-cut superheroes—with straight-laced, seemingly interchangeable, cookie-cutter personalities—were not.

The initial success of the Fantastic Four spurred Lee and Kirby on to other creations. In 1962, they combined talents to introduce the Incredible Hulk, the Mighty Thor, and the Astonishing Ant-Man, each of whom not only had super powers, but also faults. Lee perfected this formula when he teamed with artist Steve Ditko to create the Amazing Spider-Man, a character wracked with problems and plagued by doubts. As the successes piled up, out of necessity Lee moved away from providing full scripts to his artists, instead providing them with a plot and allowing them to lay out the story before he returned to insert dialogue over the artwork. This so-called "Marvel Method" allowed the artist greater freedom, input, and influence over the story, and visual storytellers, like Kirby and Ditko flourished under this arrangement. Also intriguing to the readers was that it was increasingly clear that all of these characters occupied the same world, and they, their foes, and their supporting casts started showing up in one another's titles. In 1963, Lee christened the line Marvel Comics, and he and his collaborators added Iron Man, Dr. Strange, the X-Men, and the Avengers (the latter produced quickly to fill a production gap left by a delay in the development of another series, *Daredevil*, which would arrive in 1964).

Lee would provide "the Marvel Age" with its wit and hip style. He created a narrative persona that casually spoke directly to readers and made them feel like they were part of a movement. Kirby established the visual grammar for the line, penciling a prodigious number of the titles himself but also laying out many of the others. Indeed, fans responded to a whole "Bullpen" of creators that Lee introduced them to, and the popularity of Marvel Comics, especially among an older demographic of college readers, laid a foundation for Marvel's long-term success.

Even as Marvel was redefining the superhero genre, other publishers also recognized the demand, though their products were not necessarily as innovative or ultimately enduring. In addition to initial forays from Archie and Charlton a few years earlier, Gold Key got into the genre with *Doctor Solar; Man of the Atom* in 1962;

and *Magnus, Robert Fighter* in 1963. Charlton tried for another revival of the Blue Beetle in 1964 and expanded into a line of "Action Heroes" in 1965. By that time, even more publishers were jumping on the bandwagon, including American Comics Group (Nemesis and Magicman), Harvey (*Pirana*), and M. F. Enterprises (*Captain Marvel*). In 1966, at the very height of the resurgence, Tower Comics debuted with creator Wally Wood's *T.H.U.N.D.E.R. Agents*, and Archie expanded its Mighty Comics imprint with poor imitations of Marvel's style (e.g., *Mighty Crusaders*). This was, of course, the same time that ABC-TV had a phenomenal hit on its hands with the *Batman* television series (January 1966–March 1968). In addition, numerous superhero parodies arrived at this time, including transformations such as the Fat Fury and Pureheart Powerful. But by 1967, the trend had cooled and most of these publishers phased out their superhero lines, turning back to teenager humor and funny animals to appease their audience. That essentially left National and Marvel as chief purveyors for superhero fare from 1968 onward.

Precious Silver

Several hallmarks distinguish the Silver Age from the periods before and after it. Among these, one may count the characters, their depth of characterization, the rise of continuity, and the degree of world-building exercised during it. For one, the period is remarkable for the sheer proliferation of characters it introduced and particularly for how many of those characters are still appearing in print and, more recently, feature films today (e.g., the bulk of the characters featured in the Marvel Cinematic Universe were conceived in this era). As Silver Age fan Craig Shutt put it:

> It's a period when comics told the first stories of many heroes who still exist today, in tales that could be read and understood by readers of all ages [. . .] The excitement of so much new and unfolding material that would continue to thrill new generations of readers has never been captured in comics since The Silver Age ended. (22)

But more than just the volume or endurance of characters was the depth of characterization enjoyed by them, particularly those cast in the Marvel mold. Consider the case of *Fantastic Four's* Ben Grimm, the Thing. Exposure to cosmic rays gave him superhuman strength, but the accompanying rocky hide disfigured him, making him appear to be like many of the monstrous menaces that populated the rest of Martin Goodman's line at the time of his creation. His acts of heroism were always put into perspective with the realization that he could never lead a normal life with that appearance. Such a hero was simultaneously inspirational and tragic, and, as the Marvel saga unfolded, he began to grow in depth. For example, in *Fantastic Four* #51 (June 1966), Grimm's superpowers and monstrous form are stolen by a nameless scientist bent on infiltrating the team and destroy them from within. However, taking the Thing's form also seems to result in the villain taking on his inherent nobility. In a crucial moment, the imposter sacrifices himself, an act that preserves lives, restores Grimm's rocky visage, but deprives the tragic hero yet again of a chance at normal happiness.

Accordingly, continuity—or the interrelationships among different issues—became increasingly important (Coogan 206). Prior to the Silver Age, most comics were entirely episodic with each issue containing multiple self-contained adventures (Jenkins 20). Most comics of the era had multiple stories or features to make the casual consumer at the newsstand perceive greater value in the magazines. Jack Kirby had experimented with longer, book-length story telling (though usually still divided into four-chapters) in the pages of *Challengers of the Unknown* in the late 1950s. As his work with Stan Lee at Marvel matured, increasingly sophisticated stories spilled over from one issue to the next, culminating in the "Galactus Trilogy" in *Fantastic Four* #48–50 (1966). Webs of relationships began to extend not only from one issue to another, but from one series to another, until a complex mythology interwove the characters of a shared universe.

Indeed increasingly, both National and Marvel engaged in world-building. The Marvel Universe arguably grew to become the most extensive fictional universe ever devised and documented in human civilization. And if the early Marvel Universe was successfully building in breadth, then in the best-selling pages of Superman's magazines, editor Mort Weisinger was building in depth. Weisinger's creative team launched Lois Lane in her own ongoing series, developed back stories for villains, like Lex Luthor, Brainiac, and Bizzaro, and introduced new allies like Supergirl and a whole Legion of Superheroes for Superboy to pal around with. The culture of the lost world of Krypton was preserved in the bottled city of Kandor and a host of stories explored Superman's native planet. And if there were any changes to the mythos that might be too bold to insert into continuity, such as Superman marrying, retiring, or dying, then a series of 'imaginary stories' set outside of continuity could explore the ramifications of those life changes without altering the brand. In retrospect, superheroes became more mythic, more operatic in the Silver Age as their sagas and setting became more fully developed.

Tarnished Silver

As defined as the start of the Silver Age is, its closing is less universally acknowledged, with its demise placed somewhere between 1968 and 1971. Even if it did not end outright in 1968, the luster of the Silver Age had begun to dull as most of National and Marvel's competitors had exited the genre and those two publishers introduced far fewer new concepts—and those that were introduced were far less influential and lasting. The year 1968 brought the publication of cartoonist Robert Crumb's *Zap Comix* #1, heralding the rise of the underground comix movement. The comix were self-published magazines that typically broke every taboo of the Comics Code with freewheeling abandon. They came to represent an important alternative to the corporately produced comics from Archie, Charlton, Dell, Gold Key, National, and Marvel. On the other end of the spectrum, Peter Coogan has suggested that the era lasted until early 1971 and cites issue #31 of the *Teen Titans* as a breaking point (209). In that issue, the teen sidekicks switch back to their superheroic identities after a story line that had them confront issues of relevancy in civilian clothes. The return to formulaic storytelling marked an essential rejection of any further growth or development.

Between these two options lies a singular event that has more of a feeling that it marked the "end of an era": Jack Kirby's leaving Marvel Comics. Kirby's last issue for the publisher that he had helped make a phenomenon was *Fantastic Four* #102 (September 1970), ending one of the longest and most successful collaborations in comics history. But following on years of frustration from living in Stan Lee's shadow, Kirby decided to accept an offer from Carmine Infantino to write, draw, and edit his own series at the distinguished competition, National. Kirby's defection sent shockwaves through the professional and fan communities, many of whom openly wondered if Marvel Comics could go forward without the man who had defined the visual storytelling of the line. Of course it did, and likely so because Kirby had done his job too well. He had trained a stable of successors to carry forward his vision, and they persisted in his absence. He had also bequeathed Marvel with a collection of characters that would continue to fascinate readers for years to come. Marvel would continue to prosper, ultimately unseating National for dominance in the marketplace just a few years later, and Kirby would continue to innovate in the medium, but neither would achieve the creative zeal communicated at the height of the Silver Age. Indeed, while the so-called Bronze Age to follow opened up mainstream comics to more genres and would produce its own important characters, it would not rival the sheer creativity of the passing Silver Age.

Silver Linings

Though the Silver Age may have ended, its legacies are still apparent in comics culture today. The Silver Age began to bring greater recognition of the creative talents behind the production of comic books. Comic books of the Golden Age had followed the precedent of newspaper strips and featured limited credits, such as just the cartoonist's name. Thus, Bob Kane was the only signature appearing on Batman features for decades, even though Kane employed a production team of writing talent, such as Bill Finger and Gardner Fox, and artists, such as Sheldon Moldoff and Jerry Robinson, to actually produce the stories—uncredited. During the early days of the Silver Age, Stan Lee began to expand the credits to include inkers, colorists, and letterers, including them in the merry "bullpen" atmosphere he projected for the Marvel production offices. He even gave the contributors nicknames to enhance the appearance of comradery, such as "Joltin' Joe Sinnott." For the first time, creators' names were used on the covers to help market comics, though the practice was still rare; it would be into the 1980s before creators would receive regular cover credits. Creators also helped bring recognition to themselves through their own initiative. *Green Lantern* artist Gil Kane published one of the first graphic novels, *His Name Is . . . Savage!* in 1968. While these were small steps towards greater recognition, there was also backlash against the creators, too. A group of writers at National attempted to leverage decades of service and appeal for health insurance and retirement benefits, but found themselves frozen out of assignments when they asked. Certainly, the struggle for creator's rights still had a long way to go.

The other struggle undertaken in the Silver Age was representation for minorities in mainstream comics. Interestingly, a leading role for a Native American enjoyed a sustained run throughout the Silver Age and beyond. Turok, Son of Stone, debuted in the pages of Dell Comics' *Four Color* series in 1954 and went on to star in his own title from 1956–1982, with period revivals since. It was unheard of to have minorities even appearing in supporting casts, much less taking starring roles at this time. For blacks, achieving representation was a more protracted struggle. Stan Lee and Jack Kirby included the first regularly appearing African-American supporting character in a mainstream comic, Gabriel Jones, beginning in the war comic *Sgt. Fury and His Howling Commandos* #1 (May 1963). Historically, black and white soldiers had not served side-by-side in World War II but in separate units; that didn't stop Lee and Kirby from a bit of historical revisionism from their vantage point in the heart of the Civil Rights Era. Lee and Kirby also created the first black superhero, the Black Panther, monarch of Wakanda, a technologically advanced African nation (*Fantastic Four* #52,

July 1966), and Lee and Gene Colon introduced the first African-American superhero, the Falcon (*Captain America* #117, September 1969). Dell Comics released two issues of *Lobo,* a western series featuring a black lead in 1965–1966, but it would be into the 1970s before black leads would headline ongoing series.

The marginalized group that was more successful in finding its voice in the Silver Age was comic book fandom. Unlike their predecessor in science fiction fandom, comic book fans had not organized themselves very effectively prior to the Silver Age. That changed, though, when letters pages became a regular feature in comic books and fans could reach out to one another through the mail by following up with their printed addresses (Levitz 26). Mort Weisinger began to publish letters in the page of Superman comics in 1958 and by 1960 they were regular features in many comic books (Schelly 187). The post then became a vehicle for fans to circulate their own amateur publications, like *Alter-Ego*, started in 1961 by Jerry Bails and Roy Thomas. Bails also founded the Academy of Comic-Book Fans and Collectors, whose annual "Alley Awards" (named after the *Alley Oop* comic strip) was a precursor to the modern Eisner Awards, recognizing excellence in comic arts. Thomas would become one of the first fans to transition into the role of comics professional, eventually becoming Stan Lee's successor as editor-in-chief of Marvel Comics. This was merely the dawn of the fan as a source for future professionals. Thus, the vibrant fan community that exists today, online, in comics shops, and at comic book conventions took its first steps towards fraternity in this era.

And, of course, much of the raw storytelling printed in that era is being mined and refined for film and television audiences. For instance, the turn from friends to foes between a young Superman and Lex Luthor that was explored over several seasons in the television series *Smallville* was based on a single Silver Age story. Of course, Marvel Studio's *Iron Man, Thor, Avengers,* and *Ant-Man* feature films cast heroes, villains, supporting characters, and situations all debuting in the Silver Age of comics. As fan turned professional Paul Levitz notes:

Perhaps the essential joy of the Silver Age for its readers was coming to the newsstand confident in finding your familiar friends—the characters, each with their consistent lives, values, and ever-growing supporting casts, depicted with care by the anonymous creators the same way, month after month. There were surprises in the stories . . . but they were wonderfully familiar surprises, variations on themes the readers adored. (34)

Even into the twenty-first century those friends—and the familiar surprises they deliver—continue to shine.

In retrospect, the Silver Age represents a remarkable period of creativity and energy in comic book storytelling. Even as Americans were struggling with cultural upheaval that questioned traditional institutions, superheroes reassured readers that their faith in science and fundamental virtue remained unshaken. Other genres may have sold more comic books than superheroes in this period, but none of these genres produced more enduring contributions to American culture. The nation, its comic books, and its superheroes would undergo unforeseen changes in the eras ahead, but the foundations laid in the Silver Age would endure through them all.

Works Cited

Coogan, Peter. *Superhero: The Secret Origin of a Genre,* Austin: Monkey Brain Books, 2012.

Hamilton, Edith. *Mythology*. Boston: Little, Brown and Company, 2013.

Jenkins, Henry. "'Just Men in Tights:' Rewriting Silver Age Comics in an Era of Multiplicity." *The Contemporary Comic Book Superhero.* Ed. Angela Ndalianis. New York: Routledge, 2009. 16–43.

Jones, Gerard, & Will Jacobs. *The Comic Book Heroes.* Rocklin, CA: Prima Publishing, 1997.

Levitz, Paul. *The Silver Age of DC Comics, 1956–1970.* Los Angeles, CA: Tashen, 2013.

Schelly, Bill. *American Comic Book Chronicles: The 1950s.* Raleigh, NC: TwoMorrows, 2013.

Shutt, Craig. *Baby Boomer Comics: The Wild, Wacky, Wonderful Comic Books of the 1960s!* Iola, WI: Krause Publications, 2003.

Wells, John. *American Comic Book Chronicles: 1960–1964.* Raleigh, NC: TwoMorrows, 2012.

_____. *American Comic Book Chronicles: 1965–1969.* Raleigh, NC: TwoMorrows, 2014.

Rust and Revitalization: the So-Called Bronze and Modern Ages of Comics_____

Kyle Eveleth

The late 1960s were a troubled time for American comics. Wallowing in the latter years of the unofficially-named Silver Age of comics—so called because of its uptick during the "Silver Sixties," but also accurate for the omnipresent tarnish of the Comics Code Authority's leaden censorship—major comics houses languished under rising economic strain on production and reduced interest in the marketplace. The reputations of the major comics houses, among them Marvel and DC, were similarly tarnished by draconian restrictions to artists' and authors' rights under contract, dated to that gilded birth of the American superhero comic, the Golden Age. Moreover, comics readership was growing tired of the untouchable superhero, so far removed from real-world problems as to seem unbelievable. With the growing popularity of artist-driven underground comix, created by talented and disenchanted individuals like Robert Crumb and Art Spiegelman and taking as their subject the real lives of their creators, the vaunted industry, three decades removed from its glorious arrival, was oxidizing quickly, threatening to break apart at its weakest points.

The epoch following this tarnished crumbling of the Silver Age has been called the Bronze Age and, to a lesser extent, the Third Heroic Era of American comics. According to the *Overstreet* price guide, the Bronze Age runs from 1970 to 1984, covering numerous upheavals, disintegrations, explosions and implosions, and finally revitalizations that altered the landscape of American comics (1028). The naming convention, first used by fans and then the price guide, follows spiritually behind the Golden and Silver Ages, much as the bronze Olympic medal follows its golden and silver counterparts: still a podium spot, but largely regarded as the least impressive of the trio. However, the Bronze Age of comics is also perhaps the most innovative era of them all: it introduced significantly more complex storylines, more believable and human characters, and, following a relaxation of the hallowed Comics Code, a shift away from the Code-defined black and white morality of the Silver Age and its unwaveringly evil depictions of monsters, drugs, violence, and sex. Though the period did see unprecedented cutting away of much-loved titles perceived as unprofitable, such as DC's *Action Comics* and Marvel's *X-Men*, nonetheless the culling served to remove tarnished portions of a stronger underlying core of comics in a move that ultimately ushered in what scholars and fans now call the Modern Age. In order to see how these then-lambasted trimmings of licenses turned from marketing nightmare into a new Golden Age of Comics readership, contextualizing, and analyzing the major shifts marking the period—as well as some small reconsideration of the demarcations themselves—is in order. In so doing, this chapter hopes to demonstrate that the Bronze Age forged comics into an alloyed age, harder and more durable than its predecessors, resistant to tarnishing, and easily polished should it fall into disrepair.

"IT IS THE RUST WE VALUE, NOT THE GOLD"
(Alexander Pope, *Imitations of Horace: The First Epistle of the Second Book of Horace*)

For many fans of the Silver Age of Comics, the transition into the Bronze Age is oft seen as akin to the transition from iron to rust: weakening, disintegration, and finally destruction. Like rusting, the quintessential weakening events of the Bronze Age—Jack Kirby's brief stint at DC Comics, the retirement of Mort Weisinger, and the near-collapse of the comics industry with the DC Explosion—were the result of years of neglect. Usually considered the first major crack in the Silver Age veneer, Jack Kirby's *second* defection from Marvel to DC in late 1970 followed years of poor contract negotiations with his former employer (Ro 139). Kirby's shift in allegiances was not unprecedented given his reputation for freelancing and his renown in the industry (Evanier 163). Driven by then-common contractual limitations that prevented artists from retaining ownership and distribution rights to their art (Evanier 126–63), Kirby's deal with DC was largely inked on the basis of more creative custody over characters he had created, a distinct shift in policy from his days at Marvel. His new contract enabled Kirby to finally debut his sweeping opus of the "Fourth World" series, which introduced major heroes and villains in the form of the New Gods. These epic stories, "staged across Jungian vistas of raw symbol and storm" (Morrison 7) redefined the scope of superhero comics, from the definition of super to the idea of world- and dimension-crossing exploits. Spanning entire planets, galaxies, and dimensions, the sheer scope of Kirby's "Fourth World" made the seemingly expansive plots of the Silver Age seem puny by comparison. There had before been formed superheroic and supervillainous teams, but never of the size, scope, and power of the New Gods.

Though Kirby's time at DC came to a close in 1976 when he returned to Marvel (a prodigal return heralded by Stan Lee), Kirby's departure signaled a larger unrest among artists in the industry who were growing disillusioned by the insubstantial terms of their contracts, many of which left creators with few rights to the ownership of their intellectual property. Again dissatisfied with Marvel, Kirby left for good in 1979 in order to work on animation projects like *Thundarr the Barbarian* (1980) and *The Fantastic Four* (1978) before settling in with independent publishers Pacific Comics, who allowed Kirby to retain ownership of his works (Morrow 105), and working to end the system that had long deprived him of ownership of his ideas.

At around the same time, Mort Weisinger departed from his position at DC as primary editor of *Superman* titles (Lillian 8). Controlling the title (along with *Batman,* briefly) since the early 1940s (Lillian 2), Weisinger had been responsible for many late-Golden Age and Silver Age innovations in the series, including Supergirl and the now-canonical concept that Superman's powers were amplified by Earth's yellow sun (Lillian 2–8). Despite his many innovations and strengthening of *Superman*'s core canon, Weisinger's tenure was not without weak points that would prove susceptible to the rust of the transition from Silver to Bronze. As many of the writers and artists he oversaw, including Curt Swan (Zeno 16) and later Marvel chief Jim Shooter (Stroud), would explain, Weisinger's overbearing demeanor and strict adherence to his personal rules for writing comics—the same traits that shaped a tight, internally-consistent run of *Superman*—resulted in migraines for his underlings and considerable stagnation for the stories (Stroud). The most constraining of these rules was the guiding principle and main difference between *Batman* and *Superman* in Weisinger's estimation: Batman could be injured, while Superman was invulnerable. In order to make the comics more interesting, Weisinger often resorted to contrived situations in which Superman's considerable powers were, for one reason or another, temporarily lost, only to be renewed after using his considerable wit and intellect to get them back. His only weakness, it seemed, was the threat of his alias being discovered. This limitation was partially overcome by probable nuclear-stand-in kryptonite, but the large quantities needed to make for regular excitement became a tired trope by the time Weisinger's longtime colleague Julius Schwartz took over in 1970.

These chinks in the Silver Age armor were relatively minor in comparison to the industry-shaking "DC Explosion" of 1978, so named by then-publisher at DC Comics, Jenette Kahn (Kahn "Publishorial"). Marking the midpoint of the Bronze Age, between 1975 and 1978 DC premiered fifty-seven new titles, comprising new works, like *Steel* and *Shade the Changing Man*, as well as old favorites, like Kirby's *New Gods* and *Mister Miracle*. Largely a response to a Marvel ploy that had similarly increased the number of works on the stands—and which had netted Marvel dominance in the market—DC's expansion renewed many previously cancelled properties while also creating new ones. At the same time, DC took on a daring campaign to remedy ailing comics profitability, spurred on by rising production prices and its weakened position in the market. Cover prices were raised across the board while pages were added in an effort to show that DC had more value per page than its competitors. Unfortunately, the combination of these two marketing moves proved nearly fatal to DC, a "bloodbath that was mockingly labeled 'The DC Implosion'" (Kimball); steep production costs, made even higher by more pages per issue, combined with more product than ever and an ill-fated drop in sales, possibly due to blizzards in 1977 and 1978 (Kimball), resulted in the cancellation or merging of twenty properties, including staples *Showcase* (ended with issue #104) and *All Star Comics* #74 (McAvennie 179). However, twenty cancellations or merges do not make an implosion; coupled with the cancellation of so-called Explosion titles was the ill-fated simultaneous (but unrelated) cancellation of eleven other, more widely-read titles from DC's catalogue including *Metal Men* (#54), *Shazam!* (#35), *Our Fighting Forces* (#181), and *Teen Titans* (#53). Even DC's namesake comic, *Detective Comics*, was nearly cancelled by the implosion; instead, it was salvaged via merger with *Batman Family* in *Detective Comics* #481 as a sixty-eight-page, one-dollar comic. After fifteen issues as the goliath of the marketplace, *Detective Comics* returned to its normal price and size with issue #496. The DC Explosion lived up to its name: the conflagration had consumed sixty-five titles in all, leaving DC amidst the wreckage with a severely depleted cadre of twenty forty-cent monthlies and six one-dollar bi-monthlies, eight fewer than its pre-Explosion catalogue (Kimball).

The shockwaves of DC's implosion were felt across the industry. Marvel was affected least, thriving under Stan Lee-appointed Jim Shooter's reign and managing to only see a twenty-three percent reduction in average monthly sales between 1977 and 1980 by relying on classic titles like *Uncanny X-Men, The Amazing Spider-Man,* and *The Avengers,* along with carefully-chosen new runs, like a Frank Miller-drawn *Daredevil* (Tolworthy). DC did not fare as well; its already small average monthly sales, already only sixty percent of Marvel's in 1977, dropped by a third in the same time period—equivalent to just over half the sales Marvel made on a similar number of titles. Unfortunately, many other publishers did not have the iron-fisted ruler like Shooter at the helm, and they certainly did not have Marvel's bullpen of creators at their disposal. Smaller publishers, like Charlton Comics, could not compete with the deep talent—and deeper pockets—of large publishers like Marvel and DC. The same economic conditions and harsh winters that plagued the larger houses and nearly caused DC's collapse had a much more dire effect on smaller groups. Charlton cancelled many of its best-selling titles, like *The Six-Million Dollar Man, Bullwinkle and Rocky,* and *The Bionic Woman,* in 1976 before going on nearly full hiatus in 1977. The company finally disintegrated in 1985 after eight years of failed attempts to kick-start the ailing brand. Charlton was just one of the houses lost in the midst of the Bronze Age, but its tale–strong titles, abrupt cancellation, floundering, and finally failure–was a common one to be sung across the American comics scene. Former powers Gold Key (who published *Bugs Bunny*, *Donald Duck*, *Looney Toons*, and *Mickey Mouse*, among other related titles), Warren Publishing (*Creepy, Eerie, Vampirella*), and Fawcett Comics (*Captain Marvel, Dennis the Menace*) went belly-up; survivors scraped by on legacy titles and minimal production: Archie Comics reduced its stock to solely the Riverdale High books, and Harvey Comics continued churning out only *Casper the Friendly Ghost* and *Richie Rich* titles. Rust had set in, and the entire industry threatened to shake apart without intervention.

"DESTRUCTION, HENCE, LIKE CREATION, IS ONE OF NATURE'S MANDATES"
(The Marquis de Sade, *Philosophy in the Bedroom*)

As far as saviors go, the one who would fly in to rescue DC and the rest of the comics industry was unexpected at best and feared at worst. In 1981, Sol Harrison retired as President of stricken DC comics, and Jenette Kahn took his place at the helm. Backed into a market corner by the Explosion she had announced, reactions to Kahn's leadership were mixed at first. Her guidance, however, would prove fortuitous for both DC and the American comics scene as a whole. Tempered by the fate of the Explosion, Kahn set about refreshing the tired system that had allowed such violent collapse to occur and revitalizing the weakened core properties she now controlled. The first slag to be jettisoned was the archaic reimbursement and ownership policy that had prevented talented creators, like Kirby and up-and-comers Neal Adams and Denny O'Neal, from pledging fealty to a single publisher. Largely unchanged from its Golden Age roots and chafed at by nearly all well-known creators—not just Jack Kirby—the standing house policy at major comics publishers took ownership and production control from the creators and handed it to publishers. Even a single publishing of a character was enough to lay claim to it, as evidenced by DC's last-ditch publishing effort at the end of the implosion, the wryly-titled *Canceled Comic Cavalcade.* The *Cavalcade,* published by Warner's archiving division in extremely limited quantities, existed solely to claim ownership of the characters and titles between its nondescript blue covers. More a book of photocopies and unfinished black and white sketches than a true comic book, the Cavalcade was never meant for release into the wild, as copies of it were only sent to prove existence to the United States Copyright Office, the *Overstreet Price Guide*, and as desk copies to creators. Nonetheless, DC's foresight allowed them to make reprints and relaunches of *Cavalcade* titles, and many of the otherwise unpublished comics within it made appearances as filler material for surviving titles.

Under Kahn's aegis, a renewed and revised contract policy was drawn up, one that gave artists and writers unprecedented control over their works—and unprecedented royalties. Under the new plan, put into place in 1981, writers and artists enjoyed a percentage kickback once a comic sold more than the one-hundred-thousand-unit break-even point (Thompson 16–17). After selling the required number of issues, artisans who worked on the issue received a four percent kickback: two percent to the writer, 1.4 percent to the penciller, and .6 percent to the inker; layout artists and finishers earned one percent apiece. This replaced earlier work-for-hire models that deprived creators of adequate pay if they created titles that sold well, especially as demand for specific artists and writers grew. Under the royalty system, byline credits counted for more than just creative *palmarès*: names drove sales. Kirby's *Return of the New Gods* sold both to those who were fans of the New Gods series and to those who knew Kirby's style from his collaborative works. The opportunity to use name recognition and to be paid for it enticed many creators—including *New Teen Titans* wonder-duo Marv Wolfman, writer for *Green Lantern* and *Brave and the Bold* titles, and George Perez, freelance artist known for his work on *Avengers* and *Fantastic Four*—to jump on board and stay with DC.

This all came in tandem with a push from the other side of the table, the artists and authors, to generate support for then-impoverished *Superman* creators Jerry Siegel and Joe Shuster. Just five years after the decisive ruling in *Siegel & Shuster v. Warner Communications* against DC's parent company, which awarded the *Superman* creators each $20,000 annually and byline rights in all future publications, Kahn's policy change set the stage for renewed creator-rights fervor throughout the industry. Combined with pressure from talented underground comix authors and a surge in comix popularity in the market, creator rights and remuneration reached an all-time high, setting the stage for the increased direct market and enhanced creative control artists and writers currently enjoy. These in-house changes sent waves through the industry; shortly after DC's revision of its policies, Marvel followed suit to avoid losing any more talent to its competitor (10–11). Its compensation numbers lagged behind DC's except for artists, who could gain 1.5 percent royalties if they drew 'Marvel style' plots, but Shooter made it clear why the percentage remained lower than the competition: Marvel had the market by a margin wider than Superman's chest.

Kahn's major innovations did not stop at the battle for creator rights. In her announcement of the Explosion in 1978, Kahn alluded to a yet-unrealized enhancement of the quality of DC comics. Still printed on pulp paper via letterpress at sixty-five dots-per-inch, comic books remained an afterthought on distribution trucks because of their cheap, newsstand pulp origins. Technological advancements in printing had made one-hundred-twenty dots-per-inch offset printing more affordable to publishers, who once needed to pay triple the cover cost to produce even a single offset-printed comic. Increased dpi values meant better color fidelity, crisper lines, and more variability between artistic styles. Combined with higher-quality paper and increasing byline sales, DC's move to offset printing was sensible, if impractical, under the current system. The current system, as old as the printing method and the ancient work-for-hire contracts that were being left behind, gave distributors full refunds for unsold copies. With record inflation at the dawn of the 1980s, weakened distribution chains following the blizzards of the late 1970s, and wary consumers fearing the specter of nuclear war once again, comic books did not fly from the newsstands as they had before. Each unsold copy was returned to the publisher and turned no profit. Fortunately, the direct market specialty stores that bought a stock and held it until it was sold—always a staple in the comix scene—was moving into the mainstream. Almost overnight, now-iconic comic book shops opened across the country, carrying new and back issues of classics, new releases, and niche limited-runs—another Jenette Kahn innovation, mimicking the television miniseries model to contend with short-lived, one-off storylines and quick-to-die new heroes—on its vaunted shelves. The decision at DC to move into a direct market model as well as improve its quality was easy to make: the direct market neutered the opposition's only argument that unsold copies returned for refund would drive the publisher into the ground. Just like that, in the aftermath of the second-greatest blow to the industry (following the inception of the Comics Code), comics culture emerged reinvigorated and outside the corner of the newsstand. It had found a brick-and-mortar base of operations, and its droves of new readers flocked there for a new kind of superhero comic.

"WHAT NEVER WAS NOW COMES TO PASS"
(Ovid, *Metamorphoses*)

While major artists in the industry fought for their rights and the rights of those who came before, a similar battle of tried-and-true Golden and Silver Age storytelling versus Bronze Age grit applied significant pressure to the notion of the superhero. In 1970, Marvel released a comic book adaptation of Robert E. Howard's anti-hero Conan the Barbarian, interpreted through Roy Thomas and Barry Windsor-Smith. Highly successful in the industry, the already-dark *Conan the Barbarian* generated the even darker, more adult-oriented, *Savage Sword of Conan* in 1974. Following the critical acclaim of *Conan*, DC responded with a slew of sword-and-sorcery titles featuring anti-heroes of all types, including a reinterpretation of Anglo-Saxon legend *Beowulf* and Fritz Lieber's *Fafhrd and the Gray Mouser* (1972). The choice of these characters, in addition to Edgar Rice Burroughs' various properties (*Tarzan* [1972], *John Carter* [1977]) and darker, well-known heroes, like DC's revamped Green Arrow, marked a decisive shift to more human heroes. Indeed, Lieber's *Fafhrd and the Gray Mouser* were created specifically because the author, creating them in the late 1930s, was disillusioned by a lack of 'human' heroes, while Burroughs' Tarzan and John Carter are mere men doing amazing feats. This shift from invulnerable to eminently vulnerable manifested not only in heroes with mimetic human limitations, but also to their sidekicks, who were even more susceptible to the threats of the living realm. In April 1970, the duo of Denny O'Neil and Neal Adams—the quintessential Bronze Age duo—released a socially-conscious issue of *Green Lantern* co-starring established anti-hero Green Arrow as the gritty latter confronted the virtuous former with poverty, drug addiction, and other real world ills. This treatment, starting in #76, peaked in #85 (1971), in which it is revealed that the Green Lantern's sidekick, Speedy, has become a heroin addict. The cross-country story arc kicked off a frenetic period of socially-conscious work that was short lived as a specific subgenre. The Green duo's run only lasted until #89 (1972), at which point *Green Lantern* was cancelled and the pair was relegated to guest appearances in *The Flash*. A year after the cancellation, Julius Schwartz quipped to Ron Goulart that "relevance [in comics] is dead," and the era that saw the superhero comics version of the Public Service Announcement came to an abrupt end (Goulart 297).

Despite this quick ending, the real world refused to stay away from the alternate Earths found in the pages of DC and Marvel publications. Deaths of main characters, unheard of except in dreams or instances of fake death, exploded in the early 1970s. It began with tertiary characters: George Stacy, Gwen Stacy's father in *The Amazing Spider-Man*, dies in the collateral damage of a fight between Spidey and Doctor Octopus in #90 (1970). Three years later, Gerry Conway and Gil Kane shocked Silver Age readers with a long story arc, famously "Not Approved" by the CCA, which would rock the comics industry's approach to storytelling for decades. In #96–98, it is revealed that Harry Osborn, Peter's friend and son of arch-villain the Green Goblin, has become addicted to drugs. Harry's overdose in #98 ultimately snaps his father Norman out of a Green Goblin episode, but ultimately precipitates his final descent into madness. Grief over his son's addiction combined with financial troubles eventually drives Norman back to the Goblin suit, this time to take the ultimate revenge on Spider-Man for the troubles he has caused to the Osborn family. To enact his revenge, he kidnaps Peter's love interest Gwen Stacy, again drawing the innocent into the battles of the heroic and the villainous. Seeing his beloved hurled from a bridge tower in #121, Spider-Man manages to catch the falling girl with a webline only to find that her neck has snapped in the recoil. Assuming that her death was caused by whiplash from the web, Spider-Man vows to kill the Green Goblin, which he nearly does in #122. When Spider-Man cannot bring himself to land the killing blow, the Goblin tries to impale the hero on his goblin glider, a move that backfires and results in the Goblin's death. This kicks off a long revenge plot between Harry and Peter and ushers in one of the darkest eras of Spider-Man history.

Gwen Stacey's death arguably kicks off what would be known as "Bronze Age storytelling": death, blood, vengeance, and grit. Beginning in 1971, the Comics Code Authority relaxed its code enough to permit "sympathetic depiction of criminal behavior" and rare depictions of "corruption among public officials," so long as they were punished, and to allow monsters "when handled in the classic tradition such as Frankenstein, Dracula, and other high caliber literary works" (Thompson & Thompson 1). Following the precursor storyline depicting Harry's addiction, the Code was relaxed further to allow scenes of drug abuse as long as it was depicted as a "vicious habit." The Code continued to crumble throughout the 1970s and was essentially a specter in the 1980s as more violence became acceptable: DC's *Elvira's House of Mystery* #2 (1986) wore the "Approved" seal, yet featured decapitations, implied masturbation, and implied nudity; nonetheless, the next issue (1986) was not approved for slightly more implied nudity. Perhaps the greatest example of 1980s dodging of the code was *X-Men*'s "Dark Phoenix" saga (Dallas 8–9). The tagline on double-size #137, cover-dated September 1980, puts it simply: "PHOENIX MUST DIE!" While not the first reference to death on a comic book cover, the Dark Phoenix storyline signaled a major shift in comics during the 1980s to even more mature, dark themes than the late 1970s had produced—it was the first comic to break the unwritten rule of killing a primary protagonist in Jean Grey (Shooter), and by suicide, no less. Rather than destroying the series, the gambit "propelled the X-Men to the top for, what, two decades?" (Shooter).

Jean Grey's death (ultimately reneged in *Avengers* #263 [1986]) prophesied darkness to come in the Bronze Age's twilit 1980s. The decade would go on to see a darker, more mature, less mock-able *The New Teen Titans* from Wolfman and Perez (August 1980); the publication of a completely Frank Miller-controlled *Daredevil*, introducing anti-heroine Elektra (#168, September 1980) who would die just two years later in *Daredevil* #182; a much darker *Batman*, introducing Jason Todd (#357, Dec. 1982); rumors of a Jim Shooter-ordered death of all Marvel characters in *Comics Feature* #21 (1983); the actual deaths of nearly every DC character in *Crisis on Infinite Earths* (1985); and the infamous "Mutant Massacre" story arc in *X-Men* (July 1986). This succession of progressively darker exploits and major-character deaths in comics, fueled in part by the freedom of the direct market and the envelope-pushing of creators, meant a final darkness needed to be broached. Using heroes salvaged from the defunct Charlton comics (due to major-publisher licensing issues) Alan Moore and Dave Gibbons' *Watchmen* (1986) re-envisioned the comic book superhero as not just fallible, but capable of doing evil. Where *X-Men*'s death of Jean Grey introduced "an element of primal suspense" into comics (Whittaker), *Watchmen* introduced wholesale annihilation with Adrian Veidt's utilitarian ploy to end Cold War hostilities. Whatever little was left of the Code was shredded with the New York massacre that unfolded in *Watchmen*'s final issue in 1987.

The release of *Watchmen* dovetailed with other maturing interpretations of heroes in the United States; John Byrne's *Man of Steel* capitalized on reinvigorated Superman readership following the *Crisis* storyline to make a more human *ubermensch*, while Frank

Miller and Lynn Varley's *The Dark Knight Rises* "set the gold standard for comics in terms of both popularity and professional quality" (Sacks 170). Following their leads, the rest of the 1980s saw the introduction of anti-hero *The Punisher* (1986); the Kahn/Giordano revamp of DC comics to label their comics "For Mature Readers" and "Universal Readership" (1987); Todd McFarlane's introduction of Venom (*The Amazing Spider-Man* #300, May 1988); the "Death in the Family" *Batman* story arc (#426–9, 1988); and, closing the decade, the introduction of Neil Gaiman's *Sandman* series (1989). By 1989, the Code was all but abandoned, as the direct market gave more primary control to owners over the sale of contentious works to minors, something the newsstand had always lacked. In 2001, Marvel abandoned the Code in favor of its own system ("*X-Force*"); Bongo dropped it without fanfare in 2010 (Johnston); DC followed suit in 2011 (Lee); and one day later, the last holdout, Archie comics, announced it would no longer participate, effectively slaying the Code (Rogers).

"IF I'M GOING TO HAVE A PAST, I PREFER IT TO BE MULTIPLE-CHOICE!"
(The Joker, via Alan Moore, *The Killing Joke*)

The Bronze Age of Comics ostensibly ends in 1985 with *Crisis on Infinite Earths* and its wholesale destruction and recreation of many DC superheroes, or in 1986 with the publication of *The Dark Knight Returns* and *Watchmen,* the two comics Shawn O'Rourke explains are "generally accepted as encapsulating the spirit of the Modern Age." This Modern Age, demarcated by *Overstreet* to span from 1985 to the present, is defined by "the increase of adult-oriented content, the rise of the X-Men to the status of dominant intellectual property, and the reorganization of the industry's distribution system," as well as thematic shifts to "deconstructive and dystopian re-envisioning of iconic characters and the worlds that they live in" (O'Rourke). Both the span of this age, as O'Rourke argues, and its defining features are suspect. However, where O'Rourke seeks to mark the end of the Modern Age and the ushering in of a Postmodern Age (with DC's *Infinite Crisis* [2005–6] and Marvel's *Civil War* [2006–

7]), I might, instead, suggest shifting the Modern Age's front end (and therefore the Bronze Age's tail end) forward to 1990. Each of the defining characteristics O'Rourke lists—partly in defining both the Modern Age and the two comics he claims are encapsulations of it—is not exclusively the purview of post-Bronze Age comics. More accurately, his definition better suits the culmination of the destruction and renewal cycle, the same one performed throughout the Bronze Age. The increase in adult themes is in direct lineage to early shifts from campy superheroes to meaningful ones, such as 1970's *Conan the Barbarian*, *Fafhrd and the Gray Mouser* in 1972, the move to social significance from 1970 to 1972, and of course the villain-caused deaths of Gwen Stacey in 1973 and Aquababy in 1977. These new, darker, more mature themes required an ever-increasing deconstructive mode to sustain, peaking not with *The Dark Knight Rises* and *Watchmen*, but instead with completely deconstructed superheroes, like McFarlane's sarcastic and vengeful *Spawn* and the literal deconstruction—death—of icons: Superman in 1992 and Batman in 1993. The rise of the X-Men also has its roots in the midst of the Bronze Age, with the introduction of Wolverine in 1974 in *The Hulk* #181 and the release of revitalizing *Giant-Size X-Men* #1 in 1975, which took the series from weak-selling secondary Lee/Kirby work to socially prominent and socially relevant metaphor. The rise of independent publishing through publishers like Image Comics and by the efforts of artists like Jim Lee, Rob Liefield, and Todd McFarlane—largely considered the defining moment of the Modern Age, as it opened the door for hundreds of new, highly-talented artists and writers—was a triumph made possible only by Bronze Age efforts to amend bad policies and solve the problems of the failing newsstand sale model. Preempted by Dave Sim's *Cerebus*—the longest running limited series and completely independently published—and Eastman & Laird's *Teenage Mutant Ninja Turtles*, to say nothing of DC's embrace of the direct market, the debt Modern Age independent publishing owes to Bronze Age innovation is undeniable.

This does not mean, however, that comics never left the Bronze Age—only that one must reconsider where, when, and why it ended.

The so-called 'Dark Age,' the early days of the Modern Age, seem a better fit to the final days of the Bronze Age than the ushering in of an entirely new generation of comic books. Rather, the Modern Age seems to start spiritually with another boom, followed by collapse: the collapse of the speculation boom in the 1990s, a plague that sent Marvel into bankruptcy in 1996. At the same time, sales of comic books in monthly and bimonthly formats dropped severely during the 1990s. What kept publishers afloat were skyrocketing sales of trade paperbacks—bound editions of fully story arcs in a comic series—and graphic novels. Beginning with underground comix and rising to prominence with Will Eisner's groundbreaking semi-autobiographical *Contract with God* (1978), Jim Starlin's Marvel-sponsored *The Death of Captain Marvel* (1982), and Art Spiegelman's unflinching *Maus* (first chapter, 1980; first volume, 1986; full work, 1991), the proliferation of the graphic novel has been startling since its humble from-comix roots in the late 1970s. Once limited primarily to semi-autobiographical works (such as the aforementioned *Contract* and *Maus*), graphic novels now span as many genres as traditional novels, if not more.

Alas, the debate about beginning and ending dates, as with many fan-driven contentions, will likely never end. I would propose that the Bronze Age be defined as not just the temporal period from 1970 to 1996, but more readily by the spirit of cyclical destruction and renewal that drove its innovations, its heroes, and its artists. The Bronze Age was perhaps the first major era in superhero comics to be entirely devoted to clearing out the old and ringing in the new. The old guard of creators retired or were escorted gently out (some less gently than others) and a new crop of fresh-faced artisans, raised on superhero comics and hungry for a chance to leave their mark on the genre, exploded onto the scene. Tired properties were culled, many to be reinvigorated through reboots and redesigns; tired worlds were merged with others to make new, epic, thrilling world-, universe-, and indeed publisher-spanning collaborations. Superheroes were proven to be vulnerable, even killable, definitely fallible, and ultimately not the only topic comic books could cover. Smaller publishers perished, but in their wake were left humbled giants and a fertile space for independent publishing without which the comics industry would never have achieved the multimedia empires it now enjoys. And, most importantly, a generation of comic book readers was born and raised during this tempestuous time. Their eventual maturation paved the way for a resurgence in the alloyed properties forged from the simultaneously devastating and regenerative eruptions the Bronze Age had to offer. All in all, the comics industry showed that it, not unlike a Time Lord, has many incarnations and many faces, all of which require death to be revealed.

Works Cited

Dallas, Keith. "Dark Phoenix and the Darkness Before the Direct Market." *American Comic Book Chronicles: The 1980s*. Raleigh, NC: TwoMorrows Publishing, 2012: 8–24.

Evanier, Mark. *Kirby: King of Comics*. New York: Abrams Books, 2008.

Frankenhoff, Brent. "The Black and White Glut: A Decade Later." *Comic Buyer's Guide 1997 Annual*.

Goulart, Ron. *Ron Goulart's Great History of Comic Books*. Chicago: Contemporary Books, 1986.

Johnston, Rich. "Bongo Dropped Comics Code A Year Ago—And No One Noticed." *BleedingCool*. n.d. Web. January 21, 2011.

Kahn, Jenette. "Publishorial: Onward and Upward." *DC Comics*, September 1978.

Kimball, Kirk. "The Secret Origins of the DC Implosion, Part One." *Dial B for Blog*. March 2006. Web. 2 Aug. 2014.

Lee, Jim. "From the Co-Publishers." "The Source." *DC Comics*. January 20, 2011.

Lillian, Guy H., III. "Mort Weisinger: The Man Who Couldn't Be Superman." *The Amazing World of DC Comics* #7 (July 1975): 2–8.

McAvennie, Michael. "1970s." *DC Comics Year By Year: A Visual Chronicle*. Ed. Hannah Dolan. New York: DK Publishing, 2010.

Morrison, Grant. "Introduction. Morrison, Grant. "Introduction." *Jack Kirby's Fourth World Omnibus Volume One*. New York: DC Comics, 2007.

Morrow, John. "The Captain Victory Connection." *The Collected Jack Kirby Collector Vol. 1*. Raleigh: TwoMorrows Publishing, 2004.

O'Rourke, Shawn. "A New Era: Infinite Crisis, Civil War, and the End of the Modern Age of Comics." *PopMatters,* 21 Feb. 2008. Web. 30 July 2014.

Overstreet Price Guide 38. Timonium, MD: Gemstone Publishing, 2008.

Ro, Ronin. *Tales to Astonish: Jack Kirby, Stan Lee and the American Comic Book Revolution.* New York: Bloomsbury, 2004.

Rogers, Vaneta. "Archie Dropping Comics Code Authority Seal in February." *Newsarama,* 21 Jan. 2011. Web. 29 July 2014.

Sacks, Jason. "*Watchmen* and the Watchers of the Comics Industry." *American Comic Book Chronicles: The 1980s.* Raleigh, NC: TwoMorrows Publishing, 2012: 152–186.

Shooter, Jim. "The Origin of the Phoenix Saga." *Jim Shooter.* 2 June 2011. Web. 2 Aug. 2014.

Stroud, Bryan D. "Interview with Jim Shooter, Part 2." *The Silver Age Sage.* Bryan D. Stroud, 2007. Web. 2 Aug. 2014.

Thompson, Don, & Maggie Thompson. "Crack in the Code." *Newfangles* 44 (Feb 1971): 1.

Thompson, Kim. "DC Creates New Royalties System for Freelancers." *The Comics Journal* 69 (Dec 1981): 16–17.

Thompson, Kim. "Marvel Announces New Royalties Plan." *The Comics Journal* 70 (Winter 1982): 10–11.

Tolworthy, Chris. "Marvel and DC Sales Figures." *The Fantastic Four 1961–1988 Was The Great American Novel.* n.d. Web. 31 July 2014.

Whittaker, Richard. "Chris Claremont: Dead Should Mean Dead." *Under the Covers.* The Austin Chronicle, 14 July 2012. Web. 2 Aug. 2014.

"X-Force #116 to be Non-Code." *ICv2,* 27 April 2001. Web. April 27, 2001. 25 July 2014.

Zeno, Eddy. *Curt Swan: A Life in Comics.* Lakewood, NJ: Vanguard Productions, 2002.

From the Mainstream to the Margins: Independent Comics Find a Voice_____

Kim Munson

In recent days, readers with an interest in comics and graphic novels can find an endless variety of sequentially-told stories with myriad content ranging from personal memoirs, histories, science fiction, fantasy, and mysteries to superheroes and anti-heroes. Breaking away from the mainstream fare produced by Marvel and DC, the two dominant publishers of comics, a host of independent publishers regularly split around thirty percent of total US sales every month. Because these publishers are more willing to take chances on unknown properties and often offer comics creators greater rights and creative freedom than the 'big two', these smaller market publishers can offer an astounding array of titles. Readers can choose fantasy adventure stories like *Adventure Time, Hellboy,* and *The Mouse Guard*; fan-favorite properties like *Star Wars*, *My Little Pony*, and *Godzilla*; adult-oriented titles like *Saga*, *The Walking Dead*, *Sex Criminals*, and *Sin City*; and personal narratives such as *Blankets*, *Maus*, and *Fun Home*. No matter what format a reader may require, digital or print, there has never been a time such as this with such a vast selection of innovative work to choose from.

There was a time when public anxiety about lurid comics content proliferated, giving enormous strength to the cold hands of censorship, which had their widest reach via the Comics Code Authority in 1954, strangling the wider comics industry. The independent comics that resisted those hands and eventually broke their grip not only made space for more diverse types of stories and art, but also allowed comics creators to retain ownership of their work while fostering the direct sales business model most readers know today. This chapter will explore five breakout projects by independent publishers and creators that helped shatter those barriers and, in so doing, changed the comics industry.

As other chapters in this volume have indicated, due to the establishment of the CCA, mid-century popular horror and crime comics virtually disappeared, and comics became relatively sanitized and boring by comparison. One of the few exceptions—a publication with great art, lowbrow humor, and pointed commentary, was Harvey Kurtzman's satirical magazine *Mad*, published by EC, that was able to avoid compliance with the CCA by changing from a comic book to magazine format, thereby avoiding the CCA's purview. *Mad* was an inspiration to many young cartoonists coming of age in the counterculture movement of the 1960s, a time marked by Vietnam War protests, the Free Speech Movement, the Civil Rights Movement, and the Summer of Love. Looking for ways to break the conformity enforced by the CCA, a new group of young cartoonists created comics that dealt with issues important to them, spiced with a liberal dose of *Mad*'s scathing humor. Campus newspapers and magazines became fertile ground for this type of commentary, and several of the artists/creators that began the first wave of independent comics, known then as underground comix (ending with an "x" to denote their uncensored nature), got their start there. These cartoonists both wrote and drew their own comics and cartoons and retained ownership of the copyrights to their work—a right mainstream comic artists had to give up to publishers.

Denis Kitchen and Underground Comix

This was the case with cartoonist and publisher Denis Kitchen, who got his start in 1964 with the *University of Wisconsin–Milwaukee Post*, a college newspaper. Although Kitchen's friend and frequent collaborator R. Crumb usually gets the credit for kicking off the underground comix movement in 1967 with *Zap Comics #1*, as a publisher, Kitchen may have been even more influential. With the publication of his first comic book *Mom's Homemade Comics* in 1968, Kitchen informally entered the business that would come to dominate his life for the next 40+ years. In Kitchen's 2010 biography, *The Oddly Compelling Art of Denis Kitchen*, he identifies the audience for his comics, and explains the reason for their success:

What I had going for me was that there was a rapidly growing market amongst hippies—what we now call a niche market. And hippies included a lot of middle-class kids who had disposable income. They also had a certain fashion sense, and clearly had tastes that weren't being fulfilled by the mass market, in literature and certainly in entertainment, like comics. The handful of underground comics that were out there—like *Mom's*, or at first *Zap*, and *Bijou* . . . were being eagerly snapped up by freaks that could find them. And freaks seemed to be everywhere, not just the Bay Area. (Brownstein 24)

Kitchen's realization that there was an underserved national audience of readers who craved new and uncensored content fortified his resolve to enter into publishing; his next challenge was to figure out where to sell these new books. Because of the adult content depicted in these comics, they could not be sold at newsstands like CCA-approved comics, and so the undergrounds established their own distribution channel—the first direct market delivery system that bypassed mainstream stores—opting instead for selling books at alternative venues, like head shops, hippie street vendors, flea markets, record stores, and college bookstores.

The success of underground comix proved that there was a steady audience for mature comics material, and they wanted not only jokes about sex and drugs but also political commentary, personal stories and characters, and exposés of corporate crime. According to Charles Brownstein's biographical essay of Kitchen, he was soon editing and publishing a laundry list of titles, including *Home Grown Funnies* (R. Crumb); *Bizarre Sex*; *The Spirit* #1–87 (Will Eisner); *Dope Comix*; *Corporate Crime Comix; Wet Satin* (Trina Robbins); *Wendel Comix* (Howard Cruse); and *Comix Book* (an experiment with Marvel). Kitchen would publish anyone who had something interesting to say. He was one of the first publishers to regularly hire female artists. He published gay-themed titles, as well as work by luminaries such as R. Crumb and Art Spiegelman, and by elder statesmen like Will Eisner and Harvey Kurtzman. He gave these artists creative control and let them retain their copyrights, which allowed them both to experiment broadly with content and to collect more income from their work (Brownstein 30-43).

In 1973, the *Miller v. California* decision, which decreed that obscenity would be determined by local community standards, brought on a wave of self-censorship. By the mid-1970s, many head shops were closing, the war in Vietnam was over, the military draft ended, and President Nixon had resigned. The counterculture movement faded away and the first wave of underground titles died out. Kitchen Sink Press continued as a publisher of classic comic strip collections, art books, and graphic novels. DC and Marvel, both of whom had been revitalized by a veritable pantheon of superhero comics from the likes of folks like Neal Adams, Dennis O'Neil, Stan Lee, Jack Kirby, and Steve Ditko, et al., were riding a wave of success. They had developed a stable of popular licensed characters like *The Avengers*, *Fantastic Four*, *Spider-Man*, and *Green Arrow/Green Lantern*; identified a blueprint for the most successful types of stories, and employed a production-line style of artist management. In this "work for hire" arrangement, individual artists had no ownership rights to their work and were treated much the same as interchangeable parts. Factors such as these contributed to a feeling of homogenization and undesirable similarity in the work, as creators, artists, and writers lacked incentive to innovate and create new characters, and the major publishing houses saw no reason to fix what they did not see as broken.

Art Speigelman and 1980's Alternative Comics

This sameness was broken by the next wave of independent comics, the alternative comics of the 1980s, which were inspired by the pluralism found in the social identity movements of the 60s, the postmodern art of the era, and the raw energy of punk rock. One of the most influential publications of that time, appropriately-titled *RAW*, grew out of New York's East Village art and music scene. *RAW* appeared in 1981, published by Raw Books and Graphics, a collaboration between cartoonist Art Spiegelman and his future wife and editor, Françoise Mouly. Around the same time mainstream comics had started the move from selling books at newsstands to direct comic sales at specialty shops, *RAW* was conceived as a tabloid-sized art magazine to be sold at newsstands next to 80s

New Wave lifestyle and architecture magazines. *RAW* provided an appropriate forum for the work of both new and established artists after the demise of the undergrounds, helping to solidify the careers of artists like Bill Griffith and Gary Panter.

Another key element aiding the success of *RAW* was Speigelman's own artistic journey and experiments. *Breakdowns: Portrait of the Artist as a Young %@#$!!* contains his groundbreaking work from 1972–1977, sandwiched between a new introductory section of auto-biographical material and a new prose afterword, published in 2008 as a thirtieth-anniversary edition. *Breakdowns* includes the earliest pages of *Maus*, the illustrated story of Spiegelman's relationship with his father, a Holocaust survivor, serving as a record of his father's memories of the horrors of Auschwitz. Adopting a device from the 'funny animal' comics of his youth, Spiegelman transformed the Nazi guards into cats, and the Jewish prisoners into mice, an idea inspired by Hitler's comment that he thought of the Jews as vermin to be exterminated. The narrative constantly shifts back and forth between past and present, showing both the brutal heartbreak of the camps and the long-term effect living through this tragedy had on Spiegelman and his family. Serialized throughout the run of *RAW*, the collected *Maus* won a special Pulitzer Prize in 1992. *Breakdowns* not only included *Maus*' first pages from the 1970's, but also the story of how Spiegelman came to craft and shape the story as he did.

One of Spiegelman's long-term goals has been to advance the comics art form out of the ghetto of critical disrespect and into mainstream bookstores, libraries, and art museums, because this was where he felt they deserved to be sold and seen. In the afterword section of *Breakdowns*, Spiegelman comments on the demons that drove him in the 1970's; speaking of his younger self in the third person, he writes:

> Once underground cartoonists had unleashed their checkered demons in the cheerfully vernacular medium of comics, he was able to focus on the grammar of that vernacular and nail his own personal demons. High Art and Low. Words and Pictures. Form and Content. It all might sound dry and academic, but—Hell!—for me then it was a matter of life and death. (70)

Inspired by the wordless comics of the American artist Lynd Ward and the wordless woodcuts of the Flemish artist Frans Masereel, Spiegelman investigated the power of imagery to convey a story both with and without words, incorporating fine art motifs and theory, his own take on comics history, and biographical material in such a way that he made comics fit for serious topics. He pushed past the boundaries that had limited the comics art form, and the public and critical acceptance of these experiments helped open comics to new creative innovations and a wider range of personal expression.

Fantagraphics and the Birth of Comics Criticism

In 1974, around the same time Spiegelman was working on the comics that would be collected in *Breakdowns*, Gary Groth and Michael Catron purchased the *Nostalgia Journal (NJ)*, a tabloid adzine based in Maryland. They formed Fantagraphics Books and re-launched *NJ* as *The Comics Journal* in 1976. Kim Thompson joined the company in 1977 and became co-publisher and vice-president after Catron left to start Apple Comics in 1985. The mission of Fantagraphics from the outset was to advance the comics medium and help it realize its potential as an art form alongside more respected genres, like film, literature, and poetry. Groth and Thompson developed a three-pronged plan of attack to achieve their goal.

First, they felt that comics needed to establish a community of informed critics—so they used the pages of *The Comics Journal* to launch that dialogue. Articles in the *Journal* openly and relentlessly criticized the crass commercialization and artistic bankruptcy of the mainstream superhero formula. Next, to preserve newspaper comics and keep the memory of those artists alive, Fantagraphics published lavishly produced collected editions of titles, like *Peanuts* (Charles Schulz), *Prince Valiant* (Hal Foster), *Krazy Kat* (George Herriman), *Little Nemo in Slumberland* (Winsor McCay), *Popeye* (E. C. Segar), *Little Orphan Annie* (Harold Gray), and others. Finally, the third prong of their plan was to encourage and publish new original comics that were outside the norm. Fantagraphics met this goal by championing titles by new artists, giving many creators their first opportunity to see their work in print, such as Chris Ware's *Acme*

Novelty Library, Peter Bagge's *Hate*, Charles Burns' *Black Hole* and Daniel Clowes' *Eightball*, Linda Medley's *Castle Waiting*, and Jessica Abel's *Artbabe* (Merino and Creekmur 263, 267).

Fantagraphics found their flagship title when they began publication of the long-running series *Love and Rockets* in 1982, written and drawn by Los Brothers Hernandez—Jaime, Gilbert and, occasionally, Mario, printed in black-and-white magazine format. Although it initially had some science fiction elements, the books were always focused primarily on character and innovative storytelling. The *Love and Rockets* brand soon spun off the *Locas* storyline, in which Jaime focused on the lives, loves, and everyday experiences of Maggie and Hopey, a pair of Latinas who were in and around the punk music scene in Southern California, and Gilbert's *Heartbreak Soup* series, which centered on the mythic Latin American town of Palomar and the interconnected lives of the people who lived there. Unlike many of the mainstream superhero comics of the era, *Love and Rockets* attracted a devoted female readership–both gay and straight, pulled in by the depiction of women of all ages and sizes with realistic, curvy bodies in complex and imperfect relationships.

Los Brothers Hernandez did not flinch when it came to challenging their audience, whether it was the casually unconventional sexual identities of the characters or the need to keep track of decades-long narratives replete with detail. Like Spiegelman's avant-garde comics before them, Los Brothers visually challenged their audience by forcing them to infer much more information from panel to panel than deal in explicit exposition. Explaining this technique in his book *Alternative Comics: An Emerging Literature*, Charles Hatfield writes:

> Gilbert and Jaime freely manipulate time, space, and point of view, collapsing hours or even years into abrupt transitions, splicing together reality and fantasy, and discerning patterns in widely separated events. Relying on the cohesiveness of the total page (and the familiarity of *L&R* as a series) to guide and reassure their readers, Los Bros pushed the tension between single image and image-in-series to the extreme, transitioning from one element to the other without warning. (70)

In many ways, the rhythm of these books carried on the Punk aesthetic, employing empathy, wit, and shock to make their points, while the art itself held the readers' attention with a fast, driving beat. Over the years, Fantagraphics has overcome serious financial and legal challenges, and maintained their position as one of the strongest champions of comics as an influential art form. They have provided an ongoing forum for serious criticism, preserved comics history with their lovingly produced collections of reprints, and opened up comics to new voice by supporting the careers of many emergent writers and artists.

The Rise of Dark Horse

Meanwhile in Bend, Oregon, Mike Richardson, a successful comic shop owner, had also grown dissatisfied with the uniformity of the mainstream comics formula of the 1980s. Like Denis Kitchen, Richardson saw a market for a wider variety of higher quality comics with more mature content and themes that would appeal to adults. With this goal in mind, he launched the highly-successful Dark Horse publishing imprint in 1986 with the anthology *Dark Horse Presents,* a creator showcase featuring contributions by twenty-nine different artists, including the premiere of Paul Chadwick's *Concrete,* which soon became Dark Horse's most popular title (Durajilija). In 1988, Dark Horse expanded into books based on licensed properties, which would come to include such popular titles as *Star Wars*, *Aliens*, and *Buffy the Vampire Slayer,* lavishing first-rate work on a genre of comic books that had gotten low quality treatment from other publishers. Dark Horse also became one of the first US comics publishers to recognize that there was a market for *manga*—a style of comic art originating in Japan, beginning with a 1987 translation of *Godzilla,* followed by popular titles like *Ghost in the Machine* (Masamune Shirow), *Oh My Goddess!* (Kōsuke Fujishima), and *Blade of the Immortal* (Hiroaki Samura).

As a comics store owner who often hosted book signings, Richardson was familiar with the frustrations comics creators felt about their lack of ownership in their creations. From the beginning, Dark Horse committed to creators retaining the rights to their books and great storytelling drawing top-notch creators and helping Dark Horse build a diverse array of titles in a wide range of genres. In the early 1990s, a group of superstar comics creators, Art Adams, John Byrne, Geoff Darrow, Dave Gibbons, Frank Miller, and Mike Mignola, approached Richardson about starting an imprint of their own to develop creator-owned titles; it was eventually launched as the *Legend* imprint.

Of all the great titles and characters to grow out of the *Legend* imprint, few of them have been as beloved and enduring as that of revolutionary artist Mike Mignola's *Hellboy* (originally crafted in conjunction with John Byrne), an everyman hero in the body of a large, red, pancake-eating, cat-loving, tobacco-smoking demon. Brought to Earth from Hell in 1944 by the mad Russian monk Rasputin as part of a Nazi plot to bring about the apocalypse, young Hellboy is adopted and named by Dr. Trevor Bruttenholm, a member of a team of science adventurers that foiled the Nazis' scheme. While searching for information about his true origins and destiny, Hellboy joins forces with Dr. Bruttenholm, now his adoptive father figure and moral compass, and becomes a key agent of the Bureau of Paranormal Research and Defense (BPRD), working with other 'gifted' colleagues to protect the world from supernatural danger.

In the introduction to the first *Hellboy* collection, *Seed of Destruction* (1994), Robert Bloch writes: "*Hellboy* is a brilliant example of how to elevate the comic of the future to a higher literary level while achieving a higher pitch of excitement. Its story line combines traditional concepts with modern frames of reference, the whole being swept along by a virtuoso treatment of dazzling artistic effect" (6). Mignola's characters live in a contemporary world with mythic and steampunk overtones, illustrated in his bold, distinctive linework, paired with a rich, sophisticated color palette in contrast to mainstream superhero books of the time which still used a lot of exaggerated costumes and primary colors. *Hellboy*'s art and stories reference themes derived from folk stories and mythology, pulp magazine covers, and pre-Comics Code horror and monster comics, all updated with a modern sensibility and a mythopoeic approach

---

to history that articulates Hellboy as being part and parcel to much unwritten global history.

Hellboy has won an abundance of accolades including Eisner and Harvey Awards for Mignola as Best Artist. The title has spawned several spin-offs and has been adapted for novels, video games, and even an animated series that first aired on the Cartoon Network. It has also been adapted into two feature films. These movies, *Hellboy* and *Hellboy II: The Golden Army,* were both directed by Guillermo del Toro and starred Ron Perlman in the eponymous role. Relatively successful at the American box office, they contributed to a string of Dark Horse film projects that began initially with Dr. Giggles in 1992 and, best-remembered, with *The Mask* and *Timecop* in 1994 and continued with successful movies adapted from other properties, such as *Alien vs. Predator* (2004, 2007), *Sin City* (2005, 2014), and *300* (2006, 2014). The diversity of properties and formats in the Dark Horse universe—comics, novels, licensed merchandise, manga, games; feature films and animation has contributed to the amazing longevity of Dark Horse Comics and has helped to establish the Pacific Northwest as a Mecca for the independent comics creator community, further bolstered by the relocation of Fantagraphics to Seattle in 1989.

The Image Revolution

In the late 1980s, Marvel and DC experienced an unpredicted boom in sales of superhero comics. One reason for this increase in sales was that Marvel had found a dynamic new team of hot young artists to revitalize books featuring their best known characters, perhaps most-notably *Spider-Man* and the *X-Men* both of which raked in sales of millions on books, licensing, and general merchandise. In 1991, books by Todd McFarlane (*Spider-Man*), Jim Lee (*X-Men*), and Rob Liefeld (*X-Force*) broke all previous sales records. This fan interest was, at least, partially driven by the development of the comic book collector market—fueled by collectors' speculation that a signed book by one of these artists, kept in pristine condition, would soon grow in value. Huge crowds would show up at book signings with lines stretching around the block. The artists lived and breathed comics, and working at Marvel, in particular, was their dream job—yet, they were unhappy. The company line at Marvel, when asked about the contributions of the artists, was that it was reader interest in Marvel's characters that was driving sales and that the artists, themselves, had little impact on sales; artists could easily be, and often were, replaced. The artists felt unappreciated and frustrated that they were not sharing financially in the fruits of their labor. For some artists, remaining at Marvel and DC was simply no longer an option (Rhoades 131–135).

In *The Image Revolution*, a documentary film directed by Patrick Meaney for Respect! Films and the Sequart Organization, uses interviews, illustrations, and archival footage, to tell the story of the founding of Image Comics, which began when seven superstar artists came together and quit Marvel on the same day. The seven artists: McFarlane (the nominal leader of the pack), Liefeld, Lee, Marc Silvestri, Jim Valentino, Erik Larsen, and Whilce Portacio, agreed on three rules for the new company: 1) Image Comics would own nothing but the company name and logo. 2) The creators would own everything else. Finally, 3) each creator would be autonomous. Under this structure, the seven creator/owners each had their own imprint published under the Image banner, a loose universe that only occasionally overlapped with the other studios harbored under the larger company.

The first titles launched by Image included *Youngblood, Spawn, WildC.A.T.S., Savage Dragon, ShadowHawk,* and *Witchblade* (Portacio's *Wetworks* was long-delayed) garnered such phenomenal sales and community interest that Image temporarily displaced DC as the number two comic book publisher. As Image Comics grew exponentially, the owner/creators hired further artists and ran studios of their own, and everyone swam in a seemingly unstoppable river of money. However, there was trouble in paradise: the artist/owners, who had no real business experience or training, spent large portions of their time managing their business, and they were able to spend very little time developing their own creative projects. Books constantly shipped late, and the writing quality, already suspect by comparison to other companies, suffered. Fights broke out amongst the original seven and founders began to leave the company.

Valentino, the only one of the original founders who had previous publishing experience prior to his work with Image, became the company's new publisher. He served in that position from 1999 and 2004, during which time he opened the company up to further creator-owned titles by people who were outside of the original group of founding artists, establishing Image Comics as the most desirable place for comics creators to publish their work. One creator who came aboard Image at this time was Robert Kirkman, who had done a satirical comic called *Battle Pope* and had an idea for a new zombie book, *The Walking Dead*. Kirkman, who had developed *The Walking Dead* in collaboration with artist Terry Moore, was sure he had a hit on his hands, but Valentino and Erik Larsen (who, by that point, had taken over as publisher) were reluctant as they felt that the zombie genre had too many limitations to work as an ongoing series, ostensibly saying that it had no "hook." In *The Image Revolution*, Kirkman explains that he told them that there *was* a hook—the zombie virus was secretly unleashed by an alien invasion force to aid them in their plan to wipe out the Earth's population, and he would hide hints to this big twist throughout the series. Valentino and Larsen bit, and *The Walking Dead* was published. Later, when Valentio mentioned that he saw no hint of aliens in the book, Kirkman admitted: "I lied. I just really wanted them to publish the book."

While sales of *The Walking Dead* comic started off slowly, by the third issue, driven by Moore's ability to capture the chaotic aftermath of the Zombie Apocalypse so vividly in black and white and Kirkman's compelling and skillfully developed survivors, it exploded. It later became a blockbuster television series for AMC and Image's most visible transmedia property, incorporating a toy line from co-founder McFarlane, a spin-off series set to run in 2015, a video game, etc. The July 2012 release of *Walking Dead* #100, with thirteen different variant covers, broke sales records, selling out of the 383,612 copies ordered on the day it was released (CBR). At the time of this writing, Image's sales, boosted by *The Walking*

Dead, put them solidly in the number three spot behind Marvel and DC in total monthly sales.

Alison Bechdel and *Fun Home*

It has been the success of all the independent projects and publishers discussed that laid the groundwork for a vital new genre to enter into the world of comics—the deeply personal, individualistic graphic novel. A leading example of this genre is Alison Bechdel's *Fun Home: A Family Tragicomic,* a work that broke away from sales limited to traditional comics shops and publishers to find great success in the mainstream world of publishing. Published by Houghton Mifflin, *Fun Home* has been showered with awards, and it was *TIME* Magazine's 2006 Book of the Year. *USA Today* enthusiastically stated that "[t]he great writing of the twenty-first century may well be found in graphic novels and nonfiction. . . . Alison Bechdel's *Fun Home* is an astonishing advertisement for this emerging literary form." This triumph, arguably, would not have happened if publishers like Kitchen Sink Press and Fantagraphics had not opened the way for female cartoonists and a wider variety of stories.

Fun Home is an autobiographical memoir set in the small town of Beach Creek, PA, where Bechdel and her siblings grew up. The protagonist of this memoir is her father Bruce Bechdel, a part-time funeral director and full-time high school English teacher. Alison's mother, Helen, also an English teacher, works on her Master's degree and acts in community theatre. The title "Fun Home" actually rather sardonically refers to the family's nickname for the funeral home and comments on the emotional isolation that permeates the museum-like family home as well. The family home, an 1860's farmhouse, is the almost singular focus of Bruce's obsessive-compulsive passion for home decorating. Not a single thing can be out of place in Bruce's drive to restore the house to period grandeur, arguably shown to be compensation for the chaos and deterioration of his own family life, and his children become his glum workforce. In particular, after Alison moves away to college, she emerges as a lesbian, and is, in turn, shocked to discover that her uptight, domineering father is a closeted homosexual. Bechdel, the author, openly interrogates the notion that Bechdel's father might then become more open to his daughter now that she is an adult, has come out, and has had his secret exposed. However, shortly after these revelations are disclosed to Alison by her mother, Helen asks Bruce for a divorce. Two weeks later, Bruce dies—run over by a truck while working on a restoration project. This sequence of discovery, divorce, and death becomes the central mystery of the book: was Bruce's death an accident or a suicide? The question chews at Bechdel, and she theorizes on it throughout the book.

In one scene, when Bechdel and her brother first meet after hearing of their father's death, she says that they "greeted each other with ghastly, uncontrollable grins," which they knew were inappropriate, but they could not help themselves (Bechdel 46). This feeling of uncomfortable, oftentimes gallows humor pervades the book: everyone tried in vain to keep a tight lid on their repressed needs and emotions, yet Bechdel can't help nervously chuckling at the absurdity of it all.

Visually, Bechdel owes a great debt to the breakthroughs made by Speigelman and Los Brothers Hernandez—echoing their work; her story is not told in a linear, chronological fashion. Rather, it is told and re-told as new information comes to light or new themes require exploration. Her written text often contrasts with her drawings revealing that nothing in this family is as it seems on the carefully cultivated surface. Historian Robert C. Harvey remarks on Bechdel's incredible ability to depict the most subtle nuances of character and then offers an example that perfectly illustrates the theme of artifice versus reality through the milieu of a formal family portrait. The panel depicts a stereotypical family portrait, maintaining the illusion of a normal family. Her caption, "It's tempting to suggest, in retrospect, that our family was a sham," points out that the photo is a fraud. "Together," Harvey explains, "the picture and the words create the reality of the family as Alison understands it. Bechdel's blend of the visual and the verbal here achieves yet another dimension in thematic depth; she shows us a photograph being taken, and a photograph is yet another 'appearance'" (235).

Fun Home is a comic novel about finding identity amidst a messy, complex family life and making peace with the reality of the situation, despite knowing that there are still people who are caught up in artifice and surface appearances. In an eerie example of life imitating art, *Fun Home* has attracted critics who would like to keep Bechdel's story in the closet. In February 2014, Carolyn Kellogg of the *Los Angeles Times* reported that the budget committee of the state legislature of South Carolina recommended the denial of $52,000 in funding to the College of Charleston. Why this amount? It was the exact figure the college budgeted to buy copies of *Fun Home* for use as required reading in the college's First-Year Experience program.

In a disappointing echo of Dr. Fredric Wertham and the Comics Code Authority, the cold hand of censorship rose again in the form of South Carolina State Representative Garry Smith (R-Greenville), who said the book "goes beyond the pale of academic debate," and that the college was "promoting the gay and lesbian lifestyle" (Kellogg). Christopher Korey, who oversees the summer reading program that included *Fun Home*, defended the committee's choice, saying it "recognized the book might be controversial for a few readers, but the book asks important questions about family, identity, and transition to adulthood . . . these are important questions for all college students" (Kellogg). In response to questions by Rachel Deahl of *Publishers Weekly*, Bechdel said that she was grateful to the college for taking a stand on the book and that it was "sad and absurd that the College of Charleston is facing a funding cut for teaching my book—a book which is after all about the toll that this sort of the small-mindedness takes on people's lives" (Deahl).

Into the Future, Not on the Backs of Superman, but Superfans

While most mainstream DC and Marvel comics still focus on legacy characters, like Superman, Batman, The Avengers, and the X-Men, independent comics have opened up new worlds for readers to explore. This new openness was the theme of a keynote speech given by Image Comics publisher Eric Stephenson at ComicsPRO 2014, a convention for owners of comics specialty shops, as covered by comics journalist Heidi MacDonald. Stephenson spoke nostalgically about growing up loving superhero comics, but, nevertheless, he had developed reservations about the current publishing model used by "the big two," which he said was focused on multi-title crossover events and variant covers, maximizing income for shareholders in the short-term, but having limited appeal to an dwindling audience of collectors and fans over time (MacDonald). "This is the comic book industry," Stephenson said, "not the superhero industry, and if we want to stick around for the long haul, we need to recognize that" (MacDonald). Women had become Image's fastest growing demographic, he went on to explain, drawn in by comics and graphic novels that broke out of the superhero mold, like *Saga*, *Sex Criminals*, *Lazarus*, *Velvet*, *Pretty Deadly*, *Rocket Girl*, and *Rat Queens*, plus on-going series from other publishers, like DC's *Fables* and *Love and Rockets*. Stephenson spoke about the success Image had found with original material, like *Saga* and *The Walking Dead*, continuing with a challenge to the big two and the other publishers in attendance:

> While the rest of the entertainment industry lays back in the rut and churns out sequel after remake after reboot after sequel, we need to be on the frontline with the biggest, boldest, and best of the new ideas that will keep this industry healthy and strong for years to come. Comics are so much more than that, and this industry has existed as long as it has because of the ingenuity of men and women all over the world who yearn to share the fruits of their imaginations, not simply find new ways to prolong the life of existing intellectual properties. (MacDonald)

While some independent publishers may disagree with the details of Stephenson's claims, they would probably agree with his larger point that readers of all ages and genders are responding to the diverse voices and artistic innovations found in these new titles. According to MacDonald's monthly sales analysis on *The Comics Beat*, 151 of the 300 top-selling comics in April 2014 were titles put out by independent publishers (MacDonald).

Works Cited

Bechdel, Alison. *Fun Home: A Family Tragicomic*. New York: Mariner/ Houghton Mifflin, 2007.

Bloch, Robert. "Introduction." *Hellboy: Seed of Destruction*. By Mike Mignola & John Byrne. 3rd ed. Milwaukie, OR: Dark Horse, 2003.

Brownstein, Charles. "Who is Denis Kitchen? Snapshots from an Oddly Compelling Life." *The Oddly Compelling Art of Denis Kitchen*. Milwaukie, OR: Dark Horse, 2010.

CBR News Team. "*The Walking Dead* #100 Tops 380k In Sales." *Comic Book Resources*. 15 Jul. 2012. Web. 27 Jun. 2014.

Deahl, Rachel. "Bechdel Reacts to 'Fun Home' Controversy in So. Carolina" *Publishers Weekly*. 26 Feb. 2014. Web. 7 Jul. 2014.

Durajilija, Walter. "Undervalued Spotlight #59." *Comic Book Daily*. 18 Oct. 2010. Web. 6 Jul. 2014.

Hatfield, Charles. *Alternative Comics: an Emerging Literature*. Jackson: U of Mississippi P, 2005.

Harvey, Robert C. "Fun Home: Literary Cartooning in a Graphic Novel." *The Best American Comics Criticism*. Ed. Ben Schwartz. Seattle: Fantagraphics Books, 2010. *The Image Revolution*. Dir. Patrick Meaney. Sequart Organization (digital download), 2014. Film.

Kellogg, Carolyn. "South Carolina lawmakers OK college funding cuts over gay-themed books." *Los Angeles Times*. 1 Mar. 2014. Web. 14 Jul. 2014.

MacDonald, Heidi. "ComicsPRO: Image's Eric Stephenson addresses retailers" *Comic's Beat*. 28 Feb. 2014. Web. 27 Jun. 2014.

_____. "Indie Month-to-Month Sales: April 2014." *Comic's Beat*. 5 Jun. 2014 Web. 27 Jun. 2014.

Merino, Ana, & Corey K. Creekmur. "Fantagraphics." *Icons of the American Comic Book from Captain America to Wonder Woman, Volume 1*. Ed. Randy Duncan & Matthew J. Smith. Greenwood Icons: Santa Barbara, CA. 2013. 261–270.

Rhoades, Shirrel. *A Complete History of American Comic Books*. Peter Lang: New York, 2008.

Spiegelman, Art. *Breakdowns: Portrait of the Artist as a Young %@#$!!*. New York: Pantheon Books, 2008.

From the Page to the Tablet: Digital Media and the Comic Book

Philip Smith

In his 2000 book *Reinventing Comics*, comic book creator and scholar Scott McCloud imagined a bright future. The dawning of the digital age, he submitted, had the potential to transform the market; the Internet would drastically lower the costs of creating and distributing a comic, allowing creators to sell content directly to consumers without the support of major publishing companies (McCloud 162–3). Theoretically, creators could then operate with absolute creative freedom and maintain ownership of their work. These low barriers to entry would lead to a greater diversity of subject matter and a destabilization of superhero comics as the primary comic book form. Comic book creators would no longer be subject to the limitations of the print format, and the "infinite canvas" of digital space would provide them with almost unlimited room for creativity (200).

In some ways, McCloud was right in his predictions. The Internet certainly has transformed the ways in which comic books reach the hands of readers; comic book reader software and webcomics provide easy and immediate access (both sanctioned and unsanctioned) to comic book titles in ways that would have seemed inconceivable even twenty years ago. In 2012, the third of three years of explosive growth, digital sales represented almost nine percent of the comic book industry (ICV2 "Digital Comics"), but this figure captures only a portion of online readership. A complete survey of the readers of online and downloadable comics inclusive of webcomics would entail a count of visitor numbers across a prohibitively huge number of websites. A final number would be further complicated by the fact that many pirated, scanned versions of comics are obtained by readers through file sharing sites in numbers that likely dwarf sanctioned digital and print sales. Despite the challenges of arriving at conclusive numbers, one might reasonably assume that, thanks to the widespread availability of the Internet, the audience size for comics is now larger than it has ever been in history.

The digital revolution has changed the market for independent comic book creators; examples of functioning direct digital sales models do exist both through the independent comic branch of the vast digital comic empire that is ComiXology, through smaller operations, such as Thrillbent and the (now sadly retired) Moderntales.com. It is also the case that certain digital comics and almost all webcomics are being produced primarily (and in a small minority of cases, exclusively) to be read online. Some creators, both corporate-sponsored and independent, have been working to expand the tools of the medium beyond the limits of the printed page. The explosive proliferation of webcomics has brought forth a diversity of content, not only in terms of genres within the medium, but of creators; female and/or gay writers, who are a minority in print comics, are well-represented online.

In other ways, however, the digital age has not transformed American comics as completely or as dramatically as McCloud had once imagined. Print versions of superhero comics produced by Marvel and DC continue to dominate the market (each with a share slightly above thirty percent [Diamond Comics]). Smaller companies that lead, largely, with non-superhero titles, such as Image Comics also continue to operate using business models founded primarily on print sales. The majority of comics sold digitally across the American comic book market are electronic versions of works that were created primarily to be sold in print, and, as such, the potential of the infinite canvas is being explored only in the sidelines. The question this chapter aims to answer is why have McCloud's grand predictions for digital comics not been adopted as widely as he had hoped? By way of an answer, the economics and the content of two areas of the American comic book market shall be explored: the digital distribution of comic books inclusive of piracy and legal webcomics.

Online Distribution
The earliest forms of digital distribution for comic books were multiplatform CD and DVD sets, each of which collected a complete

archive of one Marvel title (Wershler 127). The comics sold in this format were often retouched and collected hard-to-find issues of popular series (sometimes, Wershler contends, by acquiring older copies from fans [127]). These sets were first released in 2002 and were replaced in late 2007 by online access to Marvel series through Marvel Digital Comics Unlimited (MDCU). On MDCU, comics could be viewed as an entire page or readers could zoom in to view a single panel. These comics also had a 'smart panels' navigation system, which panned from one panel to the next. Unlike the CD and DVD versions, these purchases could only be viewed through Marvel's site and could not be downloaded. MDCU could thus be better understood as a system whereby readers pay to access (in other words, rent) comics rather than purchasing them. The MDCU format has become the standard for the digital comic industry although some platforms now offer an alternative.

The website and app ComiXology has become one of the major means by which comics are accessed digitally. The company launched in 2007 and has gone from success to success. It generated a gross profit of $19 million in 2011 (Alverson "At last") and was the third highest-grossing app on Apple's American iTunes chart in 2012. In April 2014, it was acquired by Amazon, sending shockwaves throughout the digital comic book world. The site owns an estimated eighty percent share of the digital comics market (Alverson). ComiXology uses its own analogue of smart panels called Guided View. Like MDCU, the comics on ComiXology are only viewable on the ComiXology website or app. The demand for digital comics has, in some cases, been hard to meet. In March 2013, ComiXology announced that subscribers would be able to access the first issue of over seven Marvel titles for free. The company was unable to deal with the demand that followed; the huge number of subscribers who attempted to download all of the free titles caused ComiXology's servers to crash. ComiXology was forced to rescind and reinvent the offer (Cheredar).

It is noteworthy that, despite McCloud's prediction that the digital age would reduce the cost of distributing comics, digital comics sold through ComiXology generally cost the same as print at an average $1.99–$3.99 price point. This is due to the fact that ComiXology is a secondary market for works that are made primarily for print. Not only do these comics share the costs of their print counterparts, it is likely that comic book publishers do not wish to undercut their primary sales model. Nonetheless, ComiXology has brought about an approximation of the change that McCloud foresaw for independent comic books. In 2013, ComiXology began hosting the works of independent comic book creators through a portal called ComiXology Submit. Independently produced comics can be uploaded through ComiXology's site (for free) to be converted to the guided view format. ComiXology then sells the comic through their platform and splits the profits 50/50 with the creator. The creator retains ownership of their work. This business model allows independent creators to easily distribute their work to a large audience with no financial risk. The rewards, in terms of readership, can be significant; independent creator Rachel Deering stated:

> [W]hen I tweet about buying the book, ComiXology will retweet it. And they've got like, I don't know, somewhere between 30,000 and 50,000 followers [. . .] I get new followers every time ComiXology tweets about the book, and I get new sales every day. (Rogers)

One should be somewhat hesitant to describe ComiXology's work with independent creators as a complete realization of McCloud's vision, however. ComiXology does not accept all independent content; their FAQ page explains that it may dismiss anything they do not deem to be 'professional' (ComiXology). They also historically suffered pressure from the companies with whom they work; Apple previously forced ComiXology to remove 'objectionable' content from their app (Ching). The restrictions on content meant that Marvel's *Miracleman* #1 was issued without a free digital code for ComiXology; the comic was made available in a mass market and Parental Advisory version, but Marvel felt that the censorship applied represents too significant a change for them to link the censored and print versions (Burlingame). The ambiguous wording of ComiXology's (and previously also Apple's) guidelines mean that, while ComiXology does provide a valuable means of distribution for independent creators, they also incentivise the production of comics that take fewer risks in terms of content.

At the time of writing, it is too soon to tell what the Amazon acquisition will mean for the future of ComiXology Submit. An ideal scenario from the perspective of the independent comic book creator would be that, under Amazon's stewardship, ComiXology will mean more royalties now that Apple is no longer taking a cut, along with a wider readership and fewer content restrictions. A worst-case scenario would be the end of ComiXology Submit or tighter content restrictions. Interviews with a small sample of independent artists suggest that the majority are optimistic about a future working with ComiXology under Amazon (Means-Shannon).

ComiXology's growth has both reflected and brought about various changes in the industry. The year 2011 saw a diversification of digital delivery platforms that recreates the ComiXology model; comics became available through Android apps and e-readers, opening the market to readers on other platforms. Other, potentially financially viable alternatives to ComiXology have emerged. Comic book creator Mark Waid, for example, has launched his own digital comics distribution platform, Thrillbent, which includes downloadable Digital Rights Management (DRM)-free digital comics. Creators who work with Thrillbent can choose the price at which their comics will be sold, including the options of free and pay-what-you-want for potential consumers.

Digital distribution has also begun to change the industry in terms of its financial structures. In July 2014, DC changed its payment system for creators and colorists working on digital-first comics from a flat rate to a figure based on net revenue. They also ceased to consider digital and print sales separately (Wilson). At the time of this writing, it is difficult to assess who will benefit from this change and in what ways, but the change itself attests to the growing importance of digital distribution as a revenue stream.

File Sharing

Even larger, perhaps, than the growth of digital comics is the distribution of comic books through file sharing websites. A complete map of such networks is very difficult to obtain, but examples are abundant. Blogger No_Name considers one issue of *Ultimate Spiderman*, which she discovered on a file sharing site:

> [W]hile not all BitTorrent trackers track the number of times the file has been downloaded, this particular one does and it shows that the torrent for Ultimate Spider-Man #160 has been downloaded at least 11,600 times through their tracker. This number does not reflect the total number of times that same file has been downloaded through all the BitTorrent trackers combined. This number is based on only one tracking site. One of dozens of tracking sites where that same torrent file is being tracked. (No_Name)

Existing academic literature on illegal file sharing in the fields of economics, sociology, anthropology, and law is extensive, and the arguments, both in the public and academic arenas, are by no means resolved. The central arguments, with regard to file sharing and comic books, are familiar from the film and music industries: proponents of file sharing argue that pirate distribution networks are inevitable and, thus, comic book producers should be forced to adapt. These proponents also argue that file sharing allows comic book consumers to try before they buy: to sample comics in order to decide which series they wish to go on to purchase. Opponents of file sharing argue that a market where consumers are able to decide if and when they pay for content is unsustainable and that the (already fragile) industry of comics may cease to exist in its current format if consumers continue to engage in file sharing. As one writer argues:

> [I]f there is no return on the products, there is little or no incentive for the creator to continue creating and distributor to continue distributing. Pirates contribute nothing for every copy they take, and as pirates grow in number real sales diminish. And whether or not you accept it, each lost sale makes a huge impact. Every penny lost is less money to go towards innovation, quality, production speed, or creating jobs. Every penny lost is another artist not getting paid. (Comics Theory)

Some comic book creators disagree with this view; Mark Waid contends that file sharing does not result in overall damage the industry:

> [A]fter having been hip-deep in the research for the past three years, I have seen zero conclusive evidence that, on the whole, "piracy" removes more money from the system than it adds to it. Are there readers who would be buying my print comics who download them for free instead? Sure. Are there, conversely, potential readers who download one of my print comics, sample it, and then become a paying customer if they have access to ensuing print copies? Absolutely, and I've personally sold books to hundreds of them at store signings and conventions. (Waid)

Waid embraces file sharing to the extent that he makes digital copies of his comic *Insufferable* (2013–present) available online for free. Waid also embraces the infinite canvas of the web format; the digital version of *Insufferable* includes some instances where the appearance of panels and speech bubbles are staggered, pacing the acquisition of content in a way that would be impossible in print.

To measure the effects of file sharing on the comic book industry, one might look to studies in other media with a greater body of research, such as music. To cite one authoritative paper, Felix Oberholzer-Gee and Koleman Strumpf submit that, in the case of the music industry, file sharing may account for around twenty percent of a decline in sales, but this figure may be offset by an increased demand for complimentary goods, such as merchandise and concert tickets (35). They argue that the willingness of artists and publishers to create works in the fields of music, film, and print media has not diminished since the advent of file sharing and, indeed, appears to have risen; "[e]ven if file sharing were the reason that sales have fallen, the new technology does not appear to have exacted a toll on the quantity of music produced" (48–49). If the effect of file sharing on comic books resembles the music industry then Waid may be correct in his assertion that file sharing attracts as much money to comics as it takes away.

Comic book creators and distributors have attempted to counter some of the major complaints that have served as arguments in favor of file sharing. Historically, those who download comic books through such sites have argued that piracy allows faster access to content than sanctioned digital distribution. Comic book manufacturers have responded to this problem, but the efficacy of their response is debatable. The year 2011 saw a shift in digital distribution amongst comic book publishers to same-day-as-print, removing the danger that frustrated readers may choose to download a comic from a file sharing site rather than wait for a legitimate digital copy to become available. DC has gone even further than same-day-as-print with their Digital First line; issues zero and one of each Digital First comic is first released on ComiXology and then later in print format. Whether this had a significant effect is uncertain; to cite one possible measure, Google's Trends shows that the number of individuals who have searched for the term 'comics torrent' has remained relatively unchanged between 2010 and 2013, whereas the term 'download comics' has fallen since 2011.

A second problem often voiced in regard to sanctioned digital distribution concerns the rental versus purchase problem. As mentioned above, those who buy comics through ComiXology or many publishers' sites can only read their purchases through that site or app. If the website becomes unavailable (as ComiXology did in March 2013 when their servers crashed) so too does the purchased content. This complaint has been used as an argument in favor of file sharing, which allows consumers to own digital copies of comic books rather than simply pay for access. In July 2013, Image Comics announced that future electronic copies of their comics purchased through their website would be free of DRM technology (Behrenshausen). This change counters the problem described above, but serves a secondary purpose; Image Comics tacitly declared that they no longer intend to protect digital versions of their content from being shared and are, thus, giving up the digital protection aspect of the fight against illegal file sharing.

The question of file sharing has been one of the defining arguments in the digital age of comics and the future of the debate will undoubtedly continue to shape the industry in years to come. Of equal import to the method by which digital comics are delivered is the question of what is being delivered. In almost all cases discussed above, the digital comic (either sold through ComiXology or downloaded elsewhere) is typically a scan or 'guided view' conversion of a comic that was designed for print. As such, the typical digital comic is limited to the static format, 6 inch x 10 inch dimensions of an average comic book, and does not embrace the infinite canvas of online space.

Some attempts have been made to create purely digital comics. The first comics to embrace the digital appeared as early as 1996 in the form of Marvel's Cybercomics. Cybercomics included animation, sound effects, and music (Wershler 129). In 2009, they were reborn as Marvel Motion Comics, which included a fan-made element, whereby individuals could add their own audio and animation to existing comic book files. The latest incarnation of this project is Marvel's Infinite Comics, which was unveiled in 2012. Infinite Comics make use of the digital format, for example, to position panels in place of, rather than beside, previous panels and to delay the appearance of speech bubbles in an image. This format allows creators to move beyond the conventional restrictions of the printed page and control the pace at which the action appears to the reader. Such experiments are still in their early stages, however, and are certainly far from widespread. Even Infinite Comics are somewhat conservative: their creators are eager to emphasize that their comics do not deviate dramatically from the traditional format. Joe Quesada, Marvel's Chief Creative Officer, has stated that Infinite Comics "doesn't reinvent comics so completely that they become something other than what they are" (Morse). Aside from experiments such as Infinite Comics, at the time of this writing, digital comics from major presses remain firmly rooted in print. For an examination of comics that work primarily in the digital format, one must look beyond major comic book manufacturers and enter the world of independent webcomics.

Webcomics

A webcomic can be loosely defined as a comic book that uses an online format as its primary means of distribution. The number and variety of webcomics has grown exponentially in the late twentieth and early twenty-first centuries to the point that the readership of some highly successful webcomics far exceeds that of major print comics. Jerry Holkins and Mike Krahulik's *Penny Arcade* (1998–present), for example, has enjoyed a readership of as many as 2,000,000 page views per day (Holkins); by way of comparison, *Infinite Crisis*, the top-selling comic book at the time Holkins made his claim, sold 201,830 issues in one month (Comichron). In 2010, Holkins and Krahulik were voted the forty-third most influential people in the world (above President Barack Obama, Jon Stewart, and Beyoncé) by readers of *Time*.

Penny Arcade is far from representative, however; many webcomics resemble the 1960s underground comic book movement, including, in many cases, the same obscurity, dubious misogyny, and variable aesthetic quality of the early underground (Sabin 208). As was the case with the underground movement, for the average webcomic, a single individual is responsible for writing, drawing, marketing, and distributing the work. This independence undoubtedly brings benefits in terms of creative freedom, but also leads to challenges in terms of financing and distribution. Only the most successful of webcomics achieve (like *Penny Arcade*) the brand recognition and huge distribution networks which rival that of a major comic book company.

Much like the underground cartoonists of the 1960s, independent online comic book creators have harnessed new business and distribution models as a means to finance their work, although the industry as a whole has yet to arrive upon a single formula for turning a profit. In the majority of cases, the webcomic is provided for free, and income is generated through a combination of fan donations, commissions, merchandise, and advertising; Danielle Corsetto's *Girls With Slingshots* (2004–present), for example, uses all of the above. A very small minority of webcomics have successfully generated income through a paid subscription model, much like the micropayments system proposed by McCloud; in 2005, the website Moderntales.com had roughly two thousand subscribers each of whom paid $3 per month to access content. The site eventually closed its doors in April 2013. As early as 2005, Joey Manley, the site's curator, stated that, whilst the site was turning a profit, he believed that advertising space represents the medium's financial future (Walker). Other webcomic creators have experienced less success with the micropayment model; when Jonathan Rosenberg offered access to an electronic version of his two eighteen-page mini-comics (which sell for $4 in print) for $0.25, he raised just $53.25— a sum that represented, for Rosenberg, a complete failure (Walker). Perhaps the most recent example of a fan-financed webcomic is Brian K. Vaughan, Marcos Martin, and Muntsa Vicente's *The Private Eye* (2013–present) which is sold online using a pay-what-you-want model. Time will tell if this model proves to be successful, but, even if it is, it may not be easily replicable for new webcomic creators. Vaughan is an already well-established writer in television and comics and the recipient of many Eisner awards and, as such, he brings a large existing fan base to any new product.

Other webcomic creators make their work freely available and simply ask their fans for money. In 2004, Randy Milholland, creator of *Something Positive* (2001–present) asked his readers for donations to pay his annual salary (then $35,000) so that he could make comics full-time for one year (Losowsky). To his surprise, he raised the total within a month. Many webcomics employ a similar system for donations, but as an ongoing project rather than a single event. In late 2013, John Rosenberg used the Patreon platform to gather sufficient ongoing donors to sponsor his work. To name one example of many, the website for Tom Fischbach's *Twokinds* (2003–present) includes a link for Paypal donations, and the header for webcomic creator Leslie Chew's Facebook page includes his bank details and a request that readers who enjoy the site consider donating to keep it running. The main flaw in this model, Chew claims, is that donations are often inversely proportional to success:

It gets tougher as the number of fans grow and everyone thinks that someone else will support me. The amount of voluntary subscription I get keeps decreasing the more fans I get, which was why I have to stop for a month to do "real work" to pay off the bills that have been piling up. (Chew)

Other comic book artists have successfully used the Kickstarter model to finance and receive donations for their work. On the Kickstarter website, backers pledge a certain amount of money toward a project in exchange for reward. Backers are only charged if a project is fully funded. In March 2013, Aaron Diaz raised $534,994 in order to produce a print copy of his webcomic *Dresden Codak* (2005–present).

The question remains if any of these fan-funded models are truly sustainable or scalable. Certainly, the events described above were successful to different degrees and ends, but they have not been oft-repeated. Once Milholland's year of fan-funded work came to an end, for example, he began to generate funding through merchandise rather than launching a second campaign to pay his salary. Readers may be willing to give a few dollars to an independent webcomic creator for as long as that creator operates independently and with little profit; raising money for a larger-scale successful operation may not be so easy. It is further the case that *The Private Eye*, *Something Positive*, *Penny Arcade*, and *Dresden Codak* should not necessarily be taken as representative of webcomics as a whole in terms of readership and, as such, one should not assume that their crowd-funding model can be replicated by an unknown creator. One needs only to browse the category "comics" on Kickstarter.com to find a graveyard of webcomics that failed to find funding.

Many webcomic creators finance their activities through advertising. This is particularly true in the case of game-related webcomics which serve as attractive hosts for advertisements from game manufacturers. Successful webcomic creators also often take contract work; Holkins and Krahulik frequently create one-off comics for video game manufacturers, in order to promote the release of an upcoming game. In addition to advertising space, the most common source of income for webcomic creators comes through merchandise, such as T-shirts or posters, high-quality print versions of the comic, signed drawings at comic book trade shows, or (in the case of *Penny Arcade,* a series of video games). Aaron Diaz, in addition to various other forms of merchandise, invites fans to pay any amount they choose in exchange for *Dresden Codak*-themed desktop wallpapers (for examples, see Diaz, "Donation Desktop Wallpapers"). For those creators who fund their comics through merchandise, the process of packing and shipping orders can, itself, become a full-time job; in 2009 Chris Onstad of *Achewood* (2001–present) fame reported that before his business became large enough for him to hire additional staff, he and his wife would work the proverbial nine to five every day fulfilling customer's orders and only then would he be able to work on his comic (Smith).

In terms of content, the majority of webcomics, such as Kris Wilson, Rob DenBleyker, Matt Melvin, and Dave McElfatrick's *Cyanide and Happiness* (2004–present)*,* use the newspaper gag strip three-panel format. Others, such as Matthew Inman's *The Oatmeal* (2009–present) or Aaron Diaz's *Dresden Codak*, use a top-to-bottom, left-to-right format which modifies the dimensions of the standard comic book by fitting their comics to the dimensions of a scrollable browser window. Other webcomic creators have pushed deeper into the infinite canvas of virtual space. In September 2012, for example, Randall Munroe's *xkcd* (2005–present) featured a comic entitled 'Click and Drag' where the final panel served as a window into a gigantic image. The reader could explore this image by doing as instructed: clicking and dragging within the space of the panel. Other comic book artists have replaced the turning of a page with the click of a button to great effect; Emily Carroll's horror comic *His Face All Red* (2010) uses varied page sizes and a 'next' button to achieve suspense and timing which would be unavailable to a creator working in the print format. Some creators, such as the Korean horror comic writer Pick, have gone further still by using animation, (in Pick's case by taking control of the scroll function) to create motion in certain panels of their comics (see, for example, Pick, "봉천동귀신"). Such innovations test and expand the limit of what constitutes a comic and offer a new set of tools for the comic book creator.

Independent webcomics serve as the best modern representatives of creative freedom for the medium not only in terms of expanding the technical tools available to creators, but in the freedom of expression that McCloud thought possible. A typical webcomic creator, unlike his or her equivalent working in print, is not necessarily dependent upon the patronage of a larger company, nor do they not need to adhere to the style guidelines or politics of a benefactor or host. As Paul Williams and James Lyons submit, the recent celebration of alternative comics in American culture brings with it the incentive to produce a certain type of content (xxi); webcomic creators rarely suffer from such restrictions and are largely free to approach whatever subject matter they and their fans enjoy.

It is the economics of the webcomics, which place the heaviest restrictions on content in terms of both innovation and freedom of expression; the most common form of merchandise found in webcomic stores is a high-quality print version of the comic. As such, webcomic creators cannot afford to let their work drift too far from the dimensions and limitations of the printed page. Even webcomic creators who have embraced the freedom of the infinite canvas must tether their work to the print format; Charley Parker's *Argon Zark!* (1995–present) not only includes animation, but employs 'unprintable' colors that do not appear on the CMYK color range and yet Parker generates income by offering a 'deluxe portable cordless' version of his first story. Webcomic creators who depend on financial support from their readers also need to tailor their content to as wide an audience as possible; Brian King, creator of the webcomic *Mayoking.com* (2012–present), has complained that the fan response to some of his work has caused him to stick to making "safe comics" (King).

Storing Comics in the 'McCloud'

If one were being generous to McCloud, one might say (to indirectly quote William Gibson) that the future he predicted is here, but it is not evenly distributed. Marvel's experiments with Infinite Comics and its earlier incarnations, as well as the webcomics of the likes of Randall Munroe, Emily Carroll, and Pick, expand the comic book beyond the limits of the printed page. The advent of the Internet has lowered the barriers to entry for independent comic book artists, both through the independent comics arm of ComiXology and owner-made webcomics. Few examples exist of independent comics that have successfully mobilized the micropayment model imagined by McCloud, but fundraising campaigns, donations, merchandise and advertisements provide a stable income for a few. The form still remains very much tied to the print format, however; in the majority the comics that are sold or otherwise procured digitally through ComiXology and other sites are digital versions of print comics, and webcomic creators are reluctant to sacrifice the possibility of producing a (potentially lucrative) print version of their work. Because of the lingering fidelity that the market shows to print, McCloud's vision of a world filled with economically viable creator-owned comics that transcend print remains, for now, unrealized.

Acknowledgements

The author wishes to extend his thanks Leslie Chew and the staff at the Digital Comics Museum for providing information for this work. Thanks also goes to Nicholas Yanes for his invaluable feedback on an earlier version of the chapter.

Works Cited

Alverson, Brigid. "At last a digital comics number: ComiXology's sales were $19M in '11." *Comic Book Resources*, 22 Jun. 2012. Web. 10 Sept. 2014.

Behrenshausen, Bryan. "Image Comics' solution to comic book piracy: remove DRM" *Opensource*, 22 Jul. 2013. Web. 10 Sept. 2014.

Burlingame, Russ. "Miracleman Altered for ComiXology Release, Free Digital Copies Cancelled as a Result" *Comicbook.com* 18 Jan. 2014. Web. 10 Sept. 2014.

Carroll, Emily. *His Face All Red.* Emcaroll.com, n.d. Web. 10 Sept. 2014.

Cheredar, Tom. "ComiXology Resurrects 700 free Marvel Comics Promotion." *VB Media*, 8 April 2013. Web. 10 Sept. 2014.

Chew, Leslie. Personal correspondence. 26 January 2014.

Ching, Albert. "Apple Blocks 'Sex Criminals' #2 on ComiXology iOS App." *Comic Book Resources,* 5 November 2013. Web. 10 Sept. 2014.

Comichron. "March 2006 Comic Book Sales Figures." *Comichron.com,* n.d. Web. 10 Sept. 2014.

Comics Theory. "Evaluating Comic Book Piracy–Global Consequences." *Comics Theory.* Comicstheory.com, n.d. Web. 10 Sept. 2014.

ComiXology. "Why Would My Comic get Rejected?" *ComiXology,* 7 Mar. 2013. Web. 10 Sept. 2014.

Diamond Comics. "Publisher Market Share: October 2013." *Diamond Comics.com.* Diamond Comic Distributors, n.d. Web. 10 Sept. 2014.

Diaz, Aaron. "Donation Desktop Wallpapers." *Dresdencodak.com*, n.d. Web. 10 Sept. 2014.

Holkins, Jerry. "Apollogisimo." *Penny Arcade*, 13 Mar. 2006. Web. 10 Sept. 2014.

ICV2. "Digital Comics Nearly Tripled in 2012." *ICV2*, 15 Jul. 2013. Web. 10 Sept. 2014.

King, Brian. "Safe Comics." *Mayoking.com* Web. 27 March 2013.

Losowsky, Andrew. "Charity Begins on the Net." *The Guardian*, 9 Sept. 2004.Web. 10 Sept. 2014.

McCloud, Scott. *Reinventing Comics*. New York: HarperCollins, 2000.

Means-Shannon, Hannah. "ComiXology Submit Creators Respond to the Amazon Purchase–And Remain Optimistic." *Bleeding Cool*, 7 May 2014. Web. 10 Sept. 2014.

Morse, Ben. "Marvel Infinite Comics Unveiled." *Marvel.com*, 3 November 2012. Web. 10 Sept. 2014.

No_Name. "The Sad State of Comics Piracy–It's Worse than You Think." *Comics Vine*, 30 Jun. 2011. Web. 10 Sept. 2014.

Oberholzer-Gee, Felix, & Koleman Strumph. "File Sharing and Copyright*." Innovation Policy and the Economy* 10:1 (2010). 19-55.

Pick. 봉천동귀신. *Comic Naver,* n.d. Web. 10 Sept. 2014.

Rogers, Vaneta. "ComiXology Submit Launches with Anathema." *Newsarama*, 22 May 2013. Web. 10 Sept. 2014.

Sabin, Roger. *Adult Comics: An Introduction*. London: Routledge, 1993.

Smith, Julia. "The Creators of 'Trophy Wife' and 'Achewood.'" *Bullseye with Jesse Thorn*. Maximumfun.org, 4 Feb. 2014. Web. 10 Sept. 2014.

Waid, Mark. "Marketing through Piracy." *MarkWaid.com*, 24 May 2012. Web. 10 Sept. 2014.

Walker, Leslie. "Comics Looking to Spread a Little Laughter on the Web." *Washington Post*, 15 Jun. 2005. Web. 10 Sept. 2014.

Wershler, Darren. "Digital Comics, Circulation and the Importance of Being Eric Sluis." *Cinema Journal* 50.3 (2011): 27–134.

Williams, Paul, & James Lyons. "Introduction." *The Rise of the American Comics Artist: Creators and Contexts*. Ed. Paul Williams & James Jackson Lyons. Jackson, MS: UP of Mississippi, 2010. xi–xxiv.

Wilson, Matt D. "DC's New Creator Payment Plan Puts Digital Comics On Par With Print, Offers Colorists Royalties." *Comics Alliance*, 24 Jun. 2014. Web. 10 Sept. 2014.

Fantasy Elsewheres, Sutured Realities, and the End of Camp: Comics in Contemporary Film and Television

Owen R. Horton & A. J. Shackelford

At the time of this chapter's composition, four of the top six box-office earning films—*Captain America: The Winter Soldier, X-Men: Days of Future Past, Transformers: Age of* Extinction, and *The Amazing Spider-Man 2*—were from the superhero genre with the reigning champion being Cap 2 ("Comic Book"). Marvel's just-released *Guardians of the Galaxy*, is almost certain to join these other films in the top ten and has bested *The Bourne Ultimatum* with the highest-earning opening weekend in August, a time period more often than not marked as the graveyard of the Summer. While 2014 is currently experiencing a financial dearth when compared to 2013, comic book adaptations certainly appear to be outside that metric. The year 2014 may be the year of the comic book movie; however, the same could have been said for 2013 in which three of the top fifteen highest-earning films featured superheroes, not to mention 2012 where three of the top ten highest-earning films featured superheroes. While judging a film's merits based upon consumer trends in the domestic and international box office might not seem to produce the best rubric for success, comics occupy a distinct class of media (as other chapters have argued), where sales *do* matter. Superhero films are no longer relegated to *niche* status and appear to be some of the most consistently bankable films every year.

What strikes us, beyond the consistent success of the superhero film in the last fifteen years, is the ways in which this popularity also projects to the future of filmic discourse communities. Both Marvel and DC have presented an ambitious television and film slate going forward over the next decade. Fans are not simply excited about the plethora of films being released this year; they can also look forward to a sequel to *The Avengers, Superman vs. Batman: Dawn of Justice*, and *Ant-Man*, et al. in 2015. Likewise, fans can also expect sequels in the *Spider-Man* and *X-Men* franchises as well as the arrival of new franchises as DC mounts a Justice League vehicle intended to rival the Marvel Cinematic Universe's success with their films.

This lasting popularity situates the comic fan in a unique moment in popular culture: we are beyond the point of being shocked that a superhero film can be both serious and spectacular. We are beyond the point of being astonished that a superhero film could generate serious Oscar buzz beyond special effects. We now expect these films to be both fantastical and artistic achievements in equal measure. The superhero in culture is no longer something fans apologize for; it is a stable and lasting genre in American popular media. This chapter will explore how these substantial changes came out, what we see as the importance and role of the superhero in television and film, and what fans can expect as the medium grows and progresses.

Films 1978–2000: A "Fantasy Elsewhere"

In Tim Burton's *Batman* (1989), reporter Vicki Vale (Kim Bassinger) challenges Batman (Michael Keaton) on the sanity of his actions when she asks him, "You're not exactly normal, are you?" Batman's response, "It's not exactly a normal world, is it?" calls into question exactly which world he is referencing. Batman's world, after all, has occupied various positions *vis-à-vis* our world—at times, it is a reflection of our reality; at other times, it is a funhouse mirror. Likewise, there is a profound fascination with translating Gotham City into a real-world analogue: is it London? Chicago? New York City? (Uricchio 121–122). These same questions arise for the homes of other superheroes—is Superman's Metropolis an analogue New York during the daytime? Where is Flash's Central City? Green Lantern's Coast City? The desire to situate these spaces in our reality indicates a rejection of the boundaries of fantasy. Unlike Marvel, which already places its heroes in real-world spaces like New York City, DC Comic heroes occupy fictional cities that exist only in the universe of the comics themselves. Arno Meteling argues: "Superheroes are not only graphically inconsistent with a realistic backdrop when wearing spandex costumes in primary colors . . . they also seem to belong to another time and to another narrative genre" (134). This clash of timelessness and recognizable urban modernity disrupts the ability to craft a realistic superhero city. Instead, directors seemed to be stuck crafting what we call "fantasy elsewheres." We use the term "fantasy elsewhere" to describe these superheroic cityscapes—the city of the DC hero, be it Metropolis or Gotham, occupies no real space and contains no real residents, nor does it always react or interact with our world. Instead, these cities become self-contained entities that house their own narratives, people, and places. The key element of the fantasy elsewhere is that it progresses outside of reality—it is both timeless and removed from the politics of our world, occupying a distinct comics cosmology. These elements free up directors to experiment with the setting: Gotham City is always open to interpretation for each artist and need not bear any resemblance to any place on Earth. The fantasy elsewhere, then, presents a unique opportunity for a filmmaker: a modern city, with seventy-plus years of history and visuals, which requires no standard representation. This freedom of presentation allowed directors, such as Burton, to push the limits of what a city might look like, although this visual experimentation has slowly given way to a more realistic representation of the fantasy worlds of DC characters.

DC Comics held the monopoly on successful superhero franchises until 2000. For the purposes of this essay, a stark line of demarcation is drawn at 2000 because this marks a massive shift in the role of the city and the "fantasy elsewhere" in superhero films. Not coincidentally, this year also marks the beginning of Marvel Comics *successful* foray into comics films. Prior to 2000, both the *Superman* and the *Batman* franchises were incredibly successful, although both saw a sharp decline after the first two installments. Prior to Richard Donner's *Superman* (1978), superheroes in television and cinema were not serious fare. Leslie H. Martinson's *Batman* (1966), based on the television series, is a prime example of the limits of comic book cinema at the time—directors and writers were unsure how to present comic heroes in a serious way, so they emphasized the campiness of the medium to a ridiculous level.

Donner's film, then, was groundbreaking in that it treated its hero with a tender seriousness.

While Martinson's film seems to mock the idea of Batman, Donner's film earnestly holds Superman up as a paragon of virtue. Part of Superman's virtue is his timeless morality and character, and the settings of Donner's film emphasize the ways in which Superman and his world are frozen in some golden era of integrity. While the film begins on Krytpon, Superman's story starts in a romanticized 1950s Smallville, Kansas. Like other fantasy elsewheres, this Kansas is more fiction than fact—there is no Cold War, no nuclear scare; Clark's biggest challenges are a group of impotent bullies and his father's death. Contrasted against the bright and color-rich Kansas, Donner's Metropolis is mostly neon and nighttime. Again, the film is not concerned with presenting Metropolis as some modern-day analogue—there is still no Cold War and the terroristic threat Superman foils comes from one man (Gene Hackman's clownish Lex Luthor), not a national cultural foil. There is no need to situate Metropolis within these larger cultural concerns because the elements of Superman's story that Donner seeks to emphasize are those timeless and classic virtues. The role of the city, in this case, is not to function as a living breathing character, but to serve as an eager observer. Superman's spectacle is meaningless without an adoring audience, and that is the role Metropolis plays—a role even more strongly emphasized at the conclusion of the sequel, *Superman II* (1983).

Unlike Metropolis, Gotham City is very much a character in the Batman mythos. In reference to Batman's origin, the murder of his parents on the streets of Gotham, William Uricchio writes that:

> [T]hose same streets and conditions provide the locus, condition and cause for Batman's obsessive battle with crime. Gotham's value in this case is far greater than a mere setting for the adventures of a superhero: it turns on its generative relationship to the narrative, the source of the franchise's endless iteration. (120)

Whereas Superman's Metropolis serves as a means to emphasize the spectacle of his greatness, Batman's Gotham City serves as the genesis and producer of his never-ending battle; while Donner's *Superman* (1978) departed from the campiness of earlier superhero films, Burton's *Batman* (1989) was the complete antithesis: dark, gritty, violent, and psychologically-disturbed. We are so far removed from this film that it may be difficult to remember how stark Burton's changes were: an all-black, rubberized Batman suit, when all the viewer had ever known was the navy-and-grey spandex of Adam West; mobsters and gangsters instead of childish and cartoonish villains; and most importantly, a Joker (Jack Nicholson) that was more demonic psychopath than clown prince. Beyond these changes, Burton also chose to present his twisted gothic version of Gotham City—the skyscrapers reach toward the heavens (and bend and warp in the process); the streets are covered in dirt, grime, and an endless supply of industrial steam; the sky is eternally and relentlessly dark; everyone, save the Joker, dresses as if coming from or going to a funeral.

Beyond his version of the gothic, Burton also borrows heavily from noir film. The mobsters and dirty cops all wear suits and fedoras, drive classic cars, and meet in shady back alleys at night. While the main confrontation of the film is Batman versus the Joker, the strong secondary undercurrent is public and police corruption at the hands of organized crime. Some crucial noir elements are missing (who, for example, is Batman's femme fatale?), but Burton is less interested in the noir plot than he is in the noir aesthetic. The combination of the noir and the gothic is what makes Gotham City a fantasy elsewhere. Roz Kaveney argues that "Burton deliberately made a film that was set in several time periods simultaneously—the cars, the fashions and the buildings could be the 1930s, the 1950s or the near future" (238). In other words, Burton's Gotham is both timeless and outside of time, much akin to the ongoing narrative occurring in the medium of comics itself.

His sequel, *Batman Returns* (1992) carries the timeless gothic noir elements further, even going so far as to finally give the dark detective a worthy femme fatale in Catwoman (Michelle Pfeiffer), offering a tragic foil in the Penguin (Danny DeVito), and situating the plot in a public works scandal, involving the siphoning of electricity by the story's most irredeemable character, the non-supervillain, Max Shreck (Christopher Walken). As in the previous film, the reality of the audience's world is missing in Gotham—there is no Gulf War, no AIDS epidemic. This film could have released in the 1950s or in 2014 and the plot would not seem dated. Roz Kaveney, however, identifies a small crack in the fantasy elsewhere: the feminist undertones of the Catwoman. She writes:

> The Waters/Burton Catwoman is quite explicitly a reaction—not entirely a positive reaction—to feminism; at one point, rebuking a woman she has saved from muggers with the remark that "you make it too easy," she goes on to say, "I am Catwoman, hear me roar," echoing a well-known slogan. (Kaveney 242)

The crack in the façade of the fantasy elsewhere indicates that audiences and directors may not be able to work with films set in a modern world that do not at least slightly resemble contemporary culture. Is it possible to create a superhero story that does not reflect any element of our world? Burton's decision to slip this slight referent into *Batman Returns* indicates that it may not be, at least not anymore. This small breach in the wall of the fantasy elsewhere serves as a marker for where the superhero film will go, albeit not for another eight years.

The next two installments in the Batman franchise were most largely marked by the change of director—from Tim Burton to Joel Schumacher. While Burton appeared to be edging closer to the incorporation of contemporary realism, Schumacher went the complete opposite direction. The world of *Batman Forever* loses much of the dark and grimy feel of Burton's films, but it does not move toward a more realistic depiction. Instead, the world feels plastic and shiny (Schumacher himself called it "toyetic" [Kaveney 247].). There is still a darkness to Gotham City, but it feels like the controlled darkness of a theatre rather than the oppressive darkness of industrial modernity. Similarly, the characterizations in *Batman Forever* feel less darkly psychological (despite Batman's love interest, Dr. Chase Meridian [Nicole Kidman], being a psychiatrist) and more comic. The character of Two-Face (Tommy Lee Jones), for example, is meant to evoke a dark struggle between the id and the superego; instead, Schumacher offers a brightly-colored cackling jester. In short, Schumacher's film was more comic, more ridiculous, and more family-friendly. That trend toward the fantastic continued even further in *Batman and Robin* (1997). Burton's grey-and-black tones are replaced with incandescent blues and pristine silvers; it all feels clean and sterile. While the city is still perpetually in nighttime, it now offers a neon glow to the dark corners. The warped architecture of Burton's films is pushed to the uncanny—buildings no longer look real or even lived-in; rather, they are clean but devoid of human presence. Schumacher's final version of Gotham City is the ultimate fantasy elsewhere—no one seems to live in this massive city besides the principle characters.

Films 2000–2014: Suturing to Reality

The crucial difference between the heroes of the DC Universe and the Marvel Universe is that Marvel heroes inhabit real-world spaces (many of them in New York City), while their DC counterparts live in their fantasy elsewheres. The year 2000 is especially significant partially because it represents the introduction of the modern Marvel film universe, with *X-Men* (2000), and partially because it features a film that completely inverts the fantasy elsewhere mold: M. Night Shyamalan's *Unbreakable* (2000). The other element that marks 2000 as special is that it was the beginning of the superhero film as safe commercial blockbuster. While only eight films released between 1978 and 2000 featured major superhero characters, Marvel and DC have released ten such films in the last three years. Because of this acceleration, and the massive volume of comics adaptation to films released since 2000, this essay will only focus on two franchises and one film: Christopher Nolan's Dark Knight trilogy, Marvel's Iron Man trilogy, and Shyamalan's *Unbreakable*.

Unbreakable was released a few months after Bryan Singer's *X-Men* (2000), but it did more to shift the trend of the fantasy elsewhere. Shyamalan's film might have been the first to imagine a superhero not just living in a real-world city (Philadelphia) but also dealing with real-world problems. His superheroic melodrama, then, functioned as a complete rejection of the previous era's presentation of the hero and the city. While Batman and Superman operated within fantasy elsewheres—cities detached from our reality and contemporary issues—Shyamalan's David Dunn was heavily grounded in a recognizable real world. Philadelphia in this film is not a character or a genesis point; it's Philadelphia. Dunn's struggles are the existential struggles of the modern man: financial security, aging, masculinity, married life, fatherhood. It is difficult to imagine Donner's *Superman* or Burton's *Batman* spending large chunks of the narrative showing Clark Kent or Bruce Wayne working a menial job or patching together a broken marriage. In these ways, we can understand the fantasy elsewhere as more than just a physical location; rather, it is a refusal to engage with contemporary reality. Shyamalan's *Unbreakable* is ground-breaking for this genre because it not only engages with reality, it brushes away everything fantastic and otherworldly about the superhero mythos.

A better way to understand the post-2000 shift in superhero films is to examine Jason Bainbridge's concept of the city as a "suture" to reality. Although he focuses on comics, his observations apply to the film adaptations of these characters as well. Referencing Marvel superheroes' relationship to the real-life Big Apple, Jason Bainbridge writes: "New York City is therefore not only the spine of the Marvel Universe, it is a *suture*—suturing the Marvel Universe to the real world, providing a material context for these iconic forms" (172). The suture, then, is the bridge from the fantasy of the superhero to our world. While Bainbridge focuses on the role a real city like New York plays on this suture, it is also necessary to focus on the ways in which engagement with contemporary issues suture the heroes of comic films to our reality. Given the sheer number of films in this time period, this chapter could not hope to be inclusive. Rather, two franchises, launched within a few years of each other—DC's *Dark Knight* trilogy directed by Christopher Nolan and Marvel's Iron Man trilogy directed by Jon Favreau and Shane Black— illustrate both the distance superhero films have come from the fantasy elsewhere of pre-2000 and the narrative depth with which directors can suture films to our reality.

Nolan's *Batman Begins* (2005) played specifically with the concept of fear throughout the first film. The audience encounters a well-orchestrated attack on our character's home of Gotham City, an attack plotted and carried out by a headless, cell-based, intentionally-Orientalized terrorist organization designed to destroy a decadent civilization. The markers to a post-9/11 world are relatively obvious. These conceptual sutures to reality are crucial because, otherwise, Nolan borrows much from Burton's visual aesthetic—a dark, grimy, industrial city, with black and grey as the dominant colors. As the trilogy progresses, the sutures becomes more prevalent. *The Dark Knight* (2008) features a rogue terrorist villain—Heath Ledger's Joker as chaos incarnate—with a 'sins of the father' message about the consequences of over-policing. This film sutured well to the contemporary American disgust at the consequences of the War on Terror and fed into the prevailing belief that our involvement abroad had only made things worse. Finally, *The Dark Knight Rises* (2012) focused on a self-styled revolutionary, Bane (Tom Hardy), who ignites class warfare in Gotham City and uses hope as a weapon against the masses. The sutures here are with the rise of economic inequality movements such as the 99 Percent and Occupy Wall Street, which experienced growing popularity throughout the recent recession, as well as the cynical reaction to President Barack Obama's 2008 campaign slogan of "HOPE." When Bane, in a 2012 film, says "As I terrorize Gotham, I will feed its people hope to poison their souls," Nolan is making explicit connections to a political position now seen as naïve. What is crucial about the sutures in Nolan's trilogy, however, is that we never leave Gotham City. Despite the fact that Gotham does not exist, we are able to locate it in our world through the contemporary themes and struggles of its main characters. Therefore, the fantasy elsewhere becomes sutured to our world not through aesthetics but through narrative.

Marvel's Iron Man franchise functions as the studio's analogue to Batman in a number of ways. Both main characters are billionaires with no superpowers of their own, and both films engage with the American response to 9/11 more explicitly than other comic films. While the Iron Man films begin and end later than Nolan's trilogy, they offer a much less cynical view of American politics. The sutures here are more emotional and voyeuristic than in the Batman films, perhaps because Tony Stark (Robert Downey, Jr.) is meant to stand in for the audience's visceral response to contemporary problems, while Batman is engaged in a more philosophical debate. In short, the Iron Man films take themselves much less seriously, although they deal with equally serious issues. Like Nolan's trilogy, the Iron Man trilogy tracks an increasingly disillusioned response to the American reaction to terrorism. *Iron Man* (2008) acts out many Americans' fantasies of vengeance, as Stark flies around blowing up tanks and destroying terrorist safe houses. In one particular scene, Tony flies into a hostile situation in an unnamed Middle Eastern village. As he lands, the terrorists take civilian hostages. The Iron Man suit then scans the faces of everyone and instantly identifies who is a terrorist and who is an innocent. Before anyone can react, the suit fires precise missiles, killing every terrorist with zero collateral damage. This is the fantasy of the American military: the ability to quickly identify "good guys" and "bad guys" and to eliminate threats with one hundred percent accuracy and no civilian casualties. The suture here is a fantasy, but it is a fantasy that the culture understands and experiences.

On the surface, *Iron Man 2* (2010) seems relatively devoid of sutures. The film's conversations about ownership and power were not prevailing American concerns at the time. However, as in *The Dark Knight*, the film does deal with the concept of terrorism as being of our own creation. The central villain, Whiplash (Mickey Rourke), gains his hatred from a perceived wrong at the hands of the Stark family and comes to America to enact his vengeance. While *Iron Man* played to American revenge fantasies, *Iron Man 2* captured the sense that Americans felt wrongly targeted and victimized. Similarly, Tony's speech to Congress, in which he proclaims (prematurely) that he has ended terrorist threats, reflects George W. Bush's famous "Mission Accomplished" celebration. The sutures of *Iron Man 2* are both personal and political; yet, this film, apart from the first and third installments, was the least successful. The lack of engagement with the problems of the contemporary world likely contributed to this film's lukewarm reception both critically and at the box office. While *Iron Man 2* was a disappointing follow-up to the first installment, *Iron Man 3* (2013) was the most successful of the bunch. Unlike *Iron Man 2*, Shane Black's film embraced the revenge-fantasy roots of the original. In this case, the fantasy is against an entire generation's boogeyman: Osama Bin Laden. The suture here is both obvious and subtle: obvious, in that the Mandarin (Ben Kingsley) records threatening propaganda tapes reminiscent of the images of terrorists we see on regular basis; subtle, in that the plot twist reveals Mandarin to be a uniquely American "creation." Beyond these sutures, *Iron Man 3* also casts Tony in the "returning veteran with PTSD" role, now a too-common experience for too many Americans. The fantasies of this film are darker and more fragile—they revolve around guilt and brokenness, and the hope that, at the end, we can heal and return to normal like Tony does.

Television 1992–2014: The End of Camp

If one accepts the year 2000 as the line of demarcation between fantasy elsewheres and sutures to reality in comics-on-film, then perhaps a similar line might be drawn for comics-on-television. However, this line marks not the departure from fantasy elsewheres, as television settings effectively tend to be fantasy elsewheres even at their most realistic, but the departure from camp and the first attempts to create adaptations that faithfully recreate the tone and themes of the source material. Prior to 1992, comic adaptations on television were similarly colorful and goofy affairs. *Batman* (1966) is perhaps the most heinous example of a campy, kid-friendly adaptation of a tonally serious comic, but it was not the only one. Certainly, one cannot forget attempts at adaptation such as the Lynda Carter version of *Wonder Woman* (1975), The Amazing Spider-Man (1977), the better-received, but low-budgeted *The Incredible Hulk* (1977), among others of lesser acclaim to be sure. On the animated side, where returns were better, if not equally erratic, members of the Justice League received similar treatment in Hanna-Barbera's various iterations of *SuperFriends* through the seventies and eighties, as did Kevin Eastman and Peter Laird's comically-violent

Teenage Mutant Ninja Turtles in the 1988 cartoon adaptation of the same name.

However, 1992 saw the debut of two comics-based animated series that would set the stage for a whole new tone for comics on television and animated programming in general. For the first time in children's television, some of the weight and seriousness possible in modern comics came through in the adaptation. Premiering in September 1992, *Batman: The Animated Series* owed considerably to the style of Burton's *Batman* (1989) with its dark, towering cityscapes and time-in-a-blender styles of dress and transportation. Leonard Pierce has gone on record to state that it "[set] the standard for small-screen adaptations of superhero comics" (Pierce). Composer Shirley Walker's score even echoes Danny Elfman's haunting film score, maintaining the main theme from the movie for the show's introduction sequence. The show's mature themes, dramatic tone, and realistic violence (with guns that fired bullets!) were a radical departure from the colorful action cartoons of the 1980s, like *G.I. Joe: A Real American Hero* (1982) and *The Transformers* (1984). A month later, Marvel would finally achieve success in animation with *X-Men*. The costumes, characters' personalities, and team lineup were taken almost directly from the comics of the era, particularly from Jim Lee and Chris Claremont's best-selling run on *X-Men vol. 2*. In its five seasons, the series dealt with issues that were atypical for Saturday morning cartoons but central to the X-Men mythos such as prejudice, genocide, and evolution. It also featured some of the most famous X-Men storylines, such as "The Phoenix Saga" and "Days of Future Past," both of which were also adapted to film in *X-Men: The Last Stand* (2006) and *X-Men: Days of Future Past* (2014).

These two series were the spearhead of a bloom in animated adaptations of comics. The success of *Batman: The Animated Series* led to a number of sequel series and spin-offs that expanded the animated DC Universe through the next decade, including *Superman: The Animated Series* in 1996, *Batman Beyond* in 1999, *Justice League* in 2001, and *Justice League Unlimited* in 2004. On the Marvel side, a long-running *Spider-Man* cartoon arrived in 1994 devoid of the campy *Spider-Man and His Amazing Friends* vibe found in multiple incarnations from the late 1960s into the 1980s, along with *The Fantastic Four* and *Iron Man* series, followed by *The Incredible Hulk* in 1996 and *Silver Surfer* in 1998. For children who liked comics and cartoons, the 1990s were a veritable cornucopia of adaption.

The 1990s were also an interesting time for comics in live-action television, as well. DC found strange success in *Lois & Clark: The New Adventures of Superman*, a melodrama focused on the romance between Lois Lane, Clark Kent, and his caped alter-ego. This adaptation shifted the genre of Superman's tales toward romantic comedy-drama, and while it certainly held little hallmarks of the more-famous George Reeves intoned *Adventures of Superman* (1952), that's not necessarily a bad thing. DC's success with the Man of Steel continued in live action television was further cemented by the ten-season run of *Smallville* (2001), a teen drama that depicted Superman's early, mostly costumeless years. Initially set in Clark Kent's eponymous hometown, this series followed in *Lois & Clark*'s footsteps by focusing on human relationships and character development rather than super-powered action (though there was still plenty of that). The series was remarkably uneven, though, with critics mentioning that "this series, based extremely loosely on the teenage adventures of Superman, has always suffered from not knowing exactly what it wants to be. It started out as an angsty teen relationship drama; it later tossed in monster-of-the-week elements" (Pierce). Frequent nods to the *Superman* films and to the greater DC Comics universe whetted audiences' appetites for more live-action DC properties. *Arrow* (2012), for example, was a darker, sterner take on Green Arrow and took tonal cues from Christopher Nolan's *Dark Knight* trilogy to tell the toxophilite vigilante's origin story while still retaining the interest in character development and relationships that helped *Smallville* fly without a cape for ten years.

Marvel was not as successful with their live-action offerings in the 1990s. In fact, apart from two seasons of a series based on the Ultraverse comic *Night Man* and an unsuccessful pilot for a *Power Pack* series, the only live-action Marvel production from the 1990s was the made-for-TV film *Generation X* (1996). However, the success of *The Avengers* (2012) prompted Marvel to take another swing at live-action television, this time tying into the shared continuity of the films in the Marvel Cinematic Universe. *Marvel's Agents of S.H.I.E.L.D.* (2013) largely leaves the costumed superheroes on the cinema screen, instead focusing on a team of government agents led by Clark Gregg's Agent Coulson, resurrected from his death in *The Avengers*. The show's team dynamic borrows much from police procedurals and crime comedy-dramas like *CSI* and *Bones* while both working from Joss Whedon's larger mythological narrative and offering frequent references to events in the MCU films, including an extensive crossover with *Captain America: The Winter Soldier* late in the first season.

Perhaps the most popular comic book adaptation on television has no superheroes and is neither a DC nor Marvel property. Robert Kirkman's ongoing post-apocalyptic series *The Walking Dead*, published by Image Comics, serves as a reminder that comic books do not equate to superhero stories, while AMC's television adaptation, with its unflinching presentation of violence, gore, and the horrors of both zombies and humans, shows that comic adaptations on television do not have to be family-friendly. Following a group of relatable and vulnerable characters as they struggle to survive, the show is immensely popular: its fourth season premiere had 16.1 million viewers and was the top show among young adults at the time (Keveney). The success of *The Walking Dead* proves that comics—and their adaptations—are not limited to any one genre or audience.

Towards the Future

The future of comics in film and television—unlike the nightmarish futures often *depicted* in comics—is bright, shiny, and full of potential. Marvel's upcoming movie docket has been announced, with ten films to be released from 2015 through 2019 (Eisenberg). Having apparently found its confidence in live-action television again thanks to *Agents of S.H.I.E.L.D.*, Marvel's television plans include *Agent Carter* (a series set in the 1940s and focusing on the character from the *Captain America* films), plus four individual heroes' series (*Daredevil, AKA Jessica Jones, Iron Fist,* and *Luke Cage*) leading to a crossover mini-series (*The Defenders*) beginning in 2015, all existing within the Marvel Cinematic Universe (Rich). Meanwhile, animated shows, like *Avengers Assemble, Ultimate Spider-Man,* and *The Super Hero Squad Show,* introduce young viewers to Marvel properties, raising a new crop of fans for the future. Not to be outdone, DC currently has eleven comic-to-film adaptations planned according to the Wall Street Journal (Fritz). This is in addition to their television offerings, which include new series *The Flash* (an *Arrow* spin-off), *Gotham,* (a crime drama set in pre-Batman Gotham City), and *Constantine* (an occult drama focusing on the *Hellblazer* character) premiering in 2014 and two more (*iZombie* and *Preacher*) in the next year.

Even with all the film and television adaptations already produced and scheduled for production, we have only begun to scratch the surface of the deep mine of stories and characters that is the adapted American comic. If the present is any indication of the future, comic adaptations in both film and television likely will only continue to improve as studios become more willing to try adaptations of different comics genres and as more producers, directors, and writers learn how to handle the medium properly.

Works Cited

Bainbridge, Jason. "'I Am New York'— Spider-Man, New York City, and the Marvel Universe." *Comics and the City: Urban Space in Print, Picture and Sequence*. Ed. Arno Meteling & Jorn Ahrens. New York: Continuum, 2010. 163–82.

Batman. Dir. Tim Burton. Perf. Michael Keaton, Jack Nicholson, Kim Basinger, Billy Dee Williams, & Jack Palance. Warner Bros., 1989. Film.

Batman Returns. Dir. Tim Burton. Perf. Michael Keaton, Danny DeVito, & Michelle Pfeiffer. Warner Bros., 1992. Film.

The Dark Knight Rises. Dir. Christopher Nolan. Perf. Christian Bale, Michael Cane, & Gary Oldman. Warner Bros, 2012. Film.

Di Paolo, Marc. *War, Politics and Superheroes: Ethics and Propaganda in Comics and Film*. Jefferson, NC: McFarland & Co, 2011.

"Comic Book Adaptation." *Movies at the Box Office*. n.d. Web. 01 Aug. 2014.

Dittmer, Jason. *Captain America and the Nationalist Superhero: Metaphors, Narratives, and Geopolitics*. Philadelphia: Temple UP, 2013.

Eisenberg, Eric. "Marvel Studios Announces 5 New Projects Through 2019." *CinemaBlend*, 19 Jul. 2014. Web. 01 Aug. 2014.

Fingeroth, Danny. *Superman on the Couch: What Superheroes Really Tell Us About Ourselves and Our Society*. New York: Continuum, 2004.

Fritz, Ben. "Warner Bros. on a Caped Crusade DC Comics Plots Film, TV Comeback vs. Disney's Marvel." *The Wall Street Journal*. Dow Jones & Company, 27 Apr. 2014. Web. 01 Aug. 2014.

Generation X. Dir. Jack Sholder. Perf. Matt Frewer, Finola Hughes, & Jeremy Ratchford. Marvel Productions, 1996. Film.

Kaveney, Roz. *Superheroes!: Capes and Crusaders in Comics and Films*. London: I.B. Tauris, 2008.

Keveney, Bill. "AMC's 'Walking Dead' Struts to Record Ratings." *USA Today*, 14 Oct. 2013. Web. 28 July 2014.

Meteling, Arno. "A Tale of Two Cities: Politics and Superheroics in Starman and Ex Machina." *Comics and the City: Urban Space in Print, Picture and Sequence*. Ed. Jorn Ahrens & Arno Meteling. New York: Continuum, 2010. 133–49.

Morrison, Grant. *Supergods: What Masked Vigilantes, Miraculous Mutants, and a Sun God from Smallville Can Teach Us About Being Human*. New York: Spiegel & Grau, 2011.

Pierce, Leonard. "The Best and Worst Comic Book-Based TV Shows." *TV.com*, 18 Feb 2010. Web. 30 July 2014.

Rich, Katy. "Daredevil, Luke Cage And More Marvel Superheroes Getting Netflix Original Series" *CinemaBlend*, 7 Nov. 2013. Web. 01 Aug. 2014.

Uricchio, William. "The Batman's Gotham City(TM): Story, Ideology, Performance." *Comics and the City: Urban Space in Print, Picture and Sequence*. Ed. Jorn Ahrens & Arno Meteling. New York: Continuum, 2010. 119–32.

Comic Fandom throughout the Ages_____

Forrest C. Helvie

Although the nascent medium of comics began developing a population of readers, both young and old, prior to the summer of 1938, it was readers' rabid response to the release of *Action Comics* #1, marking the first appearance of Superman, when comic publishers quickly realized there were millions of fans waiting to hear more about their favorite new superhero. Seeking to capitalize on this newfound market, publishers sought to better understand the interests of their readers and deliver even more costumed characters to fill the pages of these cheap, disposable sources of action, mystery, and adventure. By reaching out to their readers through character-related promotions, letters pages, and other campaigns, comic fandom began to coalesce and grow to the heights that are seen today at comics conventions and beyond.

Fans in the Golden Age

While comic fans during the 1930s were almost exclusively children early on, this new medium quickly began to grow in popularity amongst adolescents and adults as well. Gerard Jones discusses the birth of this phenomenon in *Men of Tomorrow* when he states:

> An ever growing number of young people were driven to seek connections and meanings that life had once provided more automatically. So a particular set of personality characteristics and individual agonies became the basis for a subculture. Once in the subculture, the boys fine-tuned one another's identities around the self-definition "science fiction fan" —an indifference to clothes and appearance, a manic but unsentimental bon-homie in their meetings, an amused disdain for the drones who didn't understand them. (Jones 37)

This, according to Jones, is where the contemporary notions of geek culture first came into being.

During the year preceding and immediately following the United States' involvement in World War II, little attention was paid to comics. Superheroes were, by and large, upholders of the sanctioned status quo and exemplars of the moral right. The covers decorating newsstands showed Superman and Batman extoling children to support their country through buying war stamps and bonds, and the stories of other heroes showed these super soldiers mopping up the Germans and Italians in Europe and sinking the Japanese across the Pacific. In many regards, these comics were reinforcing the dominant cultural paradigm, and so, they were viewed with a favorable lens. It wasn't until comic book readers began to grow up and their comics began to push back against this conservative status quo that parents, community leaders, and officials began taking notice—and aim—at the medium as a whole.

Comic book fandom was dealt a significant blow during the late 1940s and 50s because of the rise of ultra-conservative politics epitomized by McCarthyism and, more directly, by Fredric Wertham's attack on the comics medium. Wertham spent the majority of his career seeking to find ways to improve conditions for youth— particularly those living in urban settings. In his studies, which have subsequently been shown to be questionable at best, if not outright disproven by comics scholar Carol Tilley, Wertham viewed comics as being responsible for the degradation of America's youth. Wertham once contended that "comic books are definitely harmful to impressionable people, and most young people are impressionable [. . .] I think Hitler was a beginner compared to the comic book industry" (Hadju 6). In some regards, the much-vilified psychiatrist was not far off the mark. In post-war America, comics were not regulated in the same ways television and cinema were, overseen by the Federal Communications Commission and the Motion Picture Association of America's Hays Code, respectively. As a result, publishers, such as William Gaines and his EC Comics brand often produced comics that were filled with graphic representations of criminal activity, horrific violence, and other illegal or disturbing content. Yet, Wertham's view on comics is clear, with no room for exception: fans of the medium needed to be educated about the dangers this four-colored pamphlet contained, and these comics needed to be banned.

David Hadju's *Ten Cent Plague* is arguably one of the most extensive sources about this period in comics and popular culture. In this text, Hadju suggests that Wertham's attack on comics represented more than just one man's efforts to save America's youth. Instead, he states:

> It is clear now that the hysteria over comic books was always about many things other than cartoons: about class and money and taste; about traditions and religions and biases rooted in time and place; about presidential politics; about the influence of a new medium called television; about how art forms, as well as people, grow up. (Hadju 7)

Matthew Costello corroborates Hadju's argument in his examination of comics and post-war American culture. Comics began to turn from looking outward towards external enemies to looking inward, as they began to see the enemy from within:

> The enemy was no longer an external entity threatening American security, but the internal problems besetting the richest society in the world. These threats involved continued racial tensions, gender inequality, poverty, and most importantly, a government that was viewed as secretive, hubristic, and controlling. (Costello 88)

Because comics previously enjoyed a sort of anonymity by flying under the radar of most adults, these transgressive comics—along with the more lurid and graphic stories being published—provided a viable scapegoat and opportunity for the conservative leaders across the country to reassert their ideological platforms. Within only a few short years following the public spectacle that Wertham helped engineer with congressional support, the comic book industry nearly collapsed as a whole: "the majority of working comics artists, writers, and editors—more than eight hundred people—lost their jobs" (Hadju 7). It would be over a decade before the industry would begin to slowly rebuild in the wake of this massive cultural purge.

Another one of the more significant effects of Wertham's assault on comics that is often overlooked is his impact on the role of women in comics, which would in turn influence the struggle women would later face getting back in as characters, creators, and fans. The greatest examples of Wertham's unintended relegation of women to the margins of comics culture can be seen in Wonder Woman. Although she is considered a peer to Superman and Batman in the DC Universe, Wonder Woman's sales—one tangible indicator of fan support—experienced a far greater drop off in the years following Wertham's condemnation of superheroes and the CCA's increasingly restrictive influence over what types of stories could be told. Not only was his crusade successful in sowing the seeds for The Comics Code Authority (CCA), he effectively closed the doors to the horror and crime genres of comics, and the superheroes didn't fare much better. Although Batman and Superman would continue to sell relatively well, Wonder Woman's sales were especially hard-hit as she began selling fifty to seventy-five percent less than her DC counterparts. In 1960, Batman and Superman sold approximately 810,000 and 502,000 issues per month respectively in 1960 compared to Wonder Woman's 213,000 (Miller). In the years to follow, her sales continued to dwindle, and this reinforced the shift towards the more heteronormative makeup of comic fandom that has, up until recent years, become the expected norm. It wasn't until the comic industry began shaking itself free from the stranglehold of the CCA that women, persons of color, and other demographics would slowly begin to trickle back into the largest genre within the medium.

Fans in the Silver Age

As the medium began to mature, so too did its readership. As a result, comics fans began to embrace those works that told stories exploring the concerns, interests, and anxieties of that era. This was most evident in Stan Lee's rise to prominence at Marvel Comics with his collaborative efforts involving Jack Kirby and Steve Ditko and their line of superhero narratives. Make no mistake, fan enthusiasm for Marvel Comics was no simple and happy accident. This increased involvement of the fan community was engineered in large part by Stan Lee's efforts to grow his readership—both in number and sophistication. He accomplished this through his "soapbox" editorials where he directly addressed his readers, the institution of letters columns wherein he engendered a dialogue with fans, and the establishment of an official Marvel Comics fan club—The Merry Marvel Marching Society—replete with a mission, newsletter, and even a song. Marvel's increased attention on its fans could arguably be seen as also giving rise to the resurgence of the comic book fanzines once popular in the pulp era of science fiction, fantasy, mystery, and adventure comics. Given the near-decade of relatively innocuous comics (by comparison) to which readers had been exposed, change was in the air.

Stan Lee's role in building a fan base for superheroes through letter columns, fan clubs, his soapbox, and even his public speaking circuit on college campuses was certainly one of the catalysts behind the growth of comic fandom. Will Eisner once related that, despite a number of creators producing quality, thought-provoking work, "nobody cared outside of comics. I felt that nobody was paying attention, except the readers, and they were mostly kids, so nobody took them seriously" (Hadju 228). When Stan Lee took over as editor-in-chief at Marvel Comics, he began speaking directly to his readership from the very first page to the last. Additionally, Lee began including a letters page where he and his readers could engage one another. Hadju writes: "The fans responded to Stan as a personality in a way they hadn't responded to any other creator of comics since the heyday of Bill Gaines," and it wasn't long after that "Marvel Maniacs were beginning to evangelize in study halls across America" (298). These comics provided readers an opportunity to be entertained, but also engage in discourse over relevant social issues of the day. Costello points to the letters pages in *Captain America* in particular as being a hotbed of discussion over identity politics where "extended debated occurred between readers discussing the meaning of patriotism, the role of violence in conflict resolution, nationalism versus global community, and the Vietnam War" (90). Within comics culture, it became clear there was an eye towards comics being more than just simple entertainment; they could also provide a vehicle for social discourse. Ditko, Kirby, and Lee took the mold created by the likes of Jerry Siegel, Joe Shuster, Bill Finger, and Bob Kane and "[t]hey'd psychologized it, with a hero who did not simply weep for his inability to change fate but also questioned, every day, whether he was even doing the right thing by being a hero" (Jones 297). Given Marvel's meteoric rise over DC during this period, it became clear that this approach was a winning formula.

It is important to point out, however, that there was a culture of comic fandom that existed prior to Stan Lee's taking the helm at Marvel, and he was certainly not the first person to innovate the letters column as a means of reaching out to fans in a more direct fashion. Bill Gaines developed an enthusiastic following surrounding his EC Comics during the 1950s prior to Fredric Wertham's shutting him out of the comic business, and some of these fans never let go of their passion for the medium. Enter Jerry Bails, Roy Thomas, and the founding of *Alter-Ego* in 1961—what is often seen as the first fanzine dedicated solely to comic books. In reality, fanzines existed for decades prior to Bails and Thomas' superhero-oriented magazine. Siegel and Shuster's original and far more menacing Superman made his first appearance in the young creators' self-published science fiction fanzine, which Gerard Jones believes may have actually been the very first fanzine dedicated to sci-fi. Although comics would be mentioned in pop culture fanzines in the pulp era, it wasn't until 1947 that Mal Willits and Jim Bradly broke ground in publishing the very first fanzine dedicated solely to comics, *The Comic Collector's News*. While limited in scope, this fanzine helped bring comic book aficionados together under a common love for collecting comics, and it helped initiate a movement that would continue in the decades to follow (Shelley 51).

When Thomas and Bails published *Alter-Ego* just prior to Marvel Comics' explosive entry into the Silver Age, they also created a new platform for fans of the medium and superhero genre to come together under the banner of a shared passion for comics. Unlike Willits and Bradley's *CCN* and the other fanzines from that era, which focused mainly on the collecting side of fan culture,

Alter-Ego aimed to stimulate discourse not only between fans of like mind, but also provided a sort of bridge between those fans of the "Golden Age" and what were then more contemporary comic book fans. Tom Spurgeon contends that:

> Bails, along with a handful of other fans he helped influenced, helped to form comics' core audience, provided a connection between readers of the Golden Age comics and the newer superhero comics that helped smooth the way for older readers of modern comics, advocated for specific characters and title concepts, provided a self-publishing model that inspired a younger generation of eventual comics pros. (Spurgeon)

When taking into account the popularity of self-publishing in comics during the late-twentieth and early twenty-first centuries, it is worth noting one of its earliest influences can be found in the fanzines.

Fans in the Bronze Age and Beyond

As the 1960s gave way to the 1970s, there was a noticeable shift away from the rigid guidelines handed down by the Comics Code Authority. Fans, long thirsty for tales of terror, began seeing horror-driven superheroes like Ghost Rider and street-level characters like Luke Cage get their own titles. Moreover, both Marvel and DC began to reflect greater elements of the real world in their comics as seen in places like *Amazing Spider-Man* #96–99 (1971) which was actually commissioned by the Nixon administration to address the rise of adolescent drug use as well as in the pages of *Green Lantern/ Green Arrow* where it was revealed that same year that Green Arrow's young ward, Speedy, was a heroin addict. These changes in the types of characters and stories readers encountered in their comics had a significant impact on fandom; however, there was yet another contribution to the industry during the 1970s and into the early 1980s that had an arguably greater impact on the development of comic fan culture: the rise of the direct market.

According to Costello, the number of comic readers declined by nearly one-third by the late 1970s, and so a decision was made to pursue a different approach: "Rather than sell through general magazine vendors, supermarkets, and drugstores" these comic book publishers "began selling through specialized retailers, known as the direct market" (Costello 21). This made sense as the shift in marketing paralleled the shift in fans. While comics were originally conceived as cheap entertainment for children that could be purchased while their parents were shopping or at those places children spent their discretionary money, these readers grew up and sought new places to purchase their favorite titles. As an increasing number of local comic shops opened across the country, and fans now had a place where they could regularly meet, talk, and immerse themselves within comics culture on a regular basis with perfect security and no fear of reproach. Not surprisingly, fan culture began to grow even more in size and number, and their interest in gathering together grew even more.

On March 21, 1970, the San Diego's Golden State Comic-Minicon (Now known ubiquitously within the greater popular culture as the San Diego Comic-Con International) provided fans with their first experience of what would become the apex of comics fan culture in the decades to follow. Although there were only about one hundred fans on that first one-day event, by the end of the first decade of the twenty-first century, the comic convention scene began to see crowds in excess of 130,000 attendees over a three-day period. Given that there are an estimated seventy-plus such conventions expected to be held in 2014, the popularity of all things comics has no discernable end in sight. These conventions have now become not only havens for comic fans, but also for legions of pop culture fans, who may or may not have any vested interest in the actual comics themselves. Charles Brownstein, the director of the Comic Book Legal Defense Fund (CBLDF), argues that:

> [C]ons are a reflection of what's happening in the larger entertainment world. . . . Comics and comics media are at the heart of our entertainment, and cons provide an incredibly attractive environment to enjoy what's happening and to understand what's coming up next. (MacDonald)

Prior to end of the 1990s, however, fans generally had to attend one of the spare few comic book conventions held across the country if they hoped to meet their favorite artists and creators. With the rise of the Internet, however, fans could engage one another from across the globe. Not only could people from different cultures come together, but these fans could also reach out and engage the actual creators through message boards, websites, email, and later, social media. Fans have the ability to reach out and communicate with these creators mere moments after a comic book is available to download from the internet, whereas, in the past, it could easily be weeks or even months in between the time a fan sent a letter and it was published with a response—assuming this happened at all, which was not likely. Without a doubt, the Internet has brought the global community closer in previously unimagined ways.

Yet, the early twenty-first century is also a strange time for comics culture. From its very beginnings, being a comic book fan often relegated one to being socially ostracized for being fixated on reading material ostensibly meant for children. Today, comic books are fueling many of Hollywood's multimillion- and even billion-dollar movie franchises. Video games stores are packed full of comic book adaptations, and even television shows are bringing in mainstream viewers for programming based on comic book source material. In many regards, comics culture is experiencing a sort of Age of Enlightenment wherein mainstream culture is taking notice of this once niche entertainment market. Producers, directors, and other mass media storytellers are discovering the medium is filled with stories that are quickly making fans out of men, women, and children who otherwise might have never picked up a comic book beforehand, and this market is one the American public has been quick to explore.

Issues Facing Comic Fandom Today

The medium is finally beginning to break out of its pop culture niche corner and is finding a place at the forefront of the mainstream through a vastly-increased presence in various media outlets. This shift, however, has not been without growing pains as readers from outside of the stereotypical white, heterosexual male paradigm began to become more active resulting in conflict between the once dominant demographic and those newer-reading audiences. Gauging reader demographics was something, historically speaking, few in the industry actively pursued; however, numbers that are more concrete began emerging in recent years. With DC Comics' 2011 reboot, the company-sweeping "New 52," comics' second-most dominant publisher commissioned Nielson to conduct a survey of its readers, which produced initially eye-opening results. Nearly ninety-three percent of respondents were male, and only a small percentage of these readers were under twenty-five. This would seem to suggest the overwhelming majority of superhero comics consumers fit this description; however, it is worth noting that this survey was a retailer survey. This means respondents were present in a comic book store and deemed regular—if not active—comic book readers. If men of this bracket were already predisposed to frequent comic book stores while women were not, this clearly skews the results of this survey, particularly in an age where online and app sales are beginning to pace paper purchases.

Comics fans benefited from this increased exposure as mass media began to incorporate the superheroes into video games, television, and cinema, which in turn, provided these fans with an increased sense of legitimacy—something often denied to the once stigmatized niche. On the other hand, this influx of new fan communities has not been without problems. The once hetero-male dominant community now faced a far more diverse population of enthusiastic devotees, who did not respond to the ways in which people of their gender, race, or orientation were depicted. Not surprisingly, comics fandom—as emblemized in the microcosm of the convention scene—continues to find itself in a place of growing pains.

Unfortunately, it is ironic that for a largely male population who—if one were to go by Jones' earlier assertions that men formed and continue to form the core of comic fans—were unsuccessful in engaging women, that now they would act in such a way as to exclude them from participating in these celebrations of all things geek. The result, then, is an increasingly noticeable conflict between some men and the women they interact with at both the smaller scale and more prominent national comic conventions across the country. At the 2013 New York Comic Convention, one major sponsor employed scantily-clad women who were hired to suggestively hock their company's wares in an overt appeal to heterosexual men— the believed-to-be stereotypical comic book fan. Although this was but one instance of many playing out in mainstream culture, one must still consider the prominence of the stage upon which it was acted over the course of a weekend in front of the near-one-hundred-thirty-thousand fans attending that one show. Moreover, these sorts of messages communicate the notion that a heterosexual man will only respond to sexual stimulation, which is a remarkably two-dimensional representation of what some women aspire to be and what some men desire (Helvie).

In an interview, Kelly Sue DeConnick discussed some of the problems facing comics, especially fans of the superhero genre. She contends that the sort of writing that objectifies women and subjects them to the male gaze—this form of communicating ideas—has a number of short- and long-term ramifications that many fans are failing to consider:

> That's an idealized female body, and that's an idealized male body! But from *whose* perspective did you decide that? And when we get into costumes? In order for the male figure to be idealized in the same way that the female figure is idealized, they would have to be wearing a thong that was glued to their half-erect penis. Literally.

> I mean, these women have wasp waists and breasts that are bulging to the point where they appear liked they would have to be painful in a way to make both of their primary and secondary sexual organs available to the viewer at the same time. It is *not* comparable. It is lazy or willfully ignorant to think that it is. . . . There is a certain kind of superhero comic that doesn't appeal to women because they are demeaned and dehumanized by them. So I would probably say *don't* give those comics to your daughter, and I'd say don't give those comics to your sons. They are not good for people–of *either* gender.

The lessons that they teach, if you were to teach with such things, what they have to say about the human condition and the relationship between the two genders are destructive and demeaning, and again, *lazy*. (DeConnick)

If comics provided its fans with a platform for engaging one another with relevant social issues, DeConnick's comments are especially poignant. Moreover, she underscores a significant reason why many women have, for many years, felt ostracized from the superhero genre of comics and have largely eschewed it in favor of more inclusive areas within the medium. Noted comics critic Kelly Thompson reiterates this problem facing comic fandom when she stated, "There's a trickledown effect in seeing these portrayals reinforced over and over again. These portrayals shape how we view and value women and contributes to everything from sexism in the work place to eating disorders," and not surprisingly, it became a genre many women have chosen to avoid (Thompson). For these reasons, there are some significant changes that need to take place in comics culture if it is going to continue to grow and develop in a way that makes it inclusive for all who want to be a part of showing their appreciation for this visually-driven genre.

For many years, fans young and old struggled under the stigma of negative stereotypes about comic book fandom. Some of these stereotypes about comic book fans include: They are typically single men; they are lacking in the way of social graces, often found living in their mothers' basements and routinely wax poetic or rage furiously about the most minute details surrounding their favorite superheroes; and so on and so forth. Arguably, the most identifiable manifestation of these negative stereotypes can be found in *The Simpsons* television character, Comic Book Guy, who runs a comic book shop and haughtily dismisses people who fail to share his intimate, if not arcane, knowledge of all things related to comics culture, while outwardly being rejected by the rest of the residents of Springfield. Although Comic Book Guy represents some of the worst aspects of fandom, it is clear there is still an undercurrent of this type of behavior in comics fandom today. This can be seen in part within the bullying, contemptuous, and possessive nature of fans dictating who can and cannot be considered a true geek and even the failure of the industry to consistently represent every demographic in meaningful ways. Although Comic Book Guy does not represent the bulk of comic fans, there are still remnants of truth behind these stereotypes that have become increasingly evident and need to be addressed.

In February of 2014, Image Comics publisher, Eric Stephenson met with hundreds of direct market retailers—whose businesses serve as a sort of epicenter for comic book fans and fan culture—and impressed upon them the need for change if the medium was going to continue to grow and remain vibrant for generations to come. Recognizing the medium's past history of catering primarily to the interests of its dominantly white male, heterosexual audience, Stephenson challenged these comic book store owners to "Be more inclusive," claiming this approach is "one of the best sales tools at [their] disposal" in their efforts to "build a community around [their] store" (Comic Book Resources). Doing so, Stephenson claims, will make comic book stores a "destination for everyone—men, women, and children of every background" (Comic Book Resources). Comics faced criticism in its early years in the culture war over the stigma of being disposable children's entertainment, unworthy of critical reception. Yet, fans from that period struggled against this stigma and the results of their efforts can be seen in many ways comics have infiltrated all levels of mainstream culture today. Once again, fans need to carry on in this tradition of struggling against limited notions of what comics can look like and who gains entry into geek culture if this culture will continue to thrive.

Works Cited

Comic Book Resources. "Image Publisher Eric Stephenson Emphasizes Direct Market Importance in ComicsPRO Speech." *Comic Book Resources*. 28 Feb. 2014. Web. 28 Feb. 2014.

DeConnick, Kelly Sue. Telephone interview. 20 Sept. 2013.

Helvie, Forrest C. "What's Wrong with This Picture? Thoughts on New York Comic Con." *NerdSpan*. 21 Oct. 2013. Web. 27 Feb. 2014.

Jones, Gerard. *Men of Tomorrow: Geeks, Gangsters, and the Birth of the Comic Book*. New York: Basic Books, 2004.

MacDonald, Heidi. "COMIC Con Culture on the Rise." *PublishersWeekly. com*. Publisher's Weekly, 25 June 2013. Web. 27 Feb. 2014. "1960." Miller, John Jackson. *Comichron*. Web. 18 August 2013.

Shelley, Bill. *Founders of Comic Fandom*. Jefferson: McFarland, 2010.

Spurgeon, Tom. "The Comics Reporter." *The Comics Reporter*. 24 Nov. 2006. Web. 27 Feb. 2014.

Thompson, Kelly. "Dear Marvel: Stop Ruining Everything." *Comic Book Resources*. 21 May 2012. Web. 24 Dec. 2012.

Tilley, Carol. "Seducing the Innocent: Fredric Wertham and the Falsifications that Helped Condemn Comics." *Information & Culture: A Journal of History* 47.4 (2012). Web. 11 Sept. 2014.

Waiting for Wonder Woman: the Problematic History of Comic Book Women and Their Cinematic Doubles_____

Katherine E. Whaley & Justin Wigard

The two largest comics publishing houses, Marvel Comics and DC Comics, have had considerable success recently with their treatment of women in comics. DC has been seen as progressive with J. H. Williams III's treatment of Batwoman, the first mainstream superhero who openly identifies as a lesbian, as shown through her relationship with both her ex-girlfriend and her current longtime girlfriend, Maggie Sawyer (Battersby). Marvel's 2014 reboot of *Ms. Marvel* stars a young Pakistani/American teenage girl in the titular role as she struggles to make sense of her identity as a superhero and determine who she is as a person. Marvel will soon be featuring an as-yet unnamed female character in the titular role of *Thor*, and it "will be the eighth title to feature a lead female protagonist and aims to speak directly to an audience that long was not the target for superhero comic books in America: women and girls" (Marvel). While this progress of featuring multiple women in their own series is commendable, it is also troubling. The superhero genre of comics has existed since 1938, and only recently have superwomen begun to be featured prominently in their own comic series, let alone drawn in a flattering light. To approach the issue of women in comics, it is necessary to understand why these successes are symptomatic of problems that have plagued women for decades.

Though the convoluted history of women in comics merits its own book-length treatment, this chapter intends to be a truncated and accessible historical overview of the position of comic book women, from their most significant beginnings in *All-Star Comics* #8 to the present day in film. In order to account for over seventy-three years of women in comics, this essay will cover both the comic books and films, the great disseminator of comics in the present moment, featuring women. For the comics books, the examples used are close readings of popular or well-known comics women, which pull back the veil on the problematic trends afflicting women in comics and on how current series challenge these trends. In the last fifteen years, a surge in popularity of superhero films warrants an examination of the women portrayed in these films. Three groups of women in superhero cinema (ordinaries, superwomen, and supervillains) will be analyzed to discern what progress, if any, has been made for women, offering unique insights into the present state of comic book women in films.

The Lady from Themyscira

Introduced in *All-Star Comics #8* in 1941, Wonder Woman exists as one of the most influential female superheroes, acting as a progenitor for female superheroes. According to creator William Moulton Marston, Wonder Woman was designed as a "feminine character with all the strength of a Superman plus all the allure of a good and beautiful woman" (Stuller 13). She became a revolutionary icon in comics as a strong and empowered woman, dominant over men, and sexually deviant as "Marston equipped Wonder Woman with her own instruments of bondage and discipline: the magic lasso and the bracelets of submission" (Call 38). Wonder Woman's magic lasso allowed her to keep bad men controlled while empowering women, and her bracelets of submission allowed her to defend the weak and accomplish superhuman feats. Essentially, Wonder Woman was designed to be a champion for female superheroes (if not a fantasy for men) and surpass the influence of Superman by inspiring both male and female comic book readers.

However, the death of Marston in 1947 transferred creative control over to a new team of writers and editors who shunted Marston's feminist ideology in lieu of conforming to the masculine direction of DC Comics of the day. After Marston's death, Wonder Woman's boyfriend Steve Trevor works tirelessly to marry her. Trevor "Won't take 'No!' for an answer" when he asks for her hand in marriage and attempts to get Wonder Woman to abdicate her superheroic nature in favor of being a domesticated housewife (Kanigher 1). Wonder Woman's feminist agency was both denied and actively combated as she became subjected to Trevor's patriarchal ideology. The era of the Comics Code Authority further crippled what little agency Wonder Woman retained through conservative ideology of the 1950s and 1960s (Johnson 81). Her bland storylines and loss of feminist advocacy made Wonder Woman a hindrance for future women to overcome, rather than a champion to emulate. The decline of Wonder Woman signified a decline for women in comics, a period of time when even their strongest icon was depowered, and the world waited for Wonder Woman to regain her footing as a hero for all people to look up to.

The Superpowers of *Not Being There* and Surviving

In the 1960s, Marvel Comics gained recognition for their portrayal of less-idealized superheroes who dealt with both real-world and fantastic issues, as in the case of Marvel's first prominent female superhero: Sue Storm, or as she was introduced in *The Fantastic Four* #1 (1961), The Invisible Girl (2). From her inception, Sue used her powers of invisibility to aid the Fantastic Four by *remaining unseen*, often acting as a support character to her more active male counterparts or as a stereotypical damsel in distress. Similarly, the second half of her title relegated Sue to a level of youthful immaturity by being known as The Invisible *Girl*, only to be given the title of "The Invisible Woman" upon marrying Mr. Fantastic in *Fantastic Four Annual* #3 (1965). This signifies the notion that only by succumbing to societal gender norms can Sue be recognized as a woman, much less have that recognition reflected in her superhero title.

One of the most distressing and sinister aspects of American comic books in recent decades is the use of sexual assault, torture, and murder of women in comics as motivation for male superheroes to become darker. The term used to describe this trope, "Women in Refrigerators," stems from a study of comics conducted in the 1990s by writer Gail Simone and was so named after the dismembered body of Alex DeWitt, girlfriend of the 90s Green Lantern (Kyle Raynor), was stuffed into a refrigerator for Green Lantern to discover (Marz 15). Motivated by the mutilation of Alex's death, Raynor evolves to suit the edgier, grittier tone of the 1990s. Another notable instance revolves around the revealed rape and death of Sue Dibny during the company-wide event known as *Identity Crisis*, which catalyzed many of the male characters to unite and rail against the villain in question, Dr. Light. The survivor's response to her rape is barely covered in the flashback, instead chronicling the superheroes trying to catch Dr. Light. In this manner, women are not seen as victims or survivors, but as plot devices.

This trend not only diminishes the impact such acts have within the comics universe, but normalizes violence against women within American society today. Rather than being seen as "social mirrors and molders that serve as barometers of the place and time in which they reside," these instances enforce detrimental aspects of American culture through repetition (Johnson 2). While the narratives themselves may deal with the violence against the women depicted, the long-standing prevalence of this issue and subsequent misuse of this trope marks it as one endemic to the problem of women in comics. Nearly seventy-six years of superhero comics have stemmed from the first appearance of Superman, yet the position of women within comics today is still unequal and inferior to the representations of men within the same medium. With the superhero genre being largely localized within American literature, the depictions of women in comics reflect dominant American attitudes toward women. The public acceptance of violence against women in comics ensures that this trope will persist, signifying comics as a literary medium that does not challenge or change issues of sexism in American culture, but instead, reinforces this ideology. The artwork of comics, however, reveals an entirely different kind of concern, namely the gratuitous sexualization and objectification of women in comics.

I'm not bad, I'm just drawn that way . . .

Over the years, female superheroes have been drawn with unnatural curves and increasingly larger bustlines while their costumes have shrunk exponentially. Rather than wear an iconic emblem or costume signifying her heritage, ideals, or powers, DC Comics' Power Girl wears a simple costume characterized by a large hole in the chest of her costume, revealing a large amount of cleavage. The origin of her costume was retroactively changed to reflect her lack of superheroic identity as she laments that "the first time I made this costume, I wanted to have a symbol . . . I just . . . I couldn't think of anything" (Johns 19). This same concept could have been reflected with a blank space where an emblem should be, as opposed to showing off the considerable amount of cleavage that is her identifying feature. An absence of a defining emblem or icon combined with the clear depiction of Power Girl's breasts seems to define the superheroine as a sex object. Conversely, one of Marvel Comics' male superheroes, Namor the Sub-Mariner, is often offered up as a male subjected to oversexualization, as his costume most often consists only of a green speedo in order to showcase his incredible physique. Yet, Namor is simply the exception to prove the trend, as the staggering amount of female superheroes who are subject to outrageously sexist costumes and poses that far outweigh one male superhero in a speedo.

In response to the objectified depictions of women in comics, fans and bloggers have devised a simple test and solution to this complex issue that has persisted in comics: "How to fix every Strong Female Character pose in superhero comics: replace the character with Hawkeye doing the same thing" (Gingerhaze). A blog entitled "The Hawkeye Initiative" formed around this concept of creating a new image by replacing a female superhero featured in a comic book cover or image with Hawkeye in the same pose: if Hawkeye does not look absurd or ridiculous in this pose (or costume), then the image in question is (probably) not sexist; if he does look absurd or ridiculous, then the image is almost certainly sexist (Glitchy). This is shown by various placements of Hawkeye showing off his male assets, such as they are, to the viewer. While this blog is intended for humorous purposes, by calling attention to the objectivist poses female characters are drawn in and the skimpy costumes worn by these female characters, comics artists and publishers can further work towards body-considerate poses and costumes. It instead exposes a trend in comics to subject women to poses in which they flaunt their breasts, bare skin, or otherwise position themselves in a sexual manner towards the reader, no matter the action in which the female superhero is engaged.

DC Comics has made recent strides towards progress with the most-recent redesign of Batgirl's costume in the latest New 52 reboot. Her costume, accompanied with design sketches from writers Cameron Stewart, Brenden Fletcher, and artist Babs Tarr, is revealed to be both functionally defensive and aesthetically flattering. In terms of design, Batgirl's costume has always been relatively conservative compared to other superwomen, which can be attributed to her consistent youthfulness throughout her history. The innovation in this costume design, however, is in its function: Batgirl's costume now features a detachable cape, snap-on gloves, a leather jacket that has been utilized in favor of the traditional form-fitting spandex, and practical leather boots in lieu of oversexualized thigh-high boots or impractical 6-inch stilettos (Zalben). It remains to be seen whether her costume will succumb to the oversexualization of most superwomen, but, as of this writing, Batgirl's costume design is one that consciously counteracts the typical female superhero costume.

Others simply abandon such costuming completely: Bill Willingham's *Fables* appropriates figures from popular fairy tales, folktales, and myths, empowering classic female characters with new identities and superpowers. The eponymous character from the classic fable Snow White is first introduced as the Deputy Mayor of Fabletown who possesses incredible powers of regeneration (*Fables: Legends in Exile* 8). Later, she marries the Big Bad Wolf and has children with him (*Fables: Wolves* 96–98). Rather than losing her agency to the role of mother, she instead becomes commander-in-chief of the largest military operation in the latter half of the comic series, elected by both the general population and the rest of the governing Fables of Fabletown as the best person for the job. Similarly, the fable Cinderella has also been revived, albeit in a less-political and more ass-kicking fashion. Cinderella first appears prominently in the role of a secret agent in the service of Fabletown (*Fables: The Mean Seasons* 21). As her narrative progresses, it is revealed that she possesses a select set of lethal martial arts training that allows her to accomplish any clandestine mission and incapacitate any enemy, both male and female, mundane human and superpowered alike (*Fables: War and Pieces* 36). These two women, along with other female characters in *Fables*, reflect recent efforts to breathe new life into older, one-dimensional characters by turning them into strong, empowered women.

Thriving on constant reinvention, in order to stay relevant and pertinent to American culture, the superhero genre's response to the issues of the past is crucial to the understanding of women operating in comics today. In recent years, many series have not only regained footholds for women in comics, but conquered new territory as comics became adapted for the film and brought women to life.

At the Movies

While the population of superheroines in comic books has grown since Wonder Woman sprang into action in the 1940s, by comparison, few superheroines have made their way onto the silver screen. Superheroines have historically had greater success on television. Lynda Carter led the way with her portrayal of Wonder Woman and her alter ego Diana Prince in the TV adaptation *Wonder Woman* (1975–1979). Beginning in the mid-90s, warrior women conquered the small screen as *Xena: Warrior Princess* (1995–2001), *Buffy the Vampire Slayer* (1997–2003), and Captain Kathryn Janeway of *Star Trek: Voyager* (1995–2001) demonstrated to audiences and critics that strong women could successfully lead a television series. Just as these shows were ending, American cinema began to embrace the superhero movie after the blockbuster box office and critical success of Sam Raimi's *Spider-Man* (2002). (Not to discount the lesser success of Bryan Singer's 2000 movie, *X-Men*.) As classic superheroes were revived, there was a call to bring back superheroines as well. Unfortunately, female driven films, like *Catwoman* (2004) and *Elektra* (2005), recorded sales significantly under their production budget compared to their male counterparts. The financial losses suffered by the studios resulted in the biggest obstacle facing superheroines today: the notion that audiences will not turn out for a superhero movie with a female lead. This concept has gone largely unchallenged by previous films and people in the industry. At present, superheroines exist as token females in groups of male superheroes and few of them have managed to shirk the normative gender expectations that require them to be love interests of the male superheroes.

Upon taking stock of blockbuster franchises, like *Batman* (in his various iterations), *Iron Man*, *Spider-Man*, and *The Amazing Spider-Man*, one finds superheroines outnumbered by ordinary women—women without superpowers who are not identified as superheroines. These ordinary characters are often lamented by many fans and scholars because they reinforce normative gender roles for women and position a female character as dependent, subservient, and/or indebted to the male superhero. While true of many of these characters, the sheer number of ordinary women characters bears closer examination than is usually given in our rush to dismiss them because they are not the superwomen we want them to be. When a superheroine does rise out of the predominantly male assemblage of heroes, even she often falls prey to these normative trappings. Female supervillains are, again, no exception. Though the path seems bleak and our superheroines are few, there is still hope for the future as audiences await the new *Wonder Woman* film expected in 2017. An examination of ordinary, heroic, and villainous women in superhero films will demonstrate that, while some progress has been made, depictions of women in superhero films continue to reaffirm normative gender expectations and normalize violence against women.

Wonderful Women Shorn of Super Wonder

While ordinary women are dwarfed by their superhero counterparts, many of these women would likely be considered exceptional outside this fantasy world. These women include scientists (Jane Foster, Betty Ross); journalists (Lois Lane, Vicki Vale); exceptional students (Gwen Stacy, Darcy Lewis); lawyers (Rachel Dawes); business executives (Pepper Potts); soldiers (Agent Peggy Carter, Agent Maria Hill); and strong, single mother-figures (May Parker, Martha Kent). Unfortunately, these women fulfill a normative gender role as love interest, mother-figure, or subordinate in the work place.

With few exceptions, the ordinary woman becomes identified by the villain as the superhero's obvious weakness, and he must gallantly ride, fly, or swing in to save her. However, just because these women need saving on occasion does not necessarily reduce them to the damsel-in-distress figure.

Many are relegated to the role of sidekick. In *The Amazing Spider-Man* (2012), after Spider-Man rescues Gwen Stacy from The Lizard's attack on the high school, he tells Gwen to go to OSCORP to make an antidote for the cross-species serum The Lizard plans to use to infect the city. Though Spider-Man gets the credit for saving the day, it is only because of Gwen's antidote that he can subdue The Lizard and save the city's citizens from being turned into giant mutant reptiles. In *Thor: The Dark World* (2013), Jane Foster remains largely inactive because she is infected by the Aether, the incarnation of one of the Infinity Stones, a power Malekith and the dark elves wish to harness. After Jane is no longer infected, she reconfigures the technology created by Dr. Erik Selvig and uses it to transport the dark elves into other realms. The technology is also Malekith's undoing as his body parts are separately transported into another realm as Thor hurtles the javelin-like tech directly into his body. Without Jane's efforts, Earth would have been doomed. Finally, Pepper Potts dons the Iron Man suit in *Iron Man 3* (2013), recalling her character of *RESCUE* from the comics, and saves Tony Stark from being crushed by falling rubble. Pepper even makes the leap from ordinary to superheroine, when she is injected with Extremis, allowing her to survive explosions, breathe fire, and defeat the villainous Mandarin. While these women are vital to the superhero's ability to save the day, their contributions are quickly forgotten because the narrative is chiefly concerned with the superhero's journey and exploits.

Then there's Mary Jane Watson in Sam Raimi's *Spider-Man* trilogy. Mary Jane is one of the worst embodiments of a leading female character in superhero films. Mary Jane endures a verbally abusive home life. She understands her own value based on the value ascribed to her in relationships and from theater reviews. She is always captured by the villain, and there are only two instances in which she actively participates in her own rescue. In *Spider-Man 2* (2004), she attempts to hit Dr. Octopus with a piece of wood, and he catches it in mid-air. In *Spider-Man 3* (2007), she manages to stay alive long enough for Harry and Peter to save her by leaping out of and dodging falling vehicles in Venom's web. Conversely, Aunt May is the only female character to successfully strike a villain in the trilogy: she hits Doc Ock with her umbrella, saving Spider-Man from being run through with a blade. Mary Jane is constantly treated poorly by male characters and objectified by the gaze of the camera.

Though many ordinary women characters are exceptional in some way, being a scientist, journalist, or soldier is not the equivalent of being a superhero. Women have entered a significantly wider array of fields since the inception of comic books and cultural standards of what makes a woman extraordinary has to change with the times. Fans do not line up to see Bruce Banner because he's an amazing scientist and researcher. They line up for the Hulk, Banner's superpowered alter ego. Tony Stark best expresses the fandom's sentiment when he meets Bruce in *The Avengers* (2012): "I'm a huge fan of the way you lose control and turn into an enormous green rage monster." While representations of smart women doing brave things are positive, audiences need to see women that are larger than life. Media scholars Elizabeth Behm-Morawitz and Hillary Pennell state that "The heroic nature of male and female superheroes and fans' connection to these characters through identification and parasocial interaction may inspire confidence in one's own ability to help others and to persevere in life" (86). If women in superhero films are always seen as the sidekick or damsel in distress, how will audiences know to expect more from the women of the world? How will women know to expect more of themselves? If we cannot imagine a more progressive and inclusive world, then we will not be able to make that world a reality. As a culture, we need to see strong, independent superheroines saving the city and fighting for those who cannot defend themselves.

The Few, The Proud . . .

Though the superheroines of the silver screen are few, their positive traits prove that women can be strong and save the day. One of the defining characteristics of the superheroine is that she is most often the only female super in the film. Black Widow, The Invisible Woman, Lady Sif, Batgirl, Liz Sherman, and, oddly enough, The Bowler are all token women in a group of men. Poison Ivy humorously references this tokenism in her fight with Batgirl in 1997's *Batman and Robin*: "As I told Lady Fries when I pulled her plug, this is a one woman show." The problem with tokenism is that it is not true representation. It is the practice of meeting the minimum requirement for a diversity quota. In both *The Avengers* and *Iron Man* 2, Black Widow has to stand in for all female superheroines, while the rest of the Avengers offer a variety of ways to embody a superhero. Despite being the lone female, these women prove invaluable to their fellow superheroes and the world. Black Widow closes the portal to Earth while Iron Man flies a nuclear warhead into the Chitauri mothership, effectively ending the Chitauri invasion together. However, Iron Man is the one who largely receives the credit (*The Avengers*). In *Hellboy*, Liz Sherman saves Hellboy and Agent Myers from an onslaught of resurrection demons by embracing her pyrokinetic powers and channeling it into a massive explosion. And while few consider 1999's *Mystery Men* in the same conversation as most of these movies, The Bowler and her haunted bowling ball destroy Casanova Frankenstein's Psycho-frakulator, saving Champion City in that spoof of comics and comics movies. Finally, in the aforementioned *Batman and Robin,* Batgirl saves the dynamic duo by defeating Poison Ivy as she figures out how to reconfigure satellites orbiting the Earth to melt the ice covering Gotham and its citizens. Again, these superheroine exploits are somewhat tantamount to overall success, yet quickly forgotten in lieu of celebrating the achievements of the superhero or predominantly male superhero team.

While these women are powerful, they are often confined to heteronormative gender roles. For example, they are often the love interest of the superhero (i.e., Elektra Natchios, Susan Storm, Liz

Sherman, Jean Grey) or considered competition for the love interest, as when Odin subtly suggests to Thor that he choose Lady Sif instead of Jane Foster (*Thor: The Dark World*). This is not to say that being in relationships is a crime. These normative gender roles become problematic when a woman's role as girlfriend or love interest surpasses her own identity as an individual and as a superheroine. Psychiatrist and film scholar Sharon Packer derisively critiques Silk Spectre II, from the film adaptation of Alan Moore's *Watchmen* (2009), for being "a parody of postfeminist independence" and generally less than super:

> The difference between Silk Spectre II and a school crossing guard is that Silk Spectre wears thigh-high fetishistic spike-heeled black boots [. . .] Otherwise, both are charged with ensuring the safety of children [. . .] She is a superheroine who depends upon men to act. If a superheroine needs such assistance, what does this say about ordinary women? (206)

Furthermore, Silk Spectre II's character arc is choosing to leave her distant lover, Dr. Manhattan, for a more attentive supersuitor, Night Owl II. Sue Storm follows a similar pattern of development in the *Fantastic Four* films. In *Fantastic Four* (2005), she wants Reed Richards to notice her and try to win her back. In *Fantastic Four: Rise of the Silver Surfer* (2007), all she wants is to get married, raise children, and give up the superhero life. She decides at the end of the film, after being brought back to life by the Silver Surfer, that she can be a superheroine, a wife, and a mother all at the same time. For all those movies' flaws, at least, in that one moment, there is *some* small growth.

Like their male counterparts, superheroines and female supervillains often emerge from a traumatic event or past. However, some of the traumas that women endure in order to propel them to their superheroine or supervillain identities seem especially fitted to their gender. Women in comic books are often victims of abuse, sexual assault, or even killed before they become stronger. Natasha Romanoff, a.k.a. Black Widow, is a former Russian spy, who knows "what it's like to be unmade" as she has "a lot of red in her ledger" (*The Avengers*). Jean Grey is crushed by a massive wave of water before she fully realizes her potential and becomes the Phoenix (*X2*). Liz Sherman is a pyrokinetic who was bullied as a child and has accidentally killed several people throughout her life because she explodes in flames when she loses control of her emotions (*Hellboy*). Patience Phillips, in certainly one of the least of all 'adaptations', is drowned before she is brought back to life by a magical cat, transforming her into Catwoman (*Catwoman*). Elektra Natichos is killed by Bullseye and brought back to life by her mentor and trainer, Stick, who teaches her to harness the powers of time (*Elektra*). Rather than be crippled by these traumas, these women emerge stronger because of them, displaying characteristics of what Packer identifies as "a positive PTSD that we will call 'post-traumatic *strength* disorder'" (238). Packer describes these "wounded warrior stories" as narratives that "instill hope that an injury may turn into a springboard for greater strength or become a conduit to untapped abilities" (238). All of these women become more powerful after their trauma and go on to help others. Audiences see these superheroines persevere over great obstacles and emulate that strength in the face of their own adversities. However, fans also experience the heightened violence towards women that is mirrored in comic books, affirming that violence against women is a normal occurrence.

How one chooses to deal with/recover from tragedy seems to be the difference between superheroines and supervillains. Rather than channeling their new powers into helping others, these supervillains seek revenge or use their new abilities for their own selfish purposes. Selina Kyle doesn't become Catwoman in *Batman Returns* until after Max Shreck pushes her out of a window. She miraculously survives the fall, but Selina/Catwoman treats the fall and all other attempts on her life as confirmed kills when she confronts Max at the end of the film: "You killed me. The Penguin killed me. Batman killed me. That's three lives down. You got enough in there," referring to the gun he's holding, "to finish me off" (*Batman Returns*). Her story arc is one of revenge against the man who killed her, or at least killed her innocence. She emerges as a confident, hypersexualized femme fatale, a skilled fighter, and an ace with a whip. Poison Ivy has much the same path in that movie's later sequel *Batman and Robin*. Dr. Pamela Isley discovers that her colleague, Dr. Jason Woodrue, was stealing the venom she was using for her cross-species experiments to create supersoldiers. He asks her to join him, as his evil business partner and lover, and Pamela adamantly rejects his proposal. He kills Pamela for rejecting him by pushing her over a table with snakes and chemicals, followed by pushing over several containers of venom on her. She emerges from the ground, transformed into Poison Ivy, another famous femme fatale.

Where Do We Go From Here?

Today, women in comics seem to be at a crossroads. The wish to be beautiful may be seen as conforming to societal beauty standards or as empowered for wanting to be beautiful in her own body. Similarly, wanting to be less complicated may be seen as shedding seventy-plus years of convoluted historical baggage, or as adhering to a male agenda of wanting to be a simple woman who is easy to dominate. Kamala Khan's struggle with her identity as Ms. Marvel reflects much of the struggle within comics for women: "I don't know what I'm supposed to do. I don't know who I'm supposed to be . . . I want to be beautiful and awesome and butt-kicking and less complicated" (Wilson 17). Marvel's recent successes with both their new female-oriented comics initiative and cinematic universe, spanning both television and film, elicit hope for the position of women in comics.

While DC's New 52 comic initiative seems less promising, the largest potential for hope may lie in the upcoming *Batman v. Superman: Dawn of Justice* (2015) and *Wonder Woman* (2017) films (Dietsch). Announced at San Diego Comic-Con 2014, a teaser image of actress Gal Gadot as Wonder Woman in *Batman v. Superman* represents the first time Wonder Woman will be shown in a live film role, and fans love it: "About seventy-three percent of reactions to the footage considered it 'amazing'; the official image of Gadot was retweeted more than seven thousand times. Wonder Woman was also the most talked-about superhero of the convention, with 149,316 mentions on Twitter" (Dietsch). Gal Gadot seems to be the Wonder

Woman fans of comics and superhero films have been waiting for, the Wonder Woman worth waiting for. Even if she still wears heels.

Work Cited

The Amazing Spider-Man. Dir. Marc Webb. Perf. Andrew Garfield, Emma Stone, & Rhys Ifans. Columbia Pictures, 2012. Film.

The Avengers. Dir. Joss Whedon. Perf. Robert Downey, Jr.; Chris Evans; & Mark Ruffalo. Walt Disney Studios Motion Pictures, 2012. Film.

Batman & Robin. Dir. Joel Schumacher. Perf. Arnold Schwarzenegger, George Clooney, & Chris O'Donnell. Warner Bros., 1997. Film.

Batman Returns. Dir. Tim Burton. Perf. Michael Keaton, Danny DeVito, & Michelle Pfeiffer. Warner Bros., 1992. Film.

Battersby, Matilda. "Batwoman Can't Have Lesbian Wedding 'Because Heroes Shouldn't Have Happy Personal Lives.'" *The Independent*. Independent Digital News and Media, 9 Sept. 2013. Web. 27 July 2014.

Behm-Morawritz, Elizabeth, & Hillary Pennell. "The Effects of Superhero Sagas on Our Gendered Selves." *Our Superheroes, Ourselves*. Ed. Robin S. Rosenberg. Oxford, U.K.: Oxford UP, 2013. 73–93.

Call, Lewis. *BDSM in American Science Fiction and Fantasy*. New York: Palgrave Macmillan, 2012.

Catwoman. Dir. Pitof Comar. Perf. Halle Berry & Sharon Stone. Warner Bros., 2004. Film.

Dietsch, TJ. "'Batman v. Superman' Most Talked-About Film of Comic-Con."*Spinoff Online*. Comic Book Resources, 29 July 2014. Web. 31 July 2014.

Elektra. Dir. Rob. Bowman. Perf. Jennifer Garner & Goran Visnjic. 20th Century Fox, 2005. Film.

Fantastic Four. Dir. Tim Story. Perf. Ioan Gruffudd, Jessica Alba, & Chris Evans. 20th Century Fox, 2005. Film.

Fantastic Four: Rise of the Silver Surfer. Dir. Tim Story. Perf. Ioan Gruffudd, Jessica Alba, & Chris Evans. Twentieth Century Fox, 2007. Film.

Gingerhaze. *How are you? I'm fine thanks*. Tumblr. 2012. Web. 28 July 2014.

Glitchy . "The Hawkeye Test." *The Hawkeye Initiative*. The Hawkeye Initiative. 2012. Web. 27 July 2014.

Hellboy. Dir. Guillermo Del Toro. Perf. Ron Perlman & Selma Blair. Columbia Pictures, 2004. Film.

Iron Man 3. Dir. Shane Black. Perf. Robert Downey, Jr. & Gwyneth Paltrow. Walt Disney Studios Motion Pictures, 2013.

Johns, Geoff. *JSA Classified Vol. 1, #2*. New York: DC Comics, 2005.

_____. Grant Morrison, Greg Rucka, & Mark Waid. *52 #11*. New York: DC Comics, 2007.

Kanigher, Robert. "S.O.S. Wonder Woman!" *Sensation Comics #94*. New York: DC Comics, 1949.

Lee, Stan. *The Fantastic Four #1*. New York: Marvel Comics, 1961.

_____. *Fantastic Four Annual #3*. New York: Marvel Comics, 1965.

Marston, William Moulton. "Introducing Wonder Woman." *All-Star Comics #8*. DC Comics, 1941.

Marvel. "Marvel Proudly Presents Thor." *Marvel*. Marvel Comics, 15 July 2014. Web. 27 July 2014.

Marz, Ron. *Green Lantern, Vol. 3, #54*. New York: DC Comics, 1994.

Mystery Men. Dir. Kinka Usher. Perf. Hank Azaria, Claire Forlani, & Janeane Garofalo. Universal Pictures, 1999. Film.

Packer, Sharon. "'What Do Women Want?'" *Superheroes and Superegos: Analyzing the Minds behind the Masks*. Santa Barbara: Praeger/ABC-CLIO, 2010. 197–221.

_____. "The Wounded Warrior: Post Traumatic *Strength* Disorder." *Superheroes and Superegos: Analyzing the Minds behind the Masks*. Santa Barbara: Praeger/ABC-CLIO, 2010. 235–43.

Robinson, Lillian S. *Wonder Women: Feminisms and Superheroes*. New York: Routledge, 2004.

Simone, Gail. *Women in Refrigerators*. Mar. 1999. Web. 29 July 2014.

Willingham, Bill. *Fables: Legends in Exile*. Vol. 1. New York: Vertigo/DC Comics, 2003.

_____. *Fables: The Mean Seasons*. Vol. 5. New York: Vertigo/DC Comics, 2005.

_____. *Fables: War and Pieces*. Vol. 11. New York: Vertigo/DC Comics, 2008.

_____. *Fables: Wolves*. Vol. 8. New York: Vertigo/DC Comics, 2006.

Wilson, G. Willow, & Adrian Alphona. *Ms. Marvel.* New York: Marvel Comics. 2014.

Zalben, Alex. "Exclusive: 'Batgirl Gets A Brand New Look From DC Comics." *MTV*. MTV News, 10 July 2014. Web. 28 July 2014.

RESOURCES

Works in the American Comic Book Genre_____

A Contract with God and Other Tenement Stories: A Graphic Novel. Will Eisner. 1978.

All-Star Superman. Grant Morrison, Frank Quitely, et al. 2005.

American Born Chinese. Gene Luen Yang. 2006.

Anya's Ghost. Vera Brosgol. 2011.

Astonishing X-Men. Joss Whedon & John Cassaday. 2005.

Batman: The Court of Owls. Scott Snyder & Greg Capullo. 2011.

Batman Chronicles. Bob Kane & Bill Finger. 2005.

Batman: The Dark Knight Returns. Frank Miller, et al. 1986.

Batman: The Long Halloween. Jeph Loeb & Tim Sale. 1996.

Batman: Year One. Frank Miller & David Mazzucchelli. 1987.

Best of Little Nemo in Slumberland. Winsor McCay. 1997.

Big Questions. Anders Nilsen. 2011.

Black Hole. Charles Burns. 1995.

Blackest Night. Geoff Johns, Ivan Reis, & Oclair Albert. 2009.

Bone. Jeff Smith. 1991.

Building Stories. Chris Ware. 2012.

The Calvin & Hobbes Tenth Anniversary Book. Bill Watterson. 1995.

Captain America: The Winter Soldier. Ed Brubaker, et al. 2010.

Complete Peanuts 1983–1986. Charles Schulz. 2012.

The Complete Persepolis. Marjane Satrapi. 2007.

The Crow. James O'Barr. 1989.

Daredevil: Born Again. Frank Miller & David Mazzucchelli. 1986.

The Death of Superman. Dan Jurgens, et al. 1992.

Essential Captain America. Stan Lee, et al. 2000.

Essential Fantastic Four Vol. 3. Stan Lee, et al. 2007.

Essential Spider-Man Vol. 1. Stan Lee. 2006.

Fables. Bill Willingham, Lan Medina, & Steve Leialoha. 2002.

Ghost World. Daniel Clowes. 1993.

Heartbreak Soup: A Love and Rockets Book. Gilbert Hernandez, et al. 2007.

Hellboy: Seed of Destruction. Mike Mignola & John Byrne. 1994.

Incognegro. Mat Johnson, Warren Pleece, & Clem Robins. 1999.

The Infinity Gauntlet. Jim Starlin & George Paerez. 1991.

Jack Kirby's New Gods. Jack Kirby. 1971.

Justice League of America/Avengers. Kurt Busiek & George Perez. 2003.

Justice League of America: Tower of Babel. Mark Waid & Howard Porter. 2000.

John Constantine, Hellblazer. Garth Ennis, et al. 1988.

Kingdom Come. Mark Waid, Alex Ross, Todd Klein, & Elliot S. Maggin. 1996.

The Life and Times of Scrooge McDuck. Don Rosa. 2007.

Locke & Key: Welcome to Lovecraft. Joe Hill & Gabriel Rodríguez. 2008.

The Maxx. Sam Kieth & William Messner-Loebs. 1993.

The New Teen Titans: The Judas Contract. George Perez, et al. 1984.

Palestine. Joe Sacco. 1996.

The Sandman. Neil Gaiman, et al. 1989.

Superman for All Seasons. Jeph Loeb & Tim Sale. 1998.

Superman, The Man of Steel. John Byrne & Marv Wolfman. 1986.

The Ultimates. Mark Millar, et al. 2002.

V for Vendetta. Alan Moore & David Lloyd. 1982.

Watchmen. Alan More & Dave Gibbons. 1986.

WE3: The Deluxe Edition. Grant Morrison, Frank Quitely, et al. 2004.

Wonder Woman Chronicles. William Moulton Marston. 2010.

Wonder Woman: Down to Earth. Greg Rucka, et al. 2003.

X-Men: The Dark Phoenix Saga. Chris Claremont & John Byrne. 1980.

Y: The Last Man. Brian K. Vaughan & Pia Guerra. 2002.

Brosgol, Vera. *Anya's Ghost*. New York: First Second, 2011.

Brubaker, Ed, Steve Epting, Mike Perkins, & Michael Lark. *Captain America: The Winter Soldier*. New York: Marvel, 2010.

Burns, Charles. *Black Hole*. New York: Pantheon, 2008.

Busiek, Kurt, & George Pérez. *JLA/Avengers*. New York: DC Comics, 2008.

Byrne, John, & Marv Wolfman. *Superman, the Man of Steel*. New York: DC Comics, 2003.

Chute, Hillary L. *Graphic Women: Life Narrative and Contemporary Comics*. New York: Columbia UP, 2010.

Claremont, Chris, & John Byrne. *X-Men: The Dark Phoenix Saga*. New York: Marvel, 2012.

Clowes, Daniel. *Ghost World*. Seattle, WA: Fantagraphics, 2001.

Duncan, Randy, & Matthew J. Smith. *Critical Approaches to Comics: An Introduction to Theories and Methods*. New York: Routledge, 2011.

_____. *The Power of Comics: History, Form and Culture*. New York: Bloomsbury, 2013.

Eisner, Will. *A Contract with God and Other Tenement Stories: A Graphic Novel*. New York: W.W. Norton, 2006.

_____. *Comics & Sequential Art*. 1985, Expanded 1990. Tamarac, FL: Poorhouse Press, 2001.

Ennis, Garth, William Simpson, et al. *John Constantine, Hellblazer*. New York: DC Comics, 2013.

Feiffer, Jules. *The Great Comic Book Heroes*. 1965. Seattle, WA: Fantagraphics Books, 2003.

Fingeroth, Danny. *Superman on the Couch: What Superheroes Really Tell Us About Ourselves and Our Society*. New York: Continuum, 2004.

Fraction, Matt, David Aja, Javier Pulido, et al . *Hawkeye*. New York, NY: Marvel Worldwide, 2013.

Gaiman, Neil, Sam Keith, Mike Dringenberg, & Malcolm Jones. *The Sandman*. New York: Vertigo, 2010.

Hatfield, Charles, Jeet Heer, & Kent Worcester. *The Superhero Reader*. Jackson: UP of Mississippi, 2013.

Hatfield, Charles. *Alternative Comics: An Emerging Literature*. Jackson: UP of Mississippi, 2005.

Heer, Jeet, & Kent Worcester, eds. *A Comics Studies Reader*. Jackson: UP of Mississippi, 2009.

_____. *Arguing Comics: Literary Masters on a Popular Medium*. Jackson: UP of Mississippi, 2004.

Hernandez, Gilbert. *Heartbreak Soup: A Love and Rockets Book*. Seattle, WA: Fantagraphics, 2007.

Hignite, Todd. *In the Studio: Visits with Contemporary Cartoonists*. New Haven & London: Yale UP, 2006.

Hill, Joe, & Gabriel Rodríguez. *Locke & Key: Welcome to Lovecraft*. San Diego, CA: IDW, 2009.

Johns, Geoff, Ivan Reis, & Oclair Albert. *Blackest Night*. New York: DC Comics, 2010.

Johnson, Mat, Warren Pleece, & Clem Robins. *Incognegro*. New York: Vertigo/DC Comics, 2008.

Jurgens, Dan, Jerry Ordway, Louise Simonson, Roger Stern, Jon Bogdanove, Tom Grummett, Jackson Guice, & Brett Breeding. *The Death of Superman*. New York, NY: DC Comics, 2013.

Kane, Bob. *Batman Chronicles*. New York: DC Comics, 2005.

Kieth, Sam, & William Messner-Loebs. *The Maxx*. La Jolla, CA: WildStorm Productions, 2003.

Kirby, Jack. *Jack Kirby's New Gods*. New York, NY: DC Comics, 1998.

Klock, Geoff. *How To Read Superhero Comics and Why*. New York: Continuum, 2006.

Kunzle, David. *Father of the Comic Strip: Rodolphe Töpffer*. Jackson: UP of Mississippi, 2007.

_____. *The History of the Comic Strip: The Nineteenth Century*. U of California P, 1990.

Lee, Stan, & Jack Kirby. *Essential Fantastic Four Volume 3*. New York, NY: Marvel Pub., 2007.

_____. *The Essential Captain America*. New York: Marvel Comics, 2000.

Lee, Stan. *The Essential Spider-Man Vol. 1*. New York: Marvel, 2002.

Loeb, Jeph, & Tim Sale. *Superman for All Seasons*. New York, NY: DC Comics, 1999.

Loeb, Jeph, Tim Sale, & Bob Kane. *Batman: The Long Halloween*. New York: DC Comics, 2011.

Lopes, Paul Douglas. *Demanding Respect: The Evolution of the American Comic Book*. Philadelphia: Temple UP, 2009.

Marston, William Moulton. *The Wonder Woman Chronicles*. New York: DC Comics, 2010.

McCay, Winsor. *The Best of Little Nemo in Slumberland*. Ed. Richard Marschall. New York: Stewart, Tabori, & Chang, 1997.

McCloud, Scott. *Making Comics*. New York: HarperCollins, 2006.

_____. *Reinventing Comics: How Imagination and Technology Are Revolutionizing an Art Form*. New York: HarperCollins, 2002.

_____. *Understanding Comics*. New York: HarperPerennial, 1994.

Mignola, Mike, & John Byrne. *Hellboy*. Milwaukie, OR: Dark Horse, 2003.

Millar, Mark, Bryan Hitch, Andrew Currie, Paul Mounts, & Chris Eliopoulos. *The Ultimates*. New York, NY: Marvel Comics, 2002.

Miller, Frank, & David Mazzucchelli. *Batman: Year One*. New York: DC Comics, 2005.

_____. *Daredevil: Born Again*. New York: Marvel, 2010.

Miller, Frank, Klaus Janson, Lynn Varley, John Costanza, & Bob Kane. *Batman: The Dark Knight Returns*. New York, NY: DC Comics, 2002.

Moore, Alan, & Dave Gibbons. *Watchmen*. New York: DC Comics, 1987.

Moore, Alan, & David Lloyd. *V for Vendetta*. New York: Dc Comics, 2008.

Morrison, Grant, Frank Quitely, Jamie Grant, & Todd Klein. *WE3: The Deluxe Edition*. New York: DC Comics, 2011.

Morrison, Grant, Frank Quitely, Jamie Grant, Phil Balsman, & Travis Lanham. *All-star Superman*. New York: DC Comics, 2011.

Nama, Adilifu. *Super Black: American Pop Culture and Black Superheroes*. Austin: U of Texas P, 2011.

Newgarden, Mark, & Paul Karasik. *How to Read Nancy*. Seattle, WA: Fantagraphics, 2013.

Nilsen, Anders. *Big Questions*. Montréal, Quebec: Drawn & Quarterly, 2011.

O'Barr, J. *The Crow*. New York: Gallery, 2011.

Rosa, Don. *The Life and Times of Scrooge McDuck*. Timonium, MD: Gemstone, 2005.

Rosenberg, Robin S., & Peter M. Coogan. *What Is a Superhero?* Oxford: Oxford UP, 2013.

Rucka, Greg, Drew Johnson, Ray Snyder, & William Moulton Marston. *Wonder Woman: Down to Earth*. New York, NY: DC Comics, 2004.

Sabin, Roger. *Comics, Comix & Graphic Novels: A History of Comic Art*. 1996. New York & London: Phaidon Press, 2002.

Sacco, Joe, Edward W. Said, & Joe Sacco. *Palestine*. Seattle, WA: Fantagraphics, 2001.

Satrapi, Marjane. *The Complete Persepolis*. New York: Pantheon, 2007.

Schulz, Charles M. *The Complete Peanuts 1983–1986*. Seattle, WA: Fantagraphics Books, 2012.

Smith, Jeff. *Bone*. Columbus, OH: Cartoon, 2004.

Snyder, Scott, & Greg Capullo. *Batman: The Court of Owls*. New York : London: DC Comics; Titan, 2012.

Starlin, Jim, George Perez, & Ron Lim. *The Infinity Gauntlet*. New York: Marvel Worldwide, 2011.

Taylor, R[ichard]. *Introduction to Cartooning: A Practical Instruction Book*. New York: Watson-Guptill Publications, 1947.

Varnum, Robin, & Christina T. Gibbons. *The Language of Comics: Word and Image*. Jackson: UP Mississippi, 2001.

Vaughan, Brian K., & Pia Guerra. *Y: The Last Man*. New York: Vertigo/ DC Comics, 2008.

Waid, Mark, & Howard Porter. *JLA: Tower of Babel*. New York, NY: DC Comics, 2001.

Waid, Mark, Alex Ross, Todd Klein, & Elliot S. Maggin. *Kingdom Come*. New York: DC Comics, 2008.

Ware, Chris. *Building Stories*. New York: Pantheon, 2012.

Watterson, Bill. *The Calvin & Hobbes Tenth Anniversary Book*. New York: Andrews & McMeel, 1995.

Whedon, Joss, & John Cassaday. *Astonishing X-Men*. New York: Marvel, 2012.

Willingham, Bill, Lan Medina, & Steve Leialoha. *Fables*. New York: DC Comics, 2012.

Wolfman, Marv, George Pérez, Dick Giordano, Adrienne Roy, Anthony Tollin, & Ben Oda. *The New Teen Titans: The Judas Contract*. New York: DC Comics, 2003.

Wolk, Douglas. *Reading Comics: How Graphic Novels Work and What They Mean*. Da Capo Press, 2007.

Yang, Gene Luen, & Lark Pien. *American Born Chinese*. New York: Square Fish, 2008.

About the Editor

Joseph Michael Sommers (PhD, University of Kansas), first and foremost, is husband to Sulynn and father to Maggie and Gwendolyn, all of whom were exceedingly patient while he completed this project. He is an associate professor at Central Michigan University, with special interest in children's and young adult literature, popular culture, illustrated texts (comics, graphic novels, and picture books), late-nineteenth-, twentieth-, and twenty-first-century literature and culture, and Bakhtinian/narrative theory. He has published many essays on comics, *The Chronicles of Narnia*, *Fahrenheit 451*, Judy Blume, *Twilight*, etc. He has co-edited two other anthologies: *Game On, Hollywood: The Intersection of Video Games and Movies* (McFarland, 2013 with Gretchen Papazian) and *Sexual Ideology in the Works of Alan Moore* (McFarland, 2012 with Todd Comer). He writes, researches, and works for his students. They may not know it, but they are more than mere fans; they are his *real* American superheroes.

Contributors

Matt Bryant Cheney (PhD candidate, University of Kentucky) lives and works in Lexington, Kentucky. He also holds a BA from Carson-Newman University and an MA in English from the University of Tennessee-Knoxville, where he wrote his thesis on Flannery O'Connor. Matt's recent work focuses on understanding the intersections among politics, morality, and cultural production in the United States from World War II to the present, with a particular interest in the different ethical demands presented by all angles of the so-called "culture wars" as they appear in literature. He has presented at numerous conferences, including the Louisville Conference on Literature Since 1900 and the Rocky Mountain Modern Language Association. When he is not requesting obscure comic titles from UK Interlibrary Loan or grading papers, you can find him sharing life with the Ashley the Beautiful, Will the Brave, and Nina the Barker.

Daniel Clark (MA in English, University of Tennessee at Chattanooga) is an associate professor of English at Cedarville University where he teaches courses in composition, advanced grammar, contemporary world literature, film, and the graphic novel. Along with Andrew Wiseman, Clark developed Cedarville's foreign film series. He also serves as co-sponsor of Alpha Kappa Delta, Cedarville's chapter of Sigma Tau Delta, the International English Honor Society. Before coming to Cedarville, he taught at the University of Maryland Asian Division in Okinawa, Japan. He also taught English as a Second Language (ESL) at the Okinawa Prefectural Language Center. Clark has been at Cedarville since 1999.

Joseph Darowski (PhD, Michigan State University) is a member of the English department at Brigham Young University, Idaho and also on the editorial review board of *The Journal of Popular Culture*. He is the editor of *The Ages of Superman: Essays on the Man of Steel in Changing Times* (McFarland, 2012) and subsequent essay collections in the series on Wonder Woman, the X-Men, and the Avengers. Most recently, he is the author of *X-Men and the Mutant Metaphor: Race and Gender in the Comic Books* (Rowman & Littlefield, 2014), and he has published additional research on popular culture, television shows, and comic books.

Kyle Eveleth (PhD candidate, University of Kentucky) specializes in twentieth- and twentieth-first-century American literature, graphic narrative, and children's literature. He has had essays published in *First Opinions, Second Reactions*, *Textual Overtures*, *Synthesis: An Anglophone Journal of Comparative Literary Studies*, and most recently in *South Central Review*. His current project re-examines the cultural and historical precedents leading to the generation of the young adult novel genre through the lens of enchantment and disenchantment.

Forrest C. Helvie (PhD, Indiana University of Pennsylvania) lives in Bristol, CT with his wife and two sons. He is an associate professor of developmental English at Norwalk Community College in Connecticut. Dr. Helvie's doctoral dissertation was entitled "Capes and the Canon: Comic Book Superheroes and Traditional American Literature," and will be published in 2015. He is a past National Lent Award recipient for his work in comics studies in addition to earning the first Connecticut State Board of Regents Award for Scholarly Excellence and the doctoral scholarly excellence award from IUP. In addition to his academic research, Helvie regularly writes for comics websites, such as *Newsarama* and *Sequart*, in addition to writing comics for a number of comic anthologies.

Owen R. Horton (PhD candidate, University of Kentucky) specializes in film, cultural studies, disability studies, and masculinity. He has a forthcoming article, "Temporal Prosthetics and Beautiful Pain: Loss, Memory, and Nostalgia in *Somewhere in Time, The Butterfly Effect,* and *Safety Not Guaranteed*," appearing in *Time Travel and the Media: Narrative, Culture and the Metaphysics of Time* (2014).

Krystal Howard (PhD candidate, Western Michigan University) teaches children's literature and writing. Her research interests include comics, children's literature, literary theory, gothic literature, and contemporary poetry. Her dissertation project is entitled "Little Terrors: A Study of Fear and Ecstasy in Children's Literature."

Daniel Lawson (PhD, Virginia Tech) is an assistant professor of English and director of the writing center at Central Michigan University. His research interests include visual rhetoric, comics, composition pedagogy, and writing center studies. His work on visual rhetoric has appeared in collections, such as *The New Work of Composing and Guns, Grenades, and Grunts: First-Person Shooter Games*.

Kim Munson (MA, San Francisco State University) is an independent art historian, writer, and curator living in the San Francisco Bay Area. Her articles on contemporary art, comic art, museum exhibitions, and labor graphics have appeared in the *International Journal of Comic Art*, the *Comics Journal*, *Icons of the American Comic Book from Captain America to Wonder Woman* and other publications. Munson has also been creative director for tech companies; production coordinator for a large manufacturer; a scenic artist for film, TV, and theatre; and a small business owner. She still writes web content and does some graphic and web design.

A. J. Shackelford (PhD candidate, University of Arkansas) specializes in both literary theory and rhetoric/composition. His current projects explore political ideologies in children's culture.

Matthew J. Smith (PhD, Ohio University) is a professor of communication at Wittenberg University in Springfield, Ohio. In collaboration with Randy Duncan of Henderson State University and Paul Levitz, former president and publisher of DC Comics, he is the author of *The Power of Comics: History, Form and Culture, 2nd Edition* (Bloomsbury Academic, 2015), which is a textbook for the comics studies classroom. Smith and Duncan have previously collaborated in editing *Critical Approaches to Comics: Theories and Methods* (Routledge, 2012), which was nominated for a Will Eisner Comic Industry Award for Best Educational/Academic Work, and *Icons of the American Comic Book* (ABC-CLIO, 2013). Smith also worked with Ben Bolling of the University of North Carolina at Chapel-Hill to edit *It Happens at Comic-Con: Ethnographic Essays on a Pop Culture Phenomenon* (McFarland, 2014).

Philip Smith (PhD candidate, Loughborough University) teaches language and literature, general English, and theory of knowledge at Sekolah Tunas Muda in Jakarta. A full list of his publications can be found on academia.edu. He endeavors to respond to any email directed to philipsmithgraduate@gmail.com.

Katherine E. Whaley (PhD candidate, University of Kentucky) teaches English, and her research interests include the works of Joss Whedon, the presence of old age and the elderly in teen television series, and representations of disability narratives in film and television. She currently serves as the area chair of Whedon Studies for the Midwest Popular Culture Association/American Culture Association. She has an article forthcoming in the winter issue of *Slayage: The Journal of the Whedon Studies Association*, entitled "'There's nothing wrong with my body': Xander as a Study in Defining Capability of the Disabled Body in *Buffy the Vampire Slayer.*"

Justin Wigard is a second-year graduate assistant in the Department of English Language and Literature at Central Michigan University (CMU). His research interests include the heroic tradition in children's literature and the works of Stephen King. He currently serves as the managing editor for *Humanorum*, an undergraduate online journal housed within the College of Humanities and Social and Behavioral Sciences at CMU. In the past, he has worked as editorial assistant on two books with Joseph Michael Sommers: *Game On, Hollywood: The Intersection of Video Games and Movies* (McFarland, 2013) and *Sexual Ideology in the Works of Alan Moore* (McFarland, 2012).

Index